Adobe® Fireworks® CS6

CLASSROOM IN A BOOK

The official training workbook from Adobe Systems

Adobe

Adobe® Fireworks® CS6 Classroom in a Book®

Adobe Press books are published by Peachpit, a division of Pearson Education located in Berkeley, California. For the latest on Adobe Press books, go to www.adobepress.com. To report errors, please send a note to errata@peachpit.com. For information on getting permission for reprints and excerpts, contact permissions@peachpit.com.

Printed and bound in the United States of America

ISBN-13:   978-0-321-82244-4
ISBN-10:   0-321-82244-7

9 8 7 6 5 4 3 2

WHAT'S ON THE DISC

Here is an overview of the contents of the Classroom in a Book disc

The *Adobe Fireworks CS6 Classroom in a Book* disc includes the lesson files that you'll need to complete the exercises in this book, as well as other content to help you learn more about Adobe Fireworks CS6 and use it with greater efficiency and ease. The diagram below represents the contents of the disc, which should help you locate the files you need.

Lesson files

Each lesson has its own folder inside the Lessons folder. You will need to copy these lesson folders to your hard drive before you can begin each lesson.

Name
▸ 📁 Lesson01
▸ 📁 Lesson02
▸ 📁 Lesson03
▸ 📁 Lesson04
▸ 📁 Lesson05
▸ 📁 Lesson06
▸ 📁 Lesson07
▸ 📁 Lesson08
▸ 📁 Lesson09
▸ 📁 Lesson10
▸ 📁 Lesson11
▸ 📁 Lesson12

Online resources

Links to Adobe Community Help, product Help and Support pages, Adobe certification programs, Adobe TV, and other useful online resources can be found inside a handy HTML file. Just open it in your Web browser and click on the links, including a special link to this book's product page where you can access updates and bonus material.

Adobe Press

Find information about other Adobe Press titles, covering the full spectrum of Adobe products, in the Online Resources file.

CONTENTS

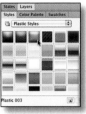

**BONUS SUPPLEMENTAL CHAPTER 14
IS LOCATED ON THE COMPANION DISC**

GETTING STARTED

Adobe Fireworks® is a professional imaging application that combines vector and bitmap imaging technologies and techniques in a single graphics application. This unique approach to imaging is due to the specific focus of Fireworks, which is creating and manipulating screen graphics for the Web or for other screen-based tools, such as mobile applications or Adobe Flash® products. Fireworks is a tool that lets you quickly and easily create, edit, or alter graphics and designs. And it's a blast to work with, too!

With the release of Adobe Fireworks CS6, the program has gained even more distinction as a unique application for *rapid prototyping*. The built-in flexibility of Fireworks and its "everything is editable all the time" mandate have been present since it was created. When you're creating mock-ups and prototypes, when client requests or design changes can come fast and furious, this type of flexibility is very important. Features such as multiple pages, Photoshop integration, CSS3 properties extraction, and jQuery Mobile workflows make Fireworks an essential tool in the design process.

About Classroom in a Book

Adobe Fireworks CS6 Classroom in a Book is part of the official training series for Adobe graphics and publishing software developed by experts in association with Adobe Systems. The lessons are designed to let you learn at your own pace. If you're new to Adobe Fireworks, you'll learn the fundamental concepts and features you'll need in order to begin to master the program. And, if you've been using Adobe Fireworks for a while, you'll find that *Classroom in a Book* teaches advanced features, including tips and techniques for using the latest version of the application and for creating web and application prototypes. Although each lesson provides step-by-step instructions for creating a specific project, there's room for exploration and experimentation. You can follow the book from start to finish, or do only the lessons that match your interests and needs. Each lesson concludes with a review section summarizing what you've covered.

What's in this book

This edition covers many new features in Adobe Fireworks CS6, such as CSS3 properties extraction, jQuery Mobile theming, enhancements to the Properties panel, the Common Library, templates, and the Styles panel.

An overview of the Adobe interface is covered in the first lesson, where you will learn how to configure the panels and document windows in Fireworks to suit your workflow. You will learn how to edit bitmap images and work with vector paths to create web interfaces. You will learn how to create and edit symbols, a powerful feature of Fireworks, and how to use such rapid prototyping tools as Master pages, shared layers, pages and states, styles, and Common Library symbols while you work on a wireframe for a tablet app and a high-fidelity prototype for a website. In addition, you will explore the art of optimizing graphics for the Web, striking that perfect balance between file size and image quality.

As you progress through the lessons, you will discover the many time-saving features Fireworks offers, such as the Batch Process Wizard, the Import command, and the Export Area command. Plus, you'll learn how Fireworks integrates with other Adobe CS6 applications like Photoshop and Bridge.

Finally, you will test out new Fireworks CS6 features, such as the CSS3 Properties extraction panel. You'll learn how to customize a jQuery Mobile website by using the new jQuery Mobile Theme command, and see how both these mobile-focused features work with Adobe Dreamweaver.

Prerequisites

Before you begin to use *Adobe Fireworks CS6 Classroom in a Book,* you should have a working knowledge of your computer and its operating system. Make sure that you know how to use the mouse and standard menus and commands, and also how to open, save, and close files. If you need to review these techniques, see the documentation included with your Microsoft Windows or Macintosh system.

Installing Adobe Fireworks

Before you begin using *Adobe Fireworks CS6 Classroom in a Book,* make sure that your computer is set up correctly and that it meets the necessary system requirements for software and hardware. You'll need a copy of Adobe Fireworks CS6, of course, but it's not included with this book. If you haven't purchased a copy, you can download a 30-day trial version from www.adobe.com/downloads. For system requirements and complete instructions on installing the software, see the

Adobe Fireworks CS6 Read Me file on the application DVD or on the Web at www. adobe.com/support.

Fireworks and Bridge are installed separately. You must install these applications from the Adobe Fireworks CS6 application DVD onto your hard disk; you cannot run the programs from the DVD. Follow the onscreen instructions. If you chose not to install Adobe Bridge, you may want to go back and install it from the DVD that Fireworks came on.

Make sure that your serial number is accessible before installing the application.

Starting Adobe Fireworks

You start Fireworks just as you do most software applications.

To start Adobe Fireworks in Windows:

Choose Start > All Programs > Adobe Fireworks CS6.

To start Adobe Fireworks in Mac OS X:

Open the Applications/Adobe Fireworks CS6 folder, and then double-click the Adobe Fireworks CS6 application icon.

Copying the Classroom in a Book files

The *Adobe Fireworks CS6 Classroom in a Book* CD includes folders containing all the electronic files for the lessons in the book. Each lesson has its own folder; you must copy the folders to your hard disk to complete the lessons. To save room on your disk, you can install only the folder necessary for each lesson as you need it, and remove it when you're done.

To install the lesson files, do the following:

1   Insert the Adobe Fireworks CS6 Classroom in a Book CD into your CD-ROM drive.

2   Browse the contents and locate the Lessons folder.

3   Do one of the following:

  • To copy all the lesson files, drag the Lessons folder from the CD onto your hard disk.

  • To copy only individual lesson files, first create a new folder on your hard disk and name it **Lessons**. Then, open the Lessons folder on the CD and drag the lesson folder or folders that you want to copy from the CD into the Lessons folder on your hard disk.

Additional resources

Adobe Fireworks CS6 Classroom in a Book is not meant to replace documentation that comes with the program or to be a comprehensive reference for every feature. Only the commands and options used in the lessons are explained in this book. For comprehensive information about program features and tutorials, please refer to these resources:

Adobe Community Help: Community Help brings together active Adobe product users, Adobe product team members, authors, and experts to give you the most useful, relevant, and up-to-date information about Adobe products.

To access Community Help: To invoke Help, press F1 or choose Help > Fireworks Help.

Adobe content is updated based on community feedback and contributions. You can add comments to content or forums—including links to web content—publish your own content using Community Publishing, or contribute Cookbook Recipes. Find out how to contribute at www.adobe.com/community/publishing/download.html.

See http://community.adobe.com/help/profile/faq.html for answers to frequently asked questions about Community Help.

Adobe Fireworks Help and Support: www.adobe.com/support/fireworks is where you can find and browse Help and Support content on adobe.com.

Adobe Forums: http://forums.adobe.com lets you tap into peer-to-peer discussions, questions, and answers on Adobe products.

Adobe TV: http://tv.adobe.com is an online video resource for expert instruction and inspiration about Adobe products, including a How To channel to get you started with your product: http://tv.adobe.com/product/fireworks/.

Adobe Design Center: www.adobe.com/designcenter offers thoughtful articles on design and design issues, a gallery showcasing the work of top-notch designers, tutorials, and more.

Adobe Developer Connection: www.adobe.com/devnet/fireworks.html is your source for technical articles, code samples, and how-to videos that cover Adobe Fireworks.

Resources for educators: www.adobe.com/education includes three free curriculums that use an integrated approach to teaching Adobe software and can be used to prepare for the Adobe Certified Associate exams.

Adobe Education Exchange: http://edexchange.adobe.com gives you access to a wealth of free resources, including course projects, tutorials, and lesson plans and also gives you, as an educator, a chance to collaborate and network with other educators.

Adobe Marketplace & Exchange: www.adobe.com/cfusion/exchange/ is a central resource for finding tools, services, extensions, code samples, and more to supplement and extend your Adobe products.

Adobe Fireworks CS6 product home page: www.adobe.com/products/fireworks

Adobe Labs: http://labs.adobe.com gives you access to early builds of cutting-edge technology, as well as forums where you can interact with both the Adobe development teams building that technology and other like-minded members of the community.

Also check out these useful sites and links:

- Community MX (www.communitymx.com): Additional free and commercial tutorials and samples

- Fireworks Zone (www.fireworkszone.com): Tutorials, art, and news on all things Fireworks

- Fireworks Guru (www.fireworksguruforum.com): Community forum where Fireworks enthusiasts share ideas, artwork, and solutions to design challenges

- John Dunning (http://johndunning.com/fireworks/): Prolific creator of Fireworks extensions

- Matt Stow (www.mattstow.com): Fireworks extension developer

- Aaron Beall (www.abeall.com): Fireworks designer and extension developer

- Darrell Heath (www.heathrowe.com): Fireworks evangelist

- Fireworks Interviews Hall of Fame (www.fireworksinterviews.com): In-depth interviews with more than 20 Fireworks designers

- Webportio (http://webportio.com): Free graphics for Adobe Fireworks

- FWPolice (http://fwpolice.com/): Free resource for Adobe Fireworks, including PNG samples and tutorials

- Adobe Fireworks Team blog (http://blogs.adobe.com/fireworks/): The latest news from the people directly responsible for bringing you Adobe Fireworks

Adobe certification

The Adobe training and certification programs are designed to help Adobe customers improve and promote their product-proficiency skills. There are four levels of certification:

- Adobe Certified Associate (ACA)
- Adobe Certified Expert (ACE)
- Adobe Certified Instructor (ACI)
- Adobe Authorized Training Center (AATC)

The Adobe Certified Associate (ACA) credential certifies that individuals have the entry-level skills to plan, design, build, and maintain effective communications using different forms of digital media.

The Adobe Certified Expert program is a way for expert users to upgrade their credentials. You can use Adobe certification as a catalyst for getting a raise, finding a job, or promoting your expertise.

If you are an ACE-level instructor, the Adobe Certified Instructor program takes your skills to the next level and gives you access to a wide range of Adobe resources.

Adobe Authorized Training Centers offer instructor-led courses and training on Adobe products, employing only Adobe Certified Instructors. A directory of AATCs is available at http://partners.adobe.com.

For information on the Adobe Certified programs, visit www.adobe.com/support/certification/main.html.

1 GETTING TO KNOW THE WORKSPACE

Lesson overview

In this lesson, you will get up to speed on the Adobe Fireworks CS6 interface. You'll learn how to do the following:

- Set up a new document

- Draw a vector shape

- Get acquainted with the Tools panel

- Use the Properties panel to change attributes of a selected object

- Customize the workspace

- Open an existing document

- Work with multiple documents in Tab view

- Combine different files into one document

- Save a file

 This lesson takes approximately 60 minutes to complete. Copy the Lesson01 folder into the Lessons folder that you created on your hard drive for these projects (or create it now, if you haven't already done so). As you work on this lesson, you won't be preserving the start files; if you need to restore the start files, copy them from the *Adobe Fireworks CS6 Classroom in a Book CD*.

Fireworks shares a similar interface to Adobe Photoshop, Adobe Dreamweaver, Adobe Flash, Adobe Illustrator, and Adobe InDesign. This common user interface makes it easy to switch from one application to another without feeling lost.

Getting started in Adobe Fireworks

Fireworks is a creative production tool, and sometimes with a creative tool, the hardest thing is figuring out where to start. We're here to help! Let's begin the process by creating a brand-new web page design and exploring the interface as we go. As you work through this exercise, refer to the figures on pages 5 and 6 to locate the main parts of the Fireworks interface.

1 Start Fireworks.

2 Choose Create New > Fireworks Document (PNG) from the Welcome screen. If you've previously changed your Preferences so that the Welcome screen does not show on startup, choose File > New.

Note: Fireworks ships with several predesigned starter templates, and you can even create your own custom templates. You'll learn more about templates in Lesson 13.

3 Set the width to 960 and the height of your document to 600 (pixels). Make sure the resolution and canvas color are at the default settings of 72 Pixels/Inch and White, and then click OK.

The New Document dialog box closes and a new blank document opens in the Fireworks work area, as shown in this screen shot of the Windows version of Fireworks.

Main Toolbar
(Windows Only)

Application Bar (Main Menus, Scroll and Zoom Tools,
Workspace Switcher, and Help Search Field)

Panel Dock

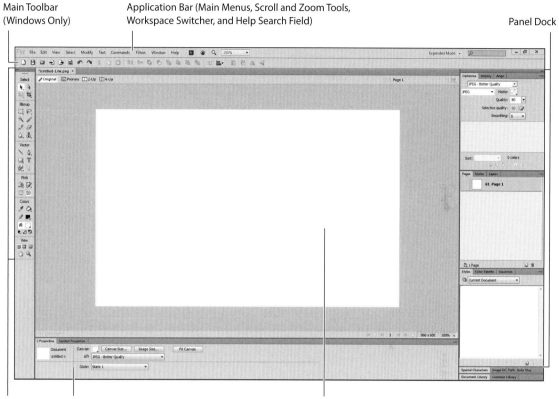

Tools Panel   Properties Panel

Document Window

The preset workspace in Fireworks for Windows consists of the Application bar and Main toolbar at the top of the screen, the Tools panel on the left, and open panels in the panel dock on the right. By default, when you have multiple documents open they appear as multiple tabs in one document window, but you can float individual documents by dragging their tabs away from the main Document window.

By default, the Mac interface is organized a little differently when compared to the Windows interface. The initial workspace for the Mac version is similar, except the Application bar is separate from the Menu bar, and there is no Main toolbar. The panels are grouped into a floating *panel dock.* In Windows, all the panels and windows that belong to an application are contained within a rectangular frame that is distinct from other applications you may have open. The area within the frame is opaque, completely obscuring any application windows that may be behind it.

Note: The Fireworks user interface is similar to the ones used in Adobe Illustrator, Adobe Photoshop, and Adobe Flash, so learning how to use the tools and organize panels in one application means that you'll know how to use them in the others.

You can create a similar appearance in the Mac version of Fireworks by turning on the Application Frame, which is disabled by default. To enable the Application Frame, choose Window > Use Application Frame (Control+Command+F). On a Mac, however, the Menu bar is always attached to the top of the screen and can't be moved, so it's not part of the Application Frame.

The default setting, for both Windows and Mac, is that multiple document windows display in a tab view. This means that only the active document (tab) is visible at any given time. To edit or view a different open document, just click on its tab to bring it to the front. If you want to detach a document window for side-by-side viewing, simply drag the tab away from the tab bar to view it in a separate, floating document window. You can also dock numerous documents above and beside each other, enabling you to see multiple files at one time. (To use this feature on the Mac, you must have the Application Frame enabled.)

Menu Bar

Application Bar

OS X Desktop

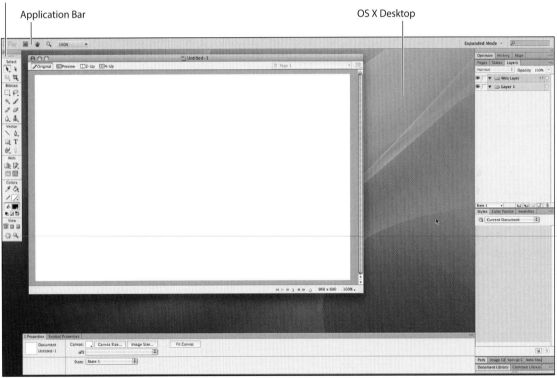

What is the right resolution?

Pixels per inch (ppi) was traditionally a unit of measure relative only to the print world. But with the growing popularity of high-resolution tablet devices and smartphones, PPI is taking on a new relevance. When dealing with most screen graphics, your concern should be the *pixel dimensions* (640 x 480, 760 x 420, and so on). The default resolution Fireworks begins with is 96 ppi (72 ppi on a Mac), and it can be left as is, unless you're specifically creating graphics for higher-resolution devices such as the iPhone4 or the BlackBerry Playbook.

If you are planning to use Fireworks for a print project, ask your printer what resolution you should be using. A general guideline for print is 300 ppi. Be aware, however, that the strengths of Fireworks lie in screen graphics, not graphics intended for the printed page. For example, you cannot change the rulers to display inches—only pixels matter on the screen, so pixels are all you get for the rulers. Likewise, Fireworks does not understand or use CMYK color or printer profiles, so your end result may not print accurately.

On the plus side, Fireworks supports PDF export, so printing your designs, for example to show to a client, has become a bit more predictable.

Preparing the canvas

You should set (activate) a couple of features before you start working. These features will remain set from this point forward when you create or open a new document.

1   If the rulers are not visible, choose View > Rulers (Ctrl+Alt+R in Windows, Command+Option+R in Mac).

2   Choose View > Tooltips (Ctrl+] in Windows, Command+] in Mac) to turn on tooltips.

Turning rulers on makes aligning objects on your canvas much easier; this is especially helpful when your work gets complex. Enabling tooltips provides you with extra information at the cursor position for the tool you're using.

Using the Tools panel

The Tools panel in Fireworks is separated into six labeled areas: Select, Bitmap, Vector, Web, Colors, and View. This arrangement helps you to quickly and easily identify the appropriate tool for the graphic object you plan to work on or create.

The *Select tools* let you select, crop, and even scale or distort objects. The main selection tool is the Pointer tool ( ).

The *Bitmap tools* are used for editing or creating new bitmap objects. You can make bitmap selections with any one of several bitmap selection tools, such as the Magic Wand or the Marquee tool. You can do basic photo editing by using the Rubber Stamp (also known as the Clone tool) or selectively sharpen, blur, lighten, darken, or smudge pixels that are part of a bitmap image. You can paint or draw bitmap objects using the Brush or Pencil tool. The only caveat is that you can't use Bitmap tools to alter vector objects.

The *Vector tools* let you create or edit vector paths and shapes. As you saw in the first exercise, you can draw vector shapes on the canvas quite easily. You can use the Pen tool to create your own custom shapes or paths. Of special note is the Text tool (T). Some people don't realize this, but text is actually a vector—be it in Photoshop, Microsoft Word, Fireworks, or many other applications. Not surprisingly, you can't use vector tools to edit bitmap objects.

The *Web toolset* is not large, but it contains two important tools that are mainstays of Fireworks and its ability to create interactive documents and optimize graphics for use on the Web. You can create interactivity such as hyperlinks with the Hotspot tools, or take things further by creating interactive visual effects such as rollovers or tap events, using the Slice tool. The Slice tool also allows you to optimize specific graphics for the Web, ensuring the best possible combination of file format, image quality and file size for a sliced graphic. The other two tools simply show or hide these web slices and hotspots on the canvas.

The *Colors tools* let you control Stroke and Fill colors. Remember, the roots of Fireworks are in the vector world, so you will not see Foreground and Background color options, as you would in primarily bitmap-editing software such as Photoshop. You can sample colors from anywhere on the desktop using the Eyedropper tool, or fill a bitmap selection with color by using the Paint Bucket or Gradient tool. You can also swap the fill and stroke colors or reset the fill and stroke to their defaults.

Last are the *View tools*. You can toggle among three views: Standard, Full Screen with Menus, and Full Screen (no menus or panels visible). The Zoom tool and Hand (scroll) tool are at the bottom of the View toolset. You can also toggle between views using the F key.

Take some time and check out the various tools. Remember, you can't break anything!

▶ Tip: Hovering your mouse cursor over any tool in the Tools panel brings up a tooltip, indicating the tool name and keyboard shortcut for that tool.

More tools than meet the eye

Take a closer look at the icons in the Tools panel. You will notice several icons have a small triangle in the bottom-right corner. This triangle indicates that multiple tools are available from within that square. To access the other tools, click and hold the icon.

Click and hold the Rectangle tool to see a flyout list of other vector tools. The three shapes at the top of the vector tools list (rectangle, ellipse, and polygon) are vector primitives, or basic shapes. Everything below the dividing line falls into the category of special vectors called Auto Shapes; they are controlled "under the hood" by JavaScript and are great for creating many common but complex vector shapes without the need of any drawing skills. You'll draw an ellipse in your document.

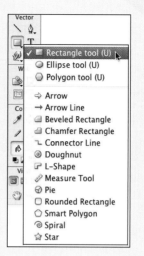

What's a primitive shape?

The word "*primitive*" borrows the same definition used in many 3D modeling applications: *a geometric form or expression from which another is derived.* In other words, the Fireworks primitive tools provide a start toward building shapes of your own.

Drawing a vector shape

Creating shapes will be an important part of almost any Fireworks project. The canvas is the visible working area for your designs. Objects that extend outside the canvas appear clipped, but the image information is not lost; just drag the object into the canvas to show the full object.

1 Select the Rectangle tool from the Vector section of the Tools panel.

2 Click the Fill color box—the one with the small paint bucket to the left of it—in the Colors section of the Tools panel to set the fill color for the rectangle. The fill color is the one that will be inside your object.

3 Using the eyedropper pointer that appears, select a medium light gray (hex value of #BBBBBB) from the Fill Color pop-up

window. After you select the color, the color picker closes automatically and the new color displays in the color box.

4   Bring the cursor over to the canvas. Note the small gray bubble, displaying X and Y coordinates. This is the Tooltips feature at work, giving you the pixel-precise location of the cursor.

5   Hold the mouse button, and drag down and to the right for at least 100 pixels. The tooltip follows the cursor, displaying the current size of the rectangle.

6   Release the mouse button when you see the coordinates reach approximately 100 pixels in height and width.

The rectangle will stay selected after you release the mouse. With most objects on the Fireworks canvas, you can tell an object is selected by the presence of a light blue border around the object and the small control boxes at each corner. The rectangle is a special, grouped vector object, however, so you won't see the blue border when it is selected (more on grouping objects in Lesson 2).

Saving the file

Before going any further, it's a good idea to save your work.

1   Choose File > Save.

2   Browse to the Lesson01 folder.

3   Change the filename to **webpage.fw.png**.

4   Click Save.

Resizing a rectangle numerically

You can resize objects using a variety of tools such as the Scale tool or even the Pointer tool, but for accurate, pixel-level control, use the dimension fields in the Properties panel, which, along with repositioning the object, is what you will do now.

1   Place your cursor in the Width field of the Properties panel.

2   Select whatever value is currently in the field and replace it with **180**.

3   Press the Tab key to move to the Height field and change its value to **400**.

● **Note:** You can also choose File > Save As to display the full Save As dialog box. Fireworks gives you many more file format options to choose from when you choose Save As, including JPEG, GIF, and Flattened PNG, as well as Photoshop PSD.

4 Press Tab again to move to the X field. This field controls the distance of an object from the left side of the canvas.

5 Replace the existing value with **20**.

6 Tab once more to the Y field and set a value of **140**.

Rounding off the rectangle

Remember that the rectangle is a special vector object? With rectangles, you can easily and symmetrically alter the corner radius of each corner with one action. Try it now.

1 In the Properties panel, locate the Roundness field and change the value from 0 to **20**.

That's it. The rectangle now has four round corners. Quick and easy, right?

Duplicating and customizing the rectangle

Creating duplicates of existing objects is also easy to do, and like many things in Fireworks, there are several ways to do it. One of the fastest methods is using keyboard commands, which you will do next.

1 Make sure the rectangle object is still selected (look for the blue control boxes on each corner). If the rectangle isn't selected, use the Pointer tool (upper-left corner of the Tools panel) to select it.

2 Press Ctrl+Shift+D (Windows) or Command+Shift+D (Mac). While it's hard to tell at the moment, you've just created a copy of the original rectangle.

3 If it's not already active, select the Pointer tool and drag the new rectangle toward the right. As you do so, you should see a red dashed line appear at the top of the rectangle. This is a Smart Guide, and it's designed to help you align objects in relation to each other or to the canvas. Notice that the Smart Guide helps you keep the new rectangle aligned to the top edge of the original rectangle. If you move too high or too low, the Guide disappears. If you get within 3 to 5 pixels of the top edge of the first rectangle, your new shape snaps to that location.

4 Drag the rectangle until the X value of the tooltip shows at or near 220. Don't worry about being precise; you've already learned in the previous exercise how to reposition an object at the pixel level, using the Properties panel.

5 If you couldn't get the rectangle to position itself at 220 pixels, use the X field in the Properties panel now to set that value.

● **Note:** You can lock the proportions of your objects from within the Properties panel by clicking on the small square to the left of the Width and Height fields. This helps you to scale objects proportionally. If the small square linking the width and height is hollow, proportions are not constrained. Clicking on the square makes it solid and adds solid connecting lines between the Width and Height fields, locking the proportions of the selected object.

6 Change the width of the rectangle to **720** pixels, using the W field.

7 Save the file by pressing Command+S (Mac) or Ctrl+S (Windows).

More about the Fireworks PNG format

Like many applications, Fireworks uses a native format that gives you access to all the creative options within the program—in this case, a modified version of the PNG format. As you add objects, effects, layers, or pages (to name a few features), this information is stored within the Fireworks PNG file so that you can open and edit the file easily at any time.

Occasionally, this causes some confusion for new users, because there is also a standard, flattened PNG format common to many graphics applications. When you're saving files, Fireworks differentiates between these "flavors" by indicating *Fireworks PNG* or *Flattened PNG* in the Save As Type field. If you just choose Save, Fireworks assumes you want to save the file as a native Fireworks PNG file, by default, and doesn't normally give you the option to choose a file type.

Fireworks CS6 augments the file name of any file that contains editable objects, adding a .fw extension prior to the true PNG file extension. You saw this when you saved the file you've been working on. This optional .fw extension is present only when you choose Save or Save As for a file that contains editable elements.

Although the .fw is not required as part of the file name, you will find using it makes differentiating editable Fireworks PNG files from flattened PNG files easier. In fact, for years, many Fireworks designers would add the .fw to an editable PNG file by choice.

Using the Properties panel

The Properties panel is context sensitive, so the contents of the panel changes based on the active selection on the canvas. As you select different tools, the Properties panel updates and displays editable attributes for the selected tool.

As you saw in the first exercise, you can easily find and add a rectangle shape and change its fill color using the Tools panel. When a shape is selected, you can change many other vector attributes in the Properties panel, was well.

1 Select the Pointer tool from the upper left of the Tools panel.

2 On the canvas, click on the left rectangle to select it.

3 In the Properties panel, click Gradient Fill icon.

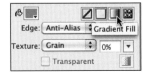

The rectangle fills with a default linear gradient, and the gradient editor opens, allowing you to edit the gradient colors. The long vertical line is called the Gradient Control Arm and lets you adjust the length, position, and angle of the gradient.

The top swatch sliders (little black boxes) control the opacity of the gradient. The swatches underneath the gradient allow you to change or add colors.

4 Click the leftmost color swatch and use the eyedropper to select the gray hex value of #BBBBBB.

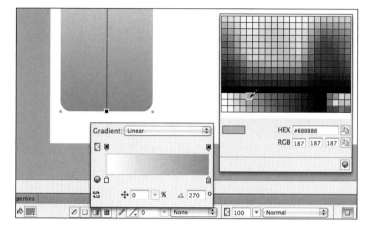

5 Click the right color swatch and change it to a dark gray, like #333333.

6 When you're done, click away from the Edit Gradient pop-up window to close it.

The other rectangle needs the same treatment, but rather than go through all those steps again, you'll save time by using the Paste Attributes features.

7 Choose Edit > Copy from the main menu bar. Make sure that the smaller rectangle is still selected.

8 Select the larger rectangle, using the Pointer tool.

9 Choose Edit > Paste Attributes. The larger rectangle takes on the same fill as the smaller one.

10 Save the file once again, by pressing Ctrl +S (Windows) or Command+S (Mac).

● **Note:** If you want to add other colors, just click the mouse directly under the gradient preview bar and choose a new color for the new swatch. Feel free to experiment with the other Fill categories, but remember to come back to the gradient style and colors indicated earlier.

● **Note:** In the Gradient Editor you can quickly reverse the gradient direction by clicking the Reverse Gradient button.

Quick access to fill types in the Properties panel

The Properties panel in Fireworks CS6 has made many features more discoverable. You've already seen how easy it is to add a gradient fill to a vector shape, but that gradient fill type is only one of four quick buttons on the Properties panel.

You can quickly change the fill of a vector object by choosing (from left to right) No Fill, Solid Fill, Gradient Fill, or Pattern Fill.

Configuring panels and panel groups

Your computer monitor is one of those places where you're always trying to make more room. No matter what size the screen is—or how many we have— we designers always want more room to build our designs. Panels take up a fair portion of the Fireworks interface by default, but you can carve yourself a little more room by customizing them. Panels contain controls that help you edit aspects of a selected object or elements of a document. Each panel is draggable, so you can group panels in custom arrangements.

Many panels are visible by default in an area on the right side of the interface called the *panel dock*. A dock is a collection of panels or panel groups displayed together, usually in a vertical arrangement. Resizing the docked panels is one way to quickly make more room for your design.

You can group and ungroup panels by dragging them into and out of the existing panel groups docked to the side of the screen.

The first time you start up Fireworks, the dock is in Expanded mode, in which the foremost panel in each group is fully expanded so you can see its features. Collapse individual panel groups by clicking once (or double-clicking on a Mac) on the empty area of the gray tab bar.

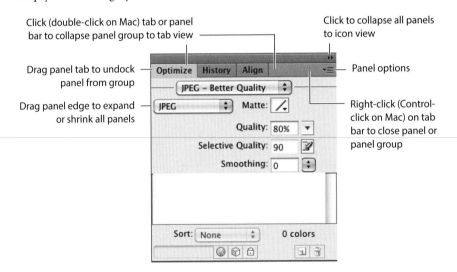

Click (double-click on Mac) tab or panel bar to collapse panel group to tab view

Click to collapse all panels to icon view

Drag panel tab to undock panel from group

Drag panel edge to expand or shrink all panels

Panel options

Right-click (Control-click on Mac) on tab bar to close panel or panel group

In the Application bar you can see the current workspace configuration in the Workspace Switcher. You can quickly reduce the dock width by choosing a different workspace.

1 Select the Workspace Switcher, and choose Iconic Mode. All panels collapse, and the dock narrows to display only panel icons.

2 Click any panel icon. The panel group expands, and the chosen panel becomes active.

3 Click the panel icon (or the double-arrow icon) to return the group to its collapsed state.

4 Position the mouse over different icons to see a tooltip that shows which panel each icon represents.

5 Choose Iconic Mode With Panel Names from the Workspace Switcher. This setting makes the docked panel groups wider, but not nearly as wide as the default Expanded mode. If you want to free up desktop space but aren't sure what the panel icons symbolize, this mode might just be perfect for you.

▶ **Tip:** You can also collapse the Properties panel by double-clicking on the empty area of the tab bar. Double-clicking again returns it to visibility.

▶ **Tip:** You can also quickly collapse the entire panel dock by double-clicking on the dark gray strip at the top of the dock.

Customizing panel arrangements

In addition to taking advantage of the existing preset workspaces, you can configure the workspace specifically to help you work the way that's best for you.

It's easy to arrange the panels and panel groups in a configuration that helps you work faster. For example, some designers like to be able to see both the Pages and Layers panels at the same time. In this exercise, you will separate the Pages panel from its current panel group.

1 Switch back to Expanded Mode.

2 Drag the Pages panel tab just above the panel group. A blue highlighted drop zone appears.

3 Release the mouse button; the Pages panel forms its own group, just above the Layers and States panel group.

4 Drag the States panel tab to the right of the Layers panel tab. Notice how easily they just slide across each other.

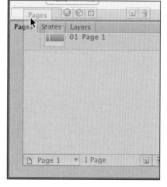

● **Note:** You can access all the available panels in Fireworks by choosing the desired panel's name from the Window menu. In some cases, these panels will appear floating above the design.

Creating custom workspaces

When you create a workspace that suits you, you then save it so that you can quickly switch from a preset, compact mode to a dual-screen mode or even just a custom panel view that holds the panels you would use most often.

Tip: Be aware that in Mac OS Lion, the Library (not the user Library, but the main library for the hard drive) is hidden from you! In order to show it, you have to go to Go > Go to Folder and type ~/Library in the field, then click Go.

To create a custom workspace, set the panels you wish to see at their desired size and visibility.

1 Select the Workspace Switcher.

2 Choose Save Current. A dialog box appears where you can name the new workspace arrangement.

3 Name the workspace and click OK, or click Cancel if you don't want to save the configuration. If you save the workspace, it will appear in the Workspace Switcher from this point on.

Deleting a custom workspace

Although you can easily *make* a custom workspace, *deleting* it isn't so easy. There is no way to remove a custom workspace within the Fireworks interface. You can overwrite the workspace by changing the panel setup and then saving the new workspace with the old name, but you're still stuck with the workspace.

To remove a custom workspace, you need to go to Application Data\Adobe\ Fireworks CS6\Commands\Workspace Layouts in Windows or ~/Library/Application Support/Adobe/Fireworks CS6/Commands/Workspace Layouts/ (where "~" represents your Home folder) on the Mac. Then delete the JSP and XML files associated with your custom workspace.

Working with multiple documents

Before we finish this lesson, let's have a look at the Fireworks CS6 document window features. Fireworks offers a variety of ways to view open document windows, and knowing how to customize the views can speed up your workflow, such as when you want to drag an object from one file to another.

When you have more than one file opened, the document windows for each are tabbed and easily accessible.

1 Choose File > Open, and browse to the Lesson01 Folder from the CD.

2 Ctrl-click (Windows) or Command-click (Mac) to select the canoe.jpg and logo.fw.png files.

3 Click the Open button. If you haven't changed your Preferences from the defaults, all three files are now open in Fireworks and you can access each one by clicking on the appropriate tab at the top of the document window.

Creating a floating document window

Tabbed documents function much like the tabbed panels. You can drag them to change the tab order. You can even drag a tabbed document out from the tab bar to float it.

Note: If you have chosen not to use the Application Frame on the Mac (Window > Use Application Frame), your document windows will still open in tabs, but you won't be able to use the docked viewing mode described in Step 2. In the classic Mac view, you can either have documents tabbed together or floating, or a combination of both.

1 Click and hold on the canoe.jpg tab, and drag it away from the other tabs. When you let go, it becomes a floating window, independent of the other document windows.

The document-arrangement options don't stop there, however.

2 Drag the logo.fw.png window to the right side of the main document window until you see a blue highlight (thin blue line) appear between the panel dock and the document window, much like you saw when you were moving the Pages panel. To make things even more obvious, the window you are dragging turns semitransparent.

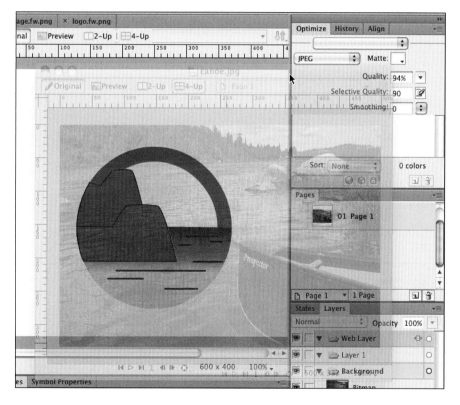

3 Release the window; you now have two sets of docked document windows. You can have as many files as you like docked in this manner.

Both floating and docked windows support tabbed documents.

4 Select the logo.fw.png file, and drag its tab over to the canoe.jpg window.

5   Move the file so the cursor appears in the tab bar. The entire bar highlights, indicating you can dock this image with the canoe.jpg file.

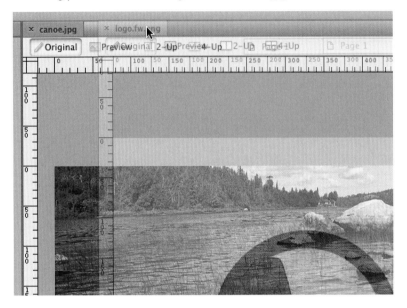

6   Release the file; it is now tabbed with the other document window.

Dragging and dropping between docked windows

With the webpage_final.fw.png now separate from the other two files, you can easily drag and drop the canoe and logo images onto the canvas area of the web page design. In any design where you need to combine elements from different files, this workflow can be helpful.

1   Select the Pointer tool (black arrow) from the upper left of the Tools panel.

2   Click to select the artwork in the logo file, and drag it over to the web page design.

3   Position the image at the top of the design, near top left. It will overlap the small rounded rectangle, but that's fine for now.

4   Release the mouse button.

5   Select the canoe.jpg file, and use the Pointer tool to drag the canoe photo from its own canvas to the web page canvas. Place it near the middle left. Don't worry about overlap.

6   Close the canoe and logo document windows, by clicking on the small **x** to the left of the file name. If prompted to save the files, choose Don't Save.

    The webpage_final.fw.png file expands to fill the available desktop area.

Scaling objects

This time you will use the Scale tool, in conjunction with the Tooltips feature, to resize the new images.

1 Select the logo image by clicking on it with the Pointer tool.

2 Choose the Scale tool (⬚). A bounding box appears around the logo.

3 Click the bottom-right corner of the bounding box and drag upward until the tooltip reads W: 90, H: 90.

4 Release the mouse and press the Enter or Return key to lock in the transformation.

5 Use the Properties panel to numerically position the logo 20 pixels from the top and left of the canvas, or the Pointer tool to drag it into place. You pick. Live dangerously.

6 Use the Scale tool to resize the canoe photo down to 160 pixels wide. If you scale from any corner, you will proportionately resize the selected object.

7 Double-click within the bounding box or press the Enter/Return key to lock in the new size.

8 Select the Pointer and position the canoe photo at X: 30, Y: 420. The tooltips will help guide you and, as always, you can use the Properties panel to make pixel-perfect adjustments.

▶ **Tip:** The default behavior in Fireworks is such that selecting an object on the canvas makes it active, unlike in Photoshop where this direct selection option must be enabled.

● **Note:** Because Fireworks moves so seamlessly between vector and bitmap artwork, you probably didn't even realize that the logo file was a vector object!

Adding placeholder text

Just to make things look a bit more complete, you'll add some placeholder text to the larger rectangle before ending this lesson. First, you'll set your text options with the Text tool, then you'll add the text using a Menu Command.

1 Select the Text tool ([T]) from the Tools panel.

The Properties panel updates, displaying options for working with the Text tool.

2 From the Font Family drop-down list, choose Arial.

3 Set the Size to 16 pixels.

4 Set the Color to White, by clicking on the Fill Color box and choosing white from the color picker. (Select the Solid fill icon from the color picker, if necessary, as Fireworks remembers the last used attributes for a given tool).

With the exception of Fill and Stroke, Fireworks will remember these text attributes. The next time you select the Text tool, the values you set in the previous steps will reappear in the Properties panel.

Fill and Stroke attributes are also tied to the vector tools (remember that text is basically vectors), so if you were to create or edit a shape and change the fill properties, those values would overwrite any text properties for the fill and stroke.

With these settings in place, you will now add some text.

5 Select Commands > Text > Lorem Ipsum.

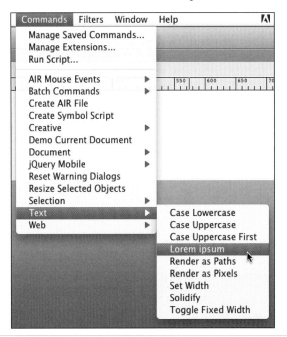

A paragraph of text appears in a text block on the canvas.

6 Use the Pointer tool to position the text block at X: 240, Y: 150.

Note that when active, the text block has a blue bounding box, indicating its size. The bounding box has control handles at all four corners and in the middle of each boundary line.

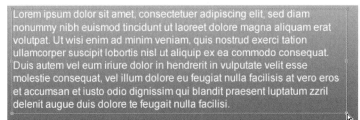

7 Using the Pointer tool, drag the bottom-right control handle to the right, until the text block size is 680 pixels wide. You can fine-tune this dimension using the W field in the Properties panel, also.

8 Double-click inside the text block. Your cursor changes to a text I-beam.

9 Click and drag to select all the text.

10 Press Ctrl+C (Windows) or Command+C (Mac) to copy the selected text to the clipboard.

11 Place the cursor at the end of the paragraph and press the Enter/Return key twice.

12 Press Ctrl+V (Windows) or Command+V (Mac) to paste the paragraph.

13 Press the Enter/Return Key twice to paste the paragraph in one more time, filling the rectangle area.

14 Save the file.

When you're done, compare the result to the figure below.

Undoing steps

The ability to reverse your actions is an all-important feature of imaging software. Fireworks gives you a couple of ways to undo an error.

Undo is, of course, the tried-and-true, familiar method:

- Ctrl+Z (Windows) or Command+Z (Mac) undoes the last action taken. To go further back, keep pressing Ctrl+Z or Command+Z.

- Ctrl+Y (Windows) or Command+Y (Mac) reapplies the last undone step.

Your other option is to use the History method. Select the History panel from your grouped panels, or choose Window > History. Dragging the History slider (left of the panel) up takes you back in time. Dragging the slider down moves you forward. The default number of history steps you can undo is 20. You can change this number in the Preferences panel (discussed later in this book), but we recommend not exceeding 50 steps to maintain stability in the application.

Review questions

1 What is the importance of the Tools panel?

2 How do you collapse panels, and why would you?

3 If you can't find a panel in the workspace, how can you locate it?

4 How does the Properties panel help when you are working on a design?

5 How can you quickly add placeholder text?

Review answers

1 The Tools panel is where all the selection, editing, and creative tools are located. From cropping an image to scaling it, whether retouching or building vector objects or adding interactive elements, everything you need begins in the Tools panel.

2 You can collapse panels by choosing a different workspace or by clicking on the dark-gray bar at the top of a panel group. This can free up a significant amount of room in your workspace, letting you see more of your design without having to zoom out as much.

3 To open a panel, choose Window > [panel name], or press the panel's shortcut (listed in the Window menu).

4 The Properties panel is a context-sensitive panel, changing its options as you select different tools or various objects on the canvas. The Properties panel provides one handy location where you can easily alter tool and object attributes.

5 To insert a paragraph of Lorem Ipsum placeholder text, select Commands > Text > Lorem Ipsum. The text takes on the last text attributes that were set in the Properties panel.

2 THE PAGES, STATES, AND LAYERS PANELS: FUNDAMENTAL WORKFLOW TOOLS

Lesson overview

Layers are probably the most important workflow and design tool you have in Fireworks. Simply put, they add structure to your document. In this lesson, you'll learn how to do the following:

- Import new pages

- Create new layers

- Create sublayers

- Change the stacking order of layers

- Rename layers

- Protect layers and objects

- Access layer options

- Edit content on different states

This lesson takes approximately 90 minutes to complete. Copy the Lesson02 folder into the Lessons folder that you created on your hard drive for these projects (or create it now, if you haven't already done so). As you work on this lesson, you won't preserve the start files. If you need to restore the start files, copy them from the *Adobe Fireworks CS6 Classroom in a Book* CD.

Understanding the relationship between pages,
layers, and states is probably the most important
concept to grasp in Fireworks. These elements add
structure to your document.

About pages, layers, and states

A Fireworks document can contain multiple pages, layers, and states. At its simplest, a brand-new Fireworks document begins with a single page (Page 1), a single state (State 1), and two layers (the Web layer and Layer 1).

Pages

The ability to add multiple pages to a Fireworks document means you can create and store multiple designs of different dimensions and resolution inside a single file.

This is a real productivity booster, because you can store several unique designs for one project all in the same file. For example, you can mock up an entire website or the horizontal and vertical layouts for a smartphone or tablet application design within a single file. You can then link pages using hotspots or slices to create a truly interactive experience for testing and proof of concept.

Each page can hold multiple layers and states.

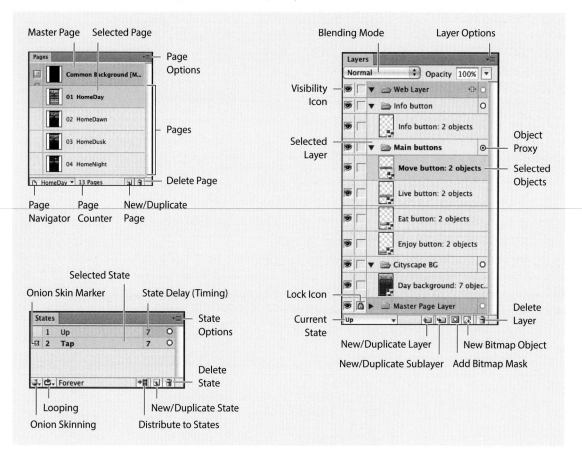

Layers

Layers help you organize and group your artwork, as well as specify which artwork is visible and how objects are stacked (overlap). Each layer can contain multiple bitmap, vector, and text objects.

With a simple design, you may be able to place all the objects in a single layer. As you add more objects to a design, however, keeping everything in a single layer becomes problematic; it becomes harder to locate specific images or text areas because you have to scroll through a very long list. Consequently, staying organized becomes a lot harder.

Layers allow related design objects to be independent from one another. Used properly, they impose a sense of order in your document. You can add or remove layers, or the objects within them, without affecting other elements in the design. You can change how objects within layers interact with other layers by changing the stacking order of layers. As you change the order of layers, objects overlap differently. You can move objects from one layer to another as well.

You can hide layers from view to make it easier to select or work with other objects, and you can lock layers so they will not be selected accidentally. You can even share layers across specific states or specific pages in a design.

States

States are useful when you need to:

- Create frame-by-frame animation.

- Show the different states of an object, such as the normal and hover states of a website navigation button.

- Control the visibility of objects based on user interaction. For example, hovering over a button displays a new button state, and then clicking that button displays new content elsewhere on the page.

Every page contains at least one state. A design requiring no interactivity may need only a single state. If you require interactivity or frame-based animation, you simply add new states. Each state represents the visibility, effects, and position of objects on each layer in that particular state, of the selected page.

Note: The interactivity described for states is controlled by adding special objects—slices or hotspots—to a special layer, called the Web layer. Regardless of your plans for the file, you cannot delete the Web layer. To learn more about hotspots and slices, read Lessons 10, 11, and 12.

Note: Web layers and regular layers can also contain sublayers that help you further organize your design. You will learn more about sublayers in this lesson.

Getting started

In this lesson, you'll be editing a mock-up for a smartphone application. You'll reorganize the file by working on the layers and adding pages for the mock-up created by another artist, as well as add a new state to show a *tap* event.

1   In Fireworks, choose File > Open and select the file localpicks_320x480_start. fw.png in the Lesson02 folder.

2   Click OK.

Remember that in Lesson 1, you separated the Pages panel from the States and Layers panels. Separating the panels will help in the coming steps.

3   Select the Pages panel. If necessary, drag the bottom of the Pages panel lower in the panel dock, so you can see all the pages.

4   Select the second page from the page list. Notice how the design changes on the canvas.

When you select a page, all you see on the canvas are the contents of that particular page.

Note: As you change the order, the sequence numbers of the affected pages also change. By default, Fireworks automatically changes the page numbers based on their stacking order, from top to bottom. To turn off numbering, choose Numbering from the Pages panel menu.

5   Drag page 09 (Meridien_back) below the page named Meridien_front. This puts the pages in a more suitable order for your next task.

You can change the order of pages in a document by dragging a page above or below another page.

New Page
Duplicate Page
Delete Page
Rename Page
Link To Master Page

Set As Master Page
Reset Master Page

Export Selected Page(s)...

• Numbering
Thumbnail Options...

Help

Pages

05 HomeNight

06 Info

07 One_Ton_Front

08 One_Ton_Back

09 Meridien_Back

10 Merdien_Front

Meridien_.▾   10 Pages

Importing pages

Next you will add pages to this mock-up. Make sure the Merdien_back page is still selected.

1   Choose File > Import, and open localpicks_320x480_restaurants.fw.png.

2   Choose Open, and the Import Page window appears. The document you're importing contains four pages, which you can preview by using the drop-down list at the top of the window or the navigation buttons below the preview image. You need to import the Gabel_front page first, so make sure that is the page currently displayed.

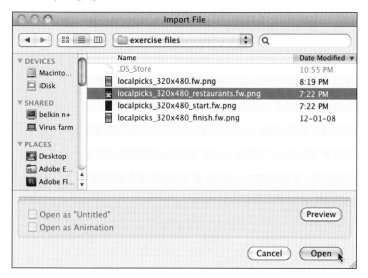

3   Select the Insert After Current Page option.

    This option creates a new page in your open file rather than importing the artwork onto the currently active page.

4 Click Insert (Windows) or Open (Mac).

5 Click Ignore when a warning message asks if you want to overwrite existing styles. This message appears because both files include the same styles. Styles are prebuilt combinations of special effects that can be added to vector objects.

Fireworks adds a new page and uses the same page name as you saw in the Import Page dialog box.

6 Select the Gabel_front page, if necessary.

7 Repeat steps 1–5, this time importing the Gabel_back page.

8 Repeat steps 1–5 for the final two pages of the restaurant file. Remember to make sure the last page of the main file is active before going through the import steps.

9 Choose File > Save As. Name the file localpicks_320x480.fw.png .

Photoshop and multipage Fireworks files

Although you can save a Fireworks document as a Photoshop file (PSD), doing so saves the currently active page only, because Photoshop has no way of interpreting multiple pages within a single document.

If you need to return to Photoshop, you can do one of the following:

- Export pages to files: Choose File > Export, and choose Pages to Files from the Export List. This produces a flattened PNG of the first state of each page.

- Save as a Photoshop file: Choose File > Save As and choose Photoshop from the Save as Type menu. This produces an editable, layered Photoshop file of the currently selected page and state.

Doug Hungarter has written a free extension called Convert Pages to PSD, which allows you to export all the pages in a Fireworks document as separate PSD files. To learn more about this extension, visit the Adobe Exchange: www.adobe.com/cfusion/exchange/index.cfm?event=extensionDetail&loc=en_us&extid=1849527#.

Note: Fireworks includes Photoshop Live Effects primarily so you can continue to edit Photoshop layer styles in Fireworks. However, the Photoshop Live Effects dialog box isn't as robust as the Layer Styles dialog box in Photoshop.

Creating a Master page

A Master page is a useful tool for sharing design elements that need to appear consistently on all pages within a design and in newly created pages. Although a powerful timesaver for designs that use consistent elements across multiple pages, a Master page is not always needed—or preferred. For this design you will designate a Master page to handle a couple of common elements: the smartphone status bar at the top and the inactive page indicators at the bottom of the screen.

1   Select the Background elements page (Page 01).

2   Right-click (Control+Click on Mac) the page to access the Pages panel options.

3   Select Set As Master Page. It's that simple.

After you set a page as the Master page, the look of its page object in the Pages panel changes slightly. The page number disappears, and Fireworks adds the additional text "[Master Page]" to the page label. A small (admittedly too small) icon displays on the left, denoting this page as the Master page.

4   Select other pages in the design. The status bar appears in all of them, as do the inactive page indicators.

5   With any page except the Master page selected, scroll to the bottom of the Layers panel.

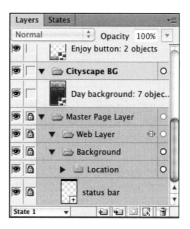

As you can see, Fireworks added a new layer called the Master Page Layer. By default, this layer is added to *all* pages in the design, appears at the bottom of the layer stack, and is locked. You cannot unlock the layer to edit the objects in the Master page. If you need to change Master page elements, you must select the Master page itself and edit the objects within the page.

6   Save the file.

● **Note:** To learn more about pages and creating links between them, read Lesson 10.

You will learn more about using a Master page in Lessons 10, 11, and 12.

Working with layers and objects

In this and the following sections, you'll continue to work with the localpicks_320x480.fw.png file. The name of the game is organization. You will be naming individual objects and layers with meaningful names, making it easier to locate and select elements within your design. You will be altering the stacking order of layers to make the layer hierarchy more visually understandable, and you will learn some time-saving workflow tips in the form of sharing layers to pages.

Naming objects

The number of objects in a Fireworks design can grow quickly as you build your design. And many objects may be quite small, especially if you're designing an application layout, making them hard to identify from the thumbnail view in the Layers panel. Fireworks helps you by highlighting independent objects in red as you move the mouse over them. This highlight indicates the independent object in that particular spot; you can then click to select that specific object. You can help yourself identify objects by giving your objects meaningful names, which is what you will do now.

1 Select the HomeDay page, and then switch to the Layers panel by clicking the Layers tab.

2 To see more of the Layers panel, and to minimize the need for scrolling, collapse the other visible panel groups by double-clicking the gray tab bar next to the panel names in other (non-Layers) panel groups.

3 On the canvas, select the red icon near the upper-right corner of the design. Fireworks highlights an object in the Layers panel.

4 In the Layers panel, double-click on this highlighted object called—none too descriptively—Group: 2 objects.

5 Rename it **Info button: 2 objects**.

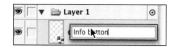

6 In the Layers panel, click the object below the Info button. Check the canvas, and you will see the Move button is highlighted, denoted by a small blue square at each corner of the button.

7 Double-click its name in the Layers panel, and change it to **Move button: 2 objects**.

8 Repeat this process for the remaining objects (the final three buttons and the background group.) You can select the objects on the canvas or just click on them in the Layers panel. Rename the other objects, from the top down, as follows:

- Live button: 2 objects
- Enjoy button: 2 objects
- Eat button: 2 objects
- Day background: 7 objects

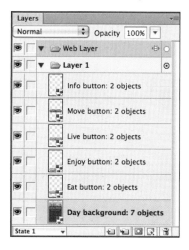

Note: In the rush to create a file, you may overlook object naming, but it's an essential part of structuring your document. When you pass a file on to coworkers, they may find a document full of unnamed objects and layers very hard to navigate and understand. On the other hand, they'll definitely appreciate a document with descriptively named objects.

▶ **Tip:** To more easily move a number of related objects around the canvas at the same time, you can temporarily group objects, so that their position in relation to each other is not affected when you move them. You'll learn how to create groups in Lesson 3.

▶ **Tip:** When renaming grouped objects, be sure to indicate that the object is still a group. Including the number of objects in the new name makes it very obvious. If you're unsure how many objects are in a group, check the object name in the Properties panel. If the object is really a group, you will see a number surrounded by parentheses. This value is the number of objects within the group.

Rearranging objects in a layer

Notice when you selected the Enjoy button that its position in the layer stack is different than the visual appearance of the buttons on the canvas.

To better match the linear display of objects between the Layer panel and the canvas, let's reposition the layer in the Layers panel.

1 Select the Eat button object in the Layers panel.

2 Drag it upward until you see a bold black line appear between the Enjoy and Live button objects in the Layers panel.

3 Release the mouse. The stacking order of the objects now matches the visual appearance on the canvas.

4 Choose File > Save to save your work so far.

Adding and naming layers

Things are a little more organized now. To help structure the file even more, you will add a new layer to the Layers panel for the HomeDay page.

1 Click the New/Duplicate Layer button at the bottom of the Layers panel. A new layer, appropriately called Layer 2, appears above the existing layer.

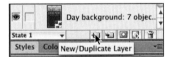

2 Double-click the new Layer 2 in the Layers panel, and change its name to **Main buttons**.

3 Create one more layer above the Main buttons layer. Rename the new layer **Info button**.

4 Double-click the original Layer 1 name, and rename it **Cityscape BG**.

Moving objects from one layer to another

Now that you have new layers, you can fill them with—you guessed it—content.

1 In the cityscape BG layer, click the Info button thumbnail object.

2 Drag the object on top of the empty Info button layer and release the mouse.

You can move single objects or multiple objects in this manner.

3 Select the Move button in the Layers panel.

4 Hold down the Shift key and click on the Enjoy button. All four main buttons are now selected in the Layers panel.

When you select an object, not only is it highlighted in the Layers panel, but an indicator icon fills in as well. You'll find this indicator at the right side of the layer name, and it looks like a radio button.

5 To move the selected objects into the Main buttons layer, drag the radio button from the Cityscape BG layer onto the radio button of the Main buttons layer.

Note: You can also cut selected objects, select a new layer, and paste the objects, or you can click and drag an object (or a series of selected objects) to a different layer.

Now all the content is in its own layer for this page. Things are much more organized. Most of this work has been done already for the other pages, but you still have work to do to complete the mock-up.

Tip: To select objects that aren't directly above or below each other, press Ctrl (Windows) or Command (Mac) as you select them.

Sharing layers to pages

Earlier, you created a Master page to share some common elements among all the pages in the design. Sometimes though, a Master page may be too rigid an option. Perhaps you want more flexibility to share content between only a few of your pages.

When you have content that needs to appear in the same location on multiple, but not all pages, sharing layers can be a real timesaver. Normally, you might copy and paste content from one page to another, but this can cause workflow issues; the positioning of the pasted elements may not be exactly the same, so the objects appear to jog around from page to page. Or perhaps you need to make changes to one or more objects. If the objects were independently placed on numerous pages in a mock-up, you would have to locate and edit each individual object. Not a very efficient use of your time.

A better solution is to share a layer between pages. With this method, you can edit objects in a *single shared layer* and those changes propagate instantly across all the pages that use the shared layer. You will do this now by sharing elements on the One-Ton front page with the newly added restaurant pages.

1 Select the Coupon background layer. Select the Layers Options menu (upper-right corner of the Layers panel) to drop down the menu.

2 From the Layers Options menu, choose Share Layer To Pages.

The Share Layer to Pages dialog box appears.

3 In the left column of the Share Layer dialog box, select One_Ton_Back.

4 Hold down the Shift key and select the last page in the list, Pierre_Back.

5 Click the Add button to move these pages to the right column.

6 Click OK.

Move through the pages now, and you will see that things look different—and not in a good way. All the restaurant pages are covered up by the background elements!

When you share a layer to another page, Fireworks automatically adds that layer to the top of the layer stack, which in this case is *not* the desired placement. The fix is easy enough, though.

7 Select the One_Ton_Back page.

8 Expand the Layers panel by dragging the bottom of the panel downward or by collapsing other panel groups.

9 Drag the shared layer (Coupon background) down so that the solid black insertion line appears between the Master Page layer and the Location Dot layers, and then release the layer.

10 Repeat this process for the other restaurant pages.

11 Save the file.

Sharing the Main and Info button layers

The pages that visualize how the app will behave at different times of day also have several common elements: the buttons. To give you more practice, you will share those layers now.

1 Select the HomeDay page.

2 In the Layers panel, select the Main buttons layer. Right-click (Control click on the Mac) the layer and choose Share Layer to Pages.

3 In the Share Layer dialog box, select the other time of day pages: HomeDawn, HomeDusk, and HomeNight.

4 Click the Add button, then click OK.

The default insertion for this Main buttons shared layer doesn't require any changes from you.

5 Right-click (Control+Click on Mac) the Info button layer from the HomeDay page, and choose Share Layer To Pages.

6 In the Share Layer dialog box, select HomeDawn, HomeDusk, HomeNight, and Info.

When a layer is shared, a new icon appears within the layer label in the Layers panel, so you can easily see which layers are shared to other pages.

7 Click the Add button.

8 Save the file.

▶ **Tip:** You can easily expand or collapse the individual layers in the Layers panel by clicking on the expansion triangle beside a layer name.

Now the main interface pages all have an information button in the upper-right corner. With these few simple steps, this file is far more organized.

Creating sublayers

For additional structure in complex files, you can use sublayers to organize related content within a single layer. This has already been done in your working file. Take a look: Select any of the restaurant pages, and expand the Coupon layer. Notice additional sublayers inside the Coupon layer, each contains its own elements.

To create a sublayer, make sure you have a main layer selected.

1 Click the New Sublayer button at the bottom of the Layers panel to add a sublayer, The sublayer name will be slightly indented when compared to the main layer name.

2 Create, drag, or paste new content into the sublayer just as you would a regular main layer.

Protecting layers

When a layer is locked, no object within it can be selected or deleted by accident.

1 Select the HomeDay page.

2 Click the Lock column in the Main buttons layer. This column is just to the left of the layer name.

3 Expand the Main buttons layer by clicking on the expansion triangle. Notice the ghost of a lock appears beside each object.

4 Try to select one of the objects in this layer or on the canvas. You can't, because they are all locked and protected.

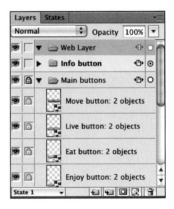

If your concern is only to protect certain objects rather than the entire layer, you can do that, too.

5 Right-click (Windows) or Control-click (Mac) the layer in the Layers panel, and choose Unlock All from the context menu.

6 Lock the Eat button.

7 On the canvas, hover over the Move button. Red highlights indicate this object is selectable.

8 Hover over the Eat button. No red indicators appear. This object is locked.

9 Unlock the Eat button by selecting the lock icon beside the object name or by selecting Unlock All again from the Options menu.

10 Save the file.

Layer options

The Layers panel has many contextual options for configuring the panel, adding new layers or sublayers, and determining how a layer interacts with other pages or states within a Fireworks design.

Access the Layers panel's options by right-clicking (or Control-clicking) any layer or by opening the Layers panel menu in the top-right corner of the panel (⊟).

Among other options, you can also enable single-layer editing. Enabling this option limits object selection on the canvas to objects in the currently active layer. To select objects in other layers, you would first have to select that parent layer from the Layers panel. This may be helpful with complicated layouts with many layers, but we recommend leaving it in its default disabled state until you need it.

Working with states

States are an important part of Fireworks. You can use them for mocking up website interaction (rollovers, Ajax emulation), for example, or to show how an application may change based on user input. States can include completely different content, or they can just indicate changes to certain elements that appear in both states. For example, a button may display a glow or drop shadow in a second state.

The local_picks file you've been working on is a mock-up of a planned smartphone application, and it needs a separate state to show what happens when a user taps on certain areas of the application. This design is still in its early stage—the interactivity has yet to be added by using slices or hotspots—but you will add a second state to the HomeDay page to represent one of the tap effects.

Note: States can also be used to create simple, state-based animations that can be exported as animate GIFs or rasterized SWF files.

Duplicating and naming states

The second state of the page will mirror the original interface but with a few alterations. The simplest way to add the necessary parts to the second state is to duplicate the existing interface from State 1.

1   Select the States tab.

2   Drag the State 1 to the New/Duplicate state icon near the bottom right of the States panel. This creates a duplicate state, including all the assets and layer hierarchy.

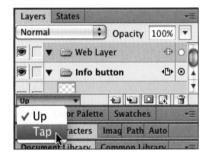

3   Double-click on the State 2 name, and rename it **Tap**.

4   Rename State 1 to **Up**.

Changing content on states

You're going to change the look of the Info button on the Tap state.

1   Select the Layers panel.

The currently selected state is displayed at the bottom-left corner of the Layers panel.

2   Click the Up state and choose the Tap state from the pop-up menu.

3   Use the Pointer tool to select the Info button on the canvas.

There are several effects applied to the Info button (gradient fill, stroke, and drop shadow), but they are not obvious in the Properties panel. The button is actually a group of objects, so the Pointer tool isn't going to help much with accessing those attributes. You could ungroup the objects, but instead you will drill into the group with the Subselection tool.

4   Select the Subselection tool (⬚).

5   Move the tool over the Info button, and notice the two objects within the group are independently highlighted now.

6 Select the circle.

The Properties panel updates to show attributes for the vector object.

7 Click on the Gradient Fill box to edit the gradient.

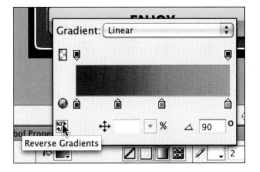

8 Click the Reverse Gradients icon to change the direction of the gradient.

9 From the Layers panel toggle back and forth between the two states. See how one simple change can make a big difference to an object's appearance?

Extra credit

As a Web or interactive designer, you will use these Fireworks elements on a regular basis, so a little practice is a good idea. Investigate the various layers and objects and see where you can improve the organization by updating object names. Experiment with the main buttons and the Tap state to create a different look for the Tap state. Try changing the fill color or type, for example. Don't forget that the buttons are grouped objects, too.

Locate the Navigation layer on the One_Ton_Front page and share it to the other restaurant pages. Be sure to check the Navigation layer's position in the layer stack and adjust it if necessary.

Note: To learn more about Web slices and optimizing graphics, read Lesson 10. To learn more about states and interactivity, read Lessons 11 and 12.

Review questions

1 What is the importance of layers?
2 What special layer does every Fireworks document have?
3 Name two benefits of using pages.
4 How do you move objects from one layer to another?
5 What are states used for?

Review answers

1 Layers add structure to your document. As you add more objects to a design, locating specific images or text areas becomes more difficult, because you have to scroll through a very long list. With objects sorted into multiple layers, you can quickly collapse layers to see your main design structure or expand a specific layer to select an individual object. Layers also allow objects to be independent from one another. You can add or remove layers or the objects within them without affecting other elements in the design. You can change how objects within layers interact with other layers by changing their stacking order.

2 Every Fireworks document has a Web layer. This is where interactive elements called *hotspots* and *slices* are stored. The Web layer does not have to be used in a design, but it cannot be deleted.

3 Pages let you create a variety of designs within a single file. This improves asset management, because you can store multiple unique designs for one project all in the same file. You can also link pages using hotspots or slices to create a truly interactive experience for testing and proof of concept.

4 You can move objects in one of several ways within the Layers panel:

   • Cut and paste a selected object from one layer to another.

   • Drag a selected object or objects from layer to layer.

   • Select an object or objects within one layer, and drag the associated radio button from the original layer to the radio button on the target layer.

5 You can use states to create simple frame-based animation or to show changes in the appearance of interactive elements, such as buttons. States can also display completely different content within the same page.

3 WORKING WITH BITMAP IMAGES

Lesson overview

In this lesson, you'll learn how to do the following:

- Use a variety of methods to crop images

- Set options for selected tools using the Properties panel

- Use guides to help position and align images

- Import bitmap images in Fireworks

- Use various bitmap tools and filters to adjust brightness, contrast, and tonality of bitmap images

- Correct images using the Rubber Stamp tool

- Align objects on the canvas using the Align panel

 This lesson takes approximately 90 minutes to complete. Copy the Lesson03 folder into the Lessons folder that you created on your hard drive for these projects (or create it now, if you haven't already done so). As you work on this lesson, you won't be preserving the start files; if you need to restore the start files, copy them from the *Adobe Fireworks CS6 Classroom in a Book* CD.

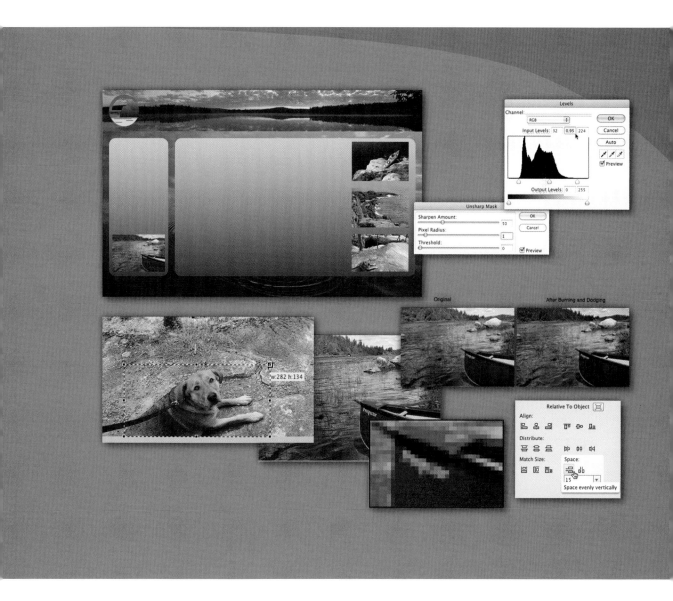

Everyone enjoys surfing through a good-looking
website or using a professionally designed interface.
Adobe Fireworks includes a solid set of tools for
creating and editing bitmap images for websites
and mobile applications.

About bitmap images

Everyone enjoys surfing through a good-looking, organized website or using a professionally designed interface. The building blocks to any effective website or app are bitmap images, and Adobe Fireworks gives you a solid set of tools for creating and editing them. You'll be more effective with those tools, however, if you understand a bit more about the structure of a bitmap.

In computer graphics, a bitmap, or *raster graphics image*, is made up of a finite rectangular grid of pixels, each of which is mapped to a specific position and color in the grid. Bitmap images are stored in image files of various formats such as JPG, PNG, TIFF, and GIF. The number of pixels in a bitmap is determined at the time of capture or creation.

A bitmap is characterized by the width and height of the image in pixels (600 pixels by 400 pixels, for example) and by the number of bits per pixel (referred to as *color depth*), which determines the number of colors it can represent. For the Web, you typically deal with images containing 32, 24, or 8 bits per pixel. An 8-bit image, for example, can display a maximum of 256 unique colors. GIF images and 8-bit PNG files are good examples. A JPEG file is a 24-bit image, which can display up to 16 million colors. A full-color transparent PNG file has 24-bit color (so it's photographically realistic) and 8 bits reserved for opacity, allowing for translucent images or drop shadows that blend with any background image or color.

Unlike true vector images, raster graphics are *resolution dependent*. This means you can't scale up to a higher resolution without loss in image quality. Vector graphics, on the other hand, easily scale up with no loss in quality. At 100% magnification, you don't normally see the pixels in a bitmap image. They become obvious only when you print the image at an incorrect resolution or when you zoom into the image on screen, as seen here in the image of the canoe and a magnified segment of its bow.

Resolution and file size

Image resolution and file size are directly related to each other. The greater the number of pixels in an image, the larger the file size will be. We're not talking about the physical dimensions of the image on a printed page; we're dealing specifically with the number of pixels that make up an image and how it relates to storing and downloading the image. For example, many current digital cameras will capture an image consisting of 4000 pixels horizontally by 3000 pixels vertically (or greater). Do the math, and you'll quickly see that an image with this resolution contains 12 million pixels in total and weighs over *40 MB*. The higher the capture resolution, the larger the file size will be.

Thinking another way, when is the last time you visited a website that sported 4000-pixel-wide images? Even background images for web pages are not this large.

Larger file sizes mean much longer downloads to a desktop or mobile device, but it's also more than a matter of patience; bandwidth consumption costs money, especially on mobile data plans. As web designers, we're regularly tasked with the balancing act of efficient file size versus acceptable image quality. You will dig deep into this topic in Lesson 10.

Image resolution versus image quality

Resolution and *quality* are two different things; you can have a high-resolution image that doesn't look very good, due to poor quality in the original scan or heavy image compression that might be set on a digital camera. *Resolution* refers to the actual number of pixels that make up the image, not the empirical or subjective quality of the image.

Tips for working with bitmaps

Good-quality graphics are key assets to many professional websites. The image-editing and layout tools in Fireworks give you the freedom to do most—if not all—of your bitmap work without leaving the application.

That said, you should keep a couple of caveats in mind:

- The maximum canvas-creation size in Fireworks is 6000 x 6000 pixels. You can work on existing files that are larger than this, but 6000 x 6000 pixels is the largest that you can create within the program.

- Fireworks was designed to work with graphics destined for screen use, and that's where its speed and flexibility really shine. Although you can open and work on very high-resolution files in Fireworks, you may find the application begins to get sluggish over time. And you may not want to have several of these files open at the same time.

Cropping an image

Cropping is a common way to remove extraneous detail, letting the viewer focus more exclusively on a specific part of an image. Cropping makes images smaller, too, removing excess baggage from your images in terms of download and storage efficiency. In this exercise, you will remove surrounding detail in a photo to help focus on the main subject.

1 Choose File > Open, and browse to the file marley.jpg in the Lesson03 folder on your hard drive. Click Open.

2 Select the Crop tool (⬚) from the Tools panel.

3 Click and drag the Crop cursor so that a bounding box surrounds Marley the dog.

4 Press Enter or Return to crop the image.

Hmm, looks like we got a bit too close; we've lost all the context for the image. We'd better go back.

5 Press Ctrl+Z (Windows) or Command+Z (Mac) to undo the crop.

6 Making sure the Crop tool is still selected, draw the crop one more time; click where Marley enters the bottom of the frame and drag the crop cursor up and to the right. You want to exclude the empty image area on the left, as well as the upper half of the trees at the top of the image.

7 Press Enter or Return to commit to the crop. Much better!

8 Save the file as **marley_cropped.jpg**, and close the file.

Cropping a single bitmap image in a design

Cropping single images is fine, but what if you need to crop an image that's already on a layer in a design? Fireworks offers a way to do this as well. And with the Tooltips feature active (View > Tooltips), you get pixel-level accuracy as well.

1 Open webpage_start.fw.png from the Lesson03 folder.

Since you last worked on the file, a new image has been added and the objects have been organized into layers in the Layers panel. Take a few minutes to examine the Layers panel before proceeding. Note that content has been placed into logical layer groupings: header, content, footer, and background.

2 Double-click on the Zoom tool in the Toolbar to view the design at 100% magnification.

3 Use the Pointer tool to select the sunrise image by clicking on the image on the canvas.

4 Choose Edit > Crop Selected Bitmap. Crop marks will appear around the sunrise image.

5 Drag the top border of the crop until the tooltip's height (h) value is 150.

6 Drag the bottom crop border until the tooltip reads h: 120.

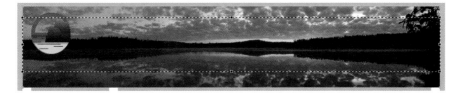

● **Note:** The small square boxes at the corners and middle of each crop line are control handles, which let you alter the crop dimensions before committing to it.

7 Press Enter or Return to commit to the crop.

▶ **Tip:** If you change your mind about cropping at all, you can press the Escape key to cancel the action.

8 Save the file.

Managing images on the canvas

When you have more than one image or object on the canvas, Fireworks gives you a variety of ways to work with those images, from showing and hiding objects to multiple selection and positioning to grouping objects for simplified asset management. You'll find that steps you take in the following exercises are a common part of most design workflows.

Adjusting the sunrise image position

After cropping the image, it's obvious that the sunrise photo is not in the correct location. Because you are dealing with a web page design, pixel precision is important. Image dimensions and X and Y coordinates may likely be needed for the true web page's Cascading Style Sheet. The goal of a mock-up design such as this is to be an accurate representation of the true HTML web page. You will use a couple of different methods to reposition the photo.

1 Select the Pointer tool, and click on the sunrise photo.

2 Tap the Up arrow key once. The image shifts position upward by a single pixel.

3 Hold down the Shift key and tap the Up arrow key once again. The image shifts by 10 pixels this time.

4 Locate the Align panel (Window > Align). In it, click the Relative To Canvas icon, so that objects align relative to the canvas.

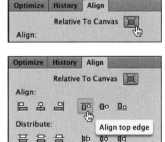

> **Tip:** You can also change a selected object's position by entering new values in the X and Y fields in the Properties panel.

5 Click the Align Top Edge icon. The sunrise snaps to the top of the canvas.

6 Save the file.

Locking objects and layers

As more elements get added to the canvas, you can unintentionally select the wrong object on the canvas or add objects to the wrong layer. You will now lock some elements to prevent this from happening.

1 In the Layers panel, locate the header layer.

2 Lock the entire layer by clicking the empty box beside the eye icon.

3 Do the same for the footer and background layers, so you don't accidentally place objects in those locations.

You will be working with the content layer in the coming exercises, so the layer needs to remain unlocked; but to avoid accidental selection, the rounded rectangles should be locked.

4 Find the canoe, mainContent, and sidebar objects in the content layer, and lock the empty box beside the eye icon.

Working with guides

In this exercise, you will use guides to help ensure an exact position for some thumbnail images you will be importing. Guides are great tools for aligning and placing objects on the canvas.

1 If rulers are not visible, choose View > Rulers.

2 Move the cursor to the ruler at the left of the document window.

3 Click and drag toward the canvas. A vertical guide appears. You will also see a tooltip appear beside the guide, with an X value. (If you don't see the tooltip, choose View > Tooltips.) This value is the horizontal position of the vertical guide.

4 When the tooltip displays near 700, release the mouse. The guide drops at that location.

Exact positioning of guides can be very important when you are aligning multiple objects. If you can't seem to get the exact pixel location by dragging a guide with the cursor, Fireworks gives you that control with the Move Guide dialog box.

5 Place your cursor on top of the guide. When you see a double-headed arrow, double-click the guide to open the Move Guide dialog box.

6 Change the current value to **750** pixels, and click OK.

The guide jumps to the desired position.

7 From the top ruler, drag a horizontal guide down to a Y value of 150.

Importing images

A very quick way to add existing images to a design is to *import* them onto the canvas. Importing gives you the ability to scale the image proportionately when you add it to the canvas. There are four key benefits to importing images:

• You can scale an image dynamically to fit a desired space in the design.

• You do not have to deal with another document window.

• You bypass the need to copy and paste or drag and drop an image from another window into a destination document.

- When importing a multipage Fireworks PNG file, you choose which page you want to import.

You will add additional thumbnails on top of the mainContent rectangle by importing images.

▶ **Tip:** A quick way to get to 100% magnification is to press Ctrl+1 (Windows) or Command+1 (Mac) or simply double-click the Zoom tool in the Tools panel.

1 Zoom to 100% using either the Zoom (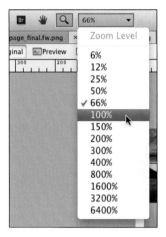) tool in the Tools panel or the Zoom Level menu in the Application bar.

2 Select the content layer from the Layers panel.

3 Choose File > Import. Browse to the Lesson03 folder, locate the kayak.jpg file, and click Open.

   Back on the canvas, notice that the cursor has changed to the import cursor, which looks like an inverted L shape (⌐). With the import cursor active, clicking and dragging the mouse draws a marquee. When you release the mouse button, Fireworks imports your image at the dimensions you created via the marquee, based on the height-to-width (aspect) ratio of the original image.

▶ **Tip:** When importing, if you click the mouse button without dragging, Fireworks will import the image at its full height and width, positioning the top-left corner at the import cursor's location.

● **Note:** By default, the import cursor automatically snaps to the nearest guide, so even if you are a couple of pixels away from the guide, the import cursor begins the marquee at the guide location.

If you simply click the mouse button without dragging, Fireworks imports the image at its full height and width, placing its top-left corner where you clicked.

4 Place the cursor near the intersection of the two guides and drag toward the right. Release the mouse when the width value in the Properties panel reaches 180.

   Check the Layers panel, and notice the new bitmap image has been added to the content layer.

5 Rename this object as **kayak** in the Layers panel.

6 Create a column of images beneath the kayak shot by repeating steps 3 to 5 for the image files superior.jpg and marley_cropped.jpg.

   Don't worry about the distance between each image. You'll adjust that next.

7 Rename the new objects to **lake** and **dog**, respectively.

Creating even space between images

A web design is usually a pretty structured layout. The Align panel makes it easy to create and maintain an organized layout in your design. For example, using the

Align panel, you can automatically add a consistent amount of space between your newly imported thumbnail images.

1   Select the Pointer tool.

2   Drag the cursor over all three thumbnail images.

3   Because you locked the rectangles earlier in this lesson, you can select only the photos when you drag your cursor over them.

4   Open the Align panel and make sure it is set to Relative to Object.

5   In the Space field, set a value of **15**.

6   Click on the **Space Evenly Vertically** icon.

    Fireworks automatically spaces the three images evenly.

7   Change the stacking order of the layers in the Layers panel so that the kayak image is at the top of the stack, and the dog photo is beneath the lake photo. While not a mandatory step, it helps visually to match the visual hierarchy in the design.

▶ **Tip:** To make it easier to move the layers, first click the mouse outside the canvas area to deselect everything.

8   Save the file.

Grouping objects together

The canvas is starting to fill up with several graphics. You're going to make your life a little easier by grouping the column of thumbnails together. Grouping temporarily turns a series of selected objects into a single object, making it easier to manipulate them.

1   Make sure the three thumbnails are still selected. If the images are not selected, be sure to select them all again.

2   Choose Modify > Group, or press Command+G (Mac) or Ctrl+G (Windows).

3   In the Layers panel, you will see that the thumbnails are now part of the same object, with a new name of Group: 3 Objects.

4   Rename the group to **thumbnails: 3 objects**.

    The column takes up a fair amount of space, with little space on the right side. You will scale the group using the Constrain Proportions option in the Properties panel.

5   Click the hollow square to the left of the width and height. The square becomes solid and you have now constrained the proportions of the group.

6   Type **170** into the Width field, and then press the Tab key. Fireworks automatically scales the height for all three images to proportionately match the width.

7 The Constrain Proportions option is *sticky*, so be sure to disable it when you no longer need it.

8 Select the Subselection tool.

Even though these photos are grouped, you can still select them as individual objects by using the Subselection tool ( ). You will use this tool now, so you can tweak the spacing between the photos.

▶ Tip: You can also choose Modify > Transform > Numeric Transform, to scale by percentage, resize by exact pixels, or rotate an object or group to a specific angle.

9 Click on the photo of Marley the dog.

10 Release the mouse and then, while pressing the Shift key, tap the Down arrow key one time. The photo moves down by 10 pixels.

11 Use the Subselection tool again to select the lake photo.

12 Tap the Down arrow key five times.

Distortion-free bitmap scaling

Scaling objects in one direction—whether they are bitmap images or vector shapes—can cause unwanted distortion. But Fireworks has a great feature called 9-slice scaling that can minimize distortion when scaling bitmaps. The trick is that this only works with images containing an area with little detail, such as a photo with a solid blue sky, for example. To learn more about 9-slice scaling, be sure to check out the Fireworks Help files.

Importing the background image

Our web page background is a little on the lackluster side, but you will fix this by bringing in a background image using the Import command again.

1 Lock the content and header layers in the Layers panel, and then hide both layers by clicking the eye icon.

2 Unlock the background layer.

3 Press Command+R (Mac) or Ctrl+R (Windows) to launch the Import Image window. This is a bit faster than choosing File > Import.

4 Locate and open the web_background.jpg image.

5 Position the import cursor at the top-left corner of the design and drag across to the right edge of the design. Make sure the Width field in the Properties panel reads 960 before you release the cursor.

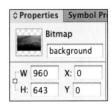

6 Rename the image to **background.**

Improving appearance using Live Filters

The background image you've imported adds a nice visual touch to the design, but it's a bit low in contrast and saturation, lacking visual impact. You will use a Live Filter to adjust the contrast. *Live Filters* are nondestructive effects you can apply to most objects (vector, bitmap, or symbol) within Fireworks. The great power and advantage of Live Filters is that you can always edit the effect at a later time. If you feel the filter is too harsh, or too subtle, just click the "*i*" icon to edit the filter properties. (Note that this icon becomes available once the Live Filter has been added to the Properties panel.)

Increasing contrast and saturation with the Levels Live Filter

Here you'll start by applying the Levels Live Filter to the background, then tweak its effect.

1 Ensure the background photo is selected (look for that blue bounding box), and then click the plus sign (+) in the Filters area of the Properties panel to add any Live Filter.

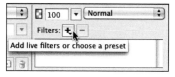

2 Choose Adjust Color > Levels. The Levels dialog box appears.

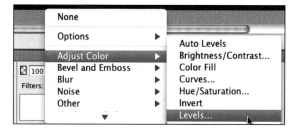

The histogram (graph) in the Levels dialog box shows you the distribution of tones in the selected image; you use it to alter shadows, midtones, and highlights. Directly below the histogram are the input level sliders: shadows on the left, highlights on the right, and midtones in the middle.

In this image, you'll notice that there is nothing displaying in the histogram for the highlights or shadows.

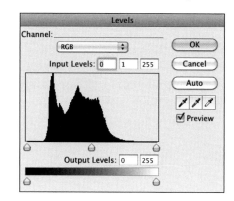

3 Drag the left slider to the right so that it almost lines up with the beginning of the histogram chart. The Input value should read about 32. Click OK.

The Levels Live Filter now appears in the Filters list in the Properties panel.

The result is definitely an improvement, but now things are too dark overall. You will reopen the Levels filter and make further adjustments.

4 Click the "*i*" icon next to the Levels filter in the Live Filters category of the Properties panel. The Levels dialog box reopens.

5 Change the highlight input value to **224** by typing the numbers into the leftmost input box above the histogram.

6 Change the midtone value to **.95** in the middle input box. Click OK.

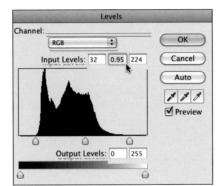

7 Press Ctrl+S (Windows) or Command+S (Mac) to save your work.

Sharpening with the Unsharp Mask Live Filter

Most images benefit from at least some sharpening, and this is especially true when you resize an image smaller than its original, as you did with the three thumbnails you imported. Fireworks, like most graphic editors, removes pixel data from an image when reducing its dimensions. This process, called *downsampling*, tends to make the image softer. You can regain some of the original crispness of the photo, however, by applying the Unsharp Mask filter, as either a permanent filter or as a Live Filter.

The Unsharp Mask filter identifies pixels that differ from surrounding pixels by the *threshold* you specify and increases the pixel contrast by the *amount* you specify. In addition, you specify the *radius* to control the degree of unsharpness the mask image will have.

● **Note:** If you research Unsharp masking, you'll often read that it should be the last adjustment you make to an image. Typically, this is true for images intended for print, so the image sharpness can be customized for a specific printer. We're not printing this image, and the only edit being applied is the Unsharp Mask. Most importantly, because we're using the nondestructive, always-editable Live Filter version, you don't really need to worry about when the filter is applied.

For the greatest flexibility, Live Filters are a better option. Try it now on the three thumbnail images.

1 Unlock the content layer, make it visible again, and select the thumbnail group from the Layers panel.

2 Press Ctrl+1 (Windows) or Command+1 (Mac) to zoom the design to 100%.

3 Click the Add Live Filters icon (+ sign) in the Properties panel.

4 Choose Sharpen > Unsharp Mask to open the Unsharp Mask dialog box. The default properties are a bit extreme for a low-resolution file, so we'll alter one slightly.

5 Change the Pixel Radius to a value of **1**.

6 Deselect the Preview option to see the images without sharpening.

7 Enable Preview again.
   Notice that there is slightly more contrast between light and dark areas and the images appear crisper. This is because Unsharp Mask increases the contrast of *edge pixels only* (the place where a dark and light pixel meet).

8 Click OK to apply the filter.

Note: Live Filters will affect all objects in a group, whether vector or bitmap. Standard bitmap filters (Filters menu) affect bitmap images only. If your try to apply a standard filter to a vector, Fireworks will prompt you to rasterize the vector object.

Unsharp Mask properties

Generally, higher-resolution images can handle (and sometimes need) higher amounts of unsharp masking than low-resolution images. The three controls for the Unsharp Masking filter are the following:

• **Sharpen Amount:** This property controls how much darker and lighter the edge borders become. Sharpen Amount can also be thought of as how much contrast is added at the edges.

• **Pixel Radius:** This property affects the size of the edges to be sharpened. A smaller radius enhances smaller-scale detail. Higher radius values can cause halos at the edges (a highlight around objects), making images look unnatural. Fine detail needs a smaller radius value. Pixel Radius and Sharpen Amount are reciprocal; reducing one allows more of the other.

• **Threshold:** This property controls how far apart adjacent tonal values have to be before the filter does anything. The threshold setting can be used to sharpen more pronounced edges while ignoring more subtle edges. Low values have a greater effect because fewer areas are excluded. Higher threshold values exclude areas of lower contrast.

Improving appearance using the bitmap tools

Fireworks is not Photoshop. There—we've said it. If you have large, high-resolution images or images that require major manipulation, chances are you should do that kind of heavy-duty work in Photoshop first. Every job has a correct tool. That said, Fireworks comes with a decent set of standard retouching tools, including the Dodge, Burn, and Rubber Stamp tools. These tools can handle most basic retouching requirements, without the need to jump back and forth between applications.

Adjusting brightness with the Dodge and Burn tools

Sometimes a photo has good general exposure, but a few areas in the image are too light or too dark. To give these areas some local adjustment, you'll find the Dodge and Burn tools come in handy.

The Dodge and Burn tools are part of the bitmap-retouching toolset; their effects are permanent (sometimes called "destructive") in that the tools completely alter pixel values. Don't let this deter you, however; just take these steps to protect your original image before experimenting with Dodge and Burn.

1 In the Layers panel, unlock the canoe image.

   This image is in pretty good shape, but the horizon is a bit overexposed and the photographer cast a shadow on the water. In the next exercises, you'll use the Dodge and Burn tools to correct these problems.

2 To keep your original safe, make a copy of the photo by dragging its thumbnail down to the New Bitmap Image icon in the Layers panel.

   With one copy of the image safe, you can always get back to the original should your adjustments not go as well as you envision.

Tip: When you select an object and zoom, Fireworks uses the active object as the central zoom point.

3 Double-click the word "Canoe" next to the selected image in the Layers panel, and rename it **Retouch**. This will help you to differentiate between the two images with a quick glance at the Layers panel at any time.

4 Press Command+(Mac) or Ctrl+(Windows) twice to magnify the photo to about 200%. It's a small image, so you'll start seeing pixels pretty quickly.

Now you're ready to delve into the different uses of Dodge and Burn.

Lightening with the Dodge tool

Dodging is an old photo darkroom term for making specific areas of a photo brighter. In Fireworks, you can lighten local areas of an image by painting over those areas with the Dodge tool.

1 Select the Dodge tool from the Tools panel. The Dodge tool is part of a collection of pixel-editing tools. You can quickly get to it by pressing the R key several times. When you see the icon that looks like a black lollipop ( ), you've got the right tool.

2 In the Properties panel, change Size to **13**. Make sure Edge is set to **100** (for a soft-edged brush) and Exposure to **20**. For Range, choose Midtones, and click the circular icon for Shape.

◇ Properties	Symbol Properties					
	Dodge tool	Size: 13 ▾	Shape: ● ■		Exposure: 20 ▾	
		Edge: ● 100 ▾	Range: Midtones ▾			

3 Carefully paint over the shadow area without releasing the mouse. Avoid painting over water areas outside the shadow.

4 To compare the original with the lightened version, press Ctrl+Z (Windows) or Command+Z (Mac) to undo the editing and view the original, then Press Ctrl+Y (Windows) or Command+Y (Mac) to reapply the dodging.

5 Toggle back and forth between before and after a few times; the effect is subtle, but noticeable. Make sure to end with a Ctrl+Y or Command+Y to keep the dodging.

Original   After Dodging

▶ **Tip:** Another option is to use the Zoom tool to drag a marquee around the area you want to magnify. When you release the mouse, Fireworks automatically centers the selected area on the canvas, and you're ready to go.

● **Note:** The pixel editing tools are found at the bottom left of the bitmap tools section of the toolbar.

Note: Each time you release the mouse and then paint again over the same area, you will further lighten an area, so it's good to apply Burning or Dodging incrementally, at low values, then toggling the visibility of the retouched version to compare with the original.

6 If you find the bottom of the shadow still too dark, try setting the Exposure to 10 and painting over that smaller area once again.

Remember, you're using a copy of the photo, so if you make mistakes, you can either undo the steps by pressing Command+Z or Ctrl+Z, or you can just delete the retouched version and make a new copy.

Darkening with the Burn tool

The Burn tool does the exact opposite of the Dodge tool; it darkens the specific areas where you apply it. For example, the horizon (sky and tree line) in the canoe photo is a bit too bright, but you can correct this quickly with the Burn tool.

1 Switch to the Burn tool, either by pressing the R key until the tool appears, or by clicking and holding the Dodge tool icon in the Tools panel until the tool flyout list appears.

2 In the Properties panel, change Size to **20** and Exposure to **30**. Leave Edge, Shape, and Range the same (100, Circular, and Midtones, respectively).

3 Paint over the horizon area in one direction only, being careful not to move the cursor into the water. Painting right to left or vice versa doesn't matter, so long as you do not release the mouse. If you release the mouse and start again, it's like adding another coat of paint to the wall.

Burning adds exposure, here making the sky and trees appear a bit darker and richer in color.

As before, if you feel the result is too subtle, simply paint over the area again.

4 Set the Zoom level to 100% again.

5 Hide the retouched version by clicking its eye icon in the Layers panel, and compare the original with the altered image. Although each of the changes you made was small, the overall effect on the image is quite substantial.

6 Click the eye icon again to redisplay the retouched image and continue to alter the image if you like, or simply save the file by pressing Ctrl+S (Windows) or Command+S (Mac).

Original   After Burning and Dodging

Repairing areas with the Rubber Stamp tool

The Rubber Stamp tool (), also known as the Clone Stamp tool, copies pixel detail from one location in a bitmap image and pastes it into another (presumably damaged or unsightly) area. Maybe there is a scratch in some packaging or a flyaway thread in some clothing. Maybe you need to smooth out skin tones in a photo or remove an unwanted highlight in a shiny object. These are all good examples of when to use the Rubber Stamp tool. Here are the general steps for using the Rubber Stamp tool:

1 Select the Rubber Stamp tool.

2 Option+Click (Mac) or Alt+Click (Windows) an area to designate it as the source (the area you want to clone from). The sampling pointer becomes a crosshair and a circle covers the retouching area. This is the stamp (or clone) cursor. The circle represents the size of the brush being used to do the retouching.

3 Move to a different part of the image, and drag the cursor. As you drag the cursor, pixels beneath the sampling are cloned to the area beneath the brush.

Now you will test this process by cleaning up the shadow area on the canoe photo.

1 Zoom in, as described earlier in the chapter, to focus in on the canoe. When retouching, it's always good to get close to your subject matter.

2 Select the Rubber Stamp tool from the Bitmap tools area of the Tools panel.

Notice that the Properties panel updates, displaying attributes for the Rubber Stamp tool. You can set the brush size and the edge softness of the brush (100 is soft, 0 is hard). You can also decide whether you want to keep your brush aligned with the original source of sampling and if you want to sample from all the layers/objects in your document, or just the active object.

> **Tip:** Depending on the brush preferences you selected, the painting cursor is shown as a rubber stamp, a crosshair, or a blue circle. You can change the cursor display for many editing tools by choosing Edit > Preferences (Windows) or Fireworks > Preferences (Mac) and then selecting the Edit category. Select or deselect the cursor options to change how the cursor is represented.

3 In the Properties panel, set your brush size to **10** pixels, the edge to **100%**, and Opacity **40**. Lowering the opacity will help blend the cloning.

4 Deselect the Source Aligned option to ensure that the sampling always begins at the same source point, no matter where you begin your actual rubber-stamping.

5 Locate an area on the canoe that is even-toned and red. Hold down Alt (Windows) or Option (Mac), and click to sample the pixels from this area.

6 Move the cursor over to the shadow area.

To Source Align or not to Source Align

When enabled, the Source Aligned option forces the sampling cursor to continuously track the position of the stamp cursor. Basically, the tool cursors are always in step with each other. If you release the mouse or move the stamp cursor somewhere else on the image, the source cursor appears at exactly the same distance and angle from the stamp cursor as when you clicked to make your original sampling point.

If you disable the Source Aligned option, the source cursor always resets itself to the original sampling location when the mouse is released, regardless of where you place the stamp cursor.

This is a context type of option; depending on what you are cloning, you may find it easier to achieve your goal by enabling or disabling Source Aligned.

7   Click and hold the mouse button, and then begin painting carefully over the area. Continue painting until the large shadow is gone. Take care not to let your sampling cursor stray into areas like the black gunnels of the canoe. Some variation in tone is fine; you want the retouching to look as realistic as possible. If necessary, release the mouse button and repeat the process to get blend the edges.

8   Save the file when you are happy with the results.

> **Note:** You are cloning pixels onto a bitmap object, so if you let your cursor slip outside the edges of the photo, you will add pixel data to an area that was originally transparent. If this happens, either undo the step or use the Eraser tool later to clean up the unwanted pixels outside the photo area.

> **Note:** To designate a different area of pixels to clone, Alt-click (Windows) or Option-click (Mac) another area of pixels.

Before Cloning   After Cloning

Rubber-stamping can take a bit of practice, which is another reason to perform the retouching on a separate or duplicate object. If your results aren't as good as you would like, you can just delete the bitmap object by selecting it and then dragging it to the Layers panel trash can icon.

Retouching an empty bitmap object

Cloning is a permanent (destructive) process; you are literally replacing pixels in one area with pixels from another. If you save and close the file, those changes become a part of the image. This is why we created a duplicate of the canoe image earlier in the lesson; the original image remains untouched.

Many professionals prefer to do this type of retouching on a separate layer. In this way, they avoid the potential for permanently ruining (or even just changing) an original image. Fireworks lets you do this kind of work in an empty bitmap object, even in the same layer as the original artwork.

An empty bitmap object is an area containing no pixel data. It gives you the opportunity to add new pixel information as a separate, unique object. Once you create this object, you must add pixel data to it in your next step, or the object will be removed from the Layers panel. You might use this object if you are planning to use the Brush or Pencil tools to add colored bitmap lines.

You create an empty bitmap object by selecting the New Bitmap Image icon in the Layers panel (▣). A transparent (empty) Bitmap object will appear in the panel, above the previously selected object.

You might also notice a blue rectangle appear on the canvas, surrounding the retouching work. This is how Fireworks indicates a selected object.

Layers *and* objects? Why?

Because the roots of Fireworks lie in the vector world—much like Adobe Illustrator— each layer can contain multiple objects. This concept may seem a little disconcerting if your experience is primarily with Photoshop, which is a layer-oriented application, but in fact, this *object-oriented* approach gives you much more control and flexibility over your designs. You can also create sublayers within a layer, which emulate the layer-groups workflow of Photoshop.

Review questions

1   What is the maximum canvas size in Fireworks, and how can this affect your workflow?

2   What is the process for cropping a specific bitmap object in a design?

3   What options do you have for adjusting the tonal range of a bitmap image?

4   What are the advantages of Live Filters over traditional filters?

5   How do you use the Rubber Stamp tool, and what is a recommended workflow for using it?

Review answers

1   The maximum canvas size you can create in Fireworks is 6000 x 6000 pixels. If you have a very large file that you want to use in Fireworks, consider scaling it to more suitable dimensions before opening it in Fireworks.

2   Select the bitmap object, and then choose Edit > Crop Selected Bitmap. This will ensure that you're cropping only one object rather than the entire design.

3   If the entire image is too dark or too light, you can use the Levels dialog box to alter overall brightness and contrast. If you want to alter specific areas in the image, you can use the Dodge tool to lighten an area, or the Burn tool to darken an area.

4   Live Filters are nondestructive and completely editable at any time. Live Filters can also be applied to both vector and bitmap objects, whereas traditional filters can be applied only to bitmap objects.

5   The Rubber Stamp tool can be used only on bitmap objects, and is designed to copy pixels from one location to another, for the purpose of correcting defects or removing unwanted elements within a photo. You must first sample the area you want to use as a source by pressing Alt (Windows) or Option (Mac) and clicking on the desired area. Then you can move the cursor to the problem area and paint over it. Ideally, this type of retouching should be done within a new bitmap object, so you do not alter the original source image.

4 WORKING WITH BITMAP SELECTIONS

Lesson overview

Making selections on a bitmap image is an important component of working with bitmaps. Bitmap selections isolate a specific area for alteration, protecting all other areas from being affected. For example, you might want to brighten a dark part of an image. By delineating a selection, you can ensure your change in pixel brightness is applied to the desired area only, *not* the entire photo. In this lesson, you'll learn how to do the following:

- Create a selection with the Magic Wand tool
- Adjust the edge of a bitmap selection
- Apply corrective filters to a selection
- Make complex selections using the Lasso and Magic Wand tools
- Modify a bitmap selection
- Save a bitmap selection for future use
- Convert a bitmap selection to a path

This lesson takes approximately 60 minutes to complete. Copy the Lesson04 folder into the Lessons folder that you created on your hard drive for these projects (or create it now, if you haven't already done so). As you work on this lesson, you won't preserve the start files. If you need to restore the start files, copy them from the *Adobe Fireworks CS6 Classroom in a Book* CD.

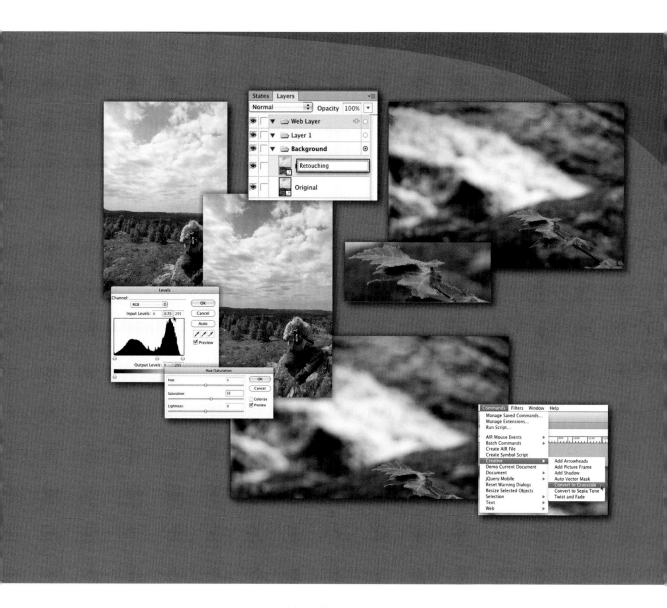

Making selections on a bitmap image is key to working with bitmaps regardless of the software application.

Understanding bitmap selections

The bitmap selection tools enable you to isolate a specific area of an image for alteration. Before you begin this lesson, though, you must also be clear on the difference between selecting an object and making a bitmap selection.

When you click an object in the Layers panel or use the Pointer tool to click an object on the canvas, you select (or activate) the entire object. You can then move, copy, edit, or cut that object from the design, without affecting anything else on the canvas. A bitmap selection differs in that you select *a specific part* of a bitmap image rather than the entire bitmap object. After you make a selection, you can copy or edit only the area within the selection border. The bitmap selection tools work on bitmap images only; you cannot use these tools on text or a vector object.

Bitmap selection tools: a primer

The selection tools in Fireworks include the Marquee and Oval Marquee tools, the Lasso and Polygon Lasso tools, and the Magic Wand tool. Each has its own strengths, and you'll need to choose the selection tool most suitable for your job.

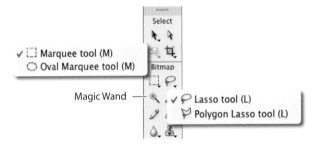

For example, choose the Marquee (⬚) or Oval Marquee (○) tool when you need to select regularly shaped areas. Simply click and drag to draw out one of these selections after choosing the appropriate tool. Holding Shift constrains the rectangular marquee to a square and the oval marquee to a circle.

One of the Lasso tools (the standard Lasso (⌒.) or the Polygon Lasso (ᖰ))may be better suited to select irregular areas when you make a freehand selection. The standard Lasso tool allows you to draw a selection on the canvas using a mouse or stylus. With the Polygon Lasso, you outline the selection by clicking to plot points around the area you want selected. You can hold down Shift to constrain Polygon Lasso marquee segments to 45-degree increments. To close the polygon selection, either click the starting point or double-click in the workspace.

If the area is primarily similar shades of colors, the Magic Wand tool (✳) may be your best choice to quickly create a selection. The Magic Wand tool selects pixels based on color. If you have an area of similarly colored pixels in your image (a blue sky, for example), the Magic Wand can quickly select that part of your image. You start the selection by clicking the wand cursor on an area of your image. The wand selects contiguous pixels of the same color range, based on the Tolerance setting in the Properties panel. You can decrease the tool's sensitivity by changing the Tolerance setting to a higher value.

Selection tool options

Most of the bitmap selection tools have the option to set the selection edge to Hard, Anti-alias, or Feather. A Hard edge gives you a jagged, pixelated selection. Anti-alias blends the selection with the area outside the selection. Feather creates a softer, less accurate, blended-edge selection. Unlike with the other two edge settings, you can apply a pixel value to Feather to increase the blend between the inside and outside of the selection.

Hard Edge   Anti-Aliased Edge   Feathered Edge

If you choose the Rectangular or Elliptical Marquee, the Properties panel offers you additional options:

- Normal creates a marquee in which the height and width are independent of each other.

- Fixed Ratio constrains the height and width to defined ratios.

- Fixed Size sets the height and width to a defined dimension, in pixels.

Select menu choices

The Select menu helps you further refine your bitmap sections. You can expand, contract, or smooth any active bitmap selection by choosing the desired action from the Select menu.

For example, the Select Inverse command toggles between the active selection and the unselected area, because sometimes selecting the unwanted part of the image is easier. Suppose you have a photo of a city scene with a clear sky in the background. You want to do some levels or filter adjustments to the city area, but using the Magic Wand tool to select the evenly colored sky will be easier (and faster). Then you can choose Select > Select Inverse to reverse the selected areas, making the city scene the active selection.

With any bitmap selection, choose Select > Select Similar to add to the current bitmap selection, based on colors within the active selection. Anywhere the colors within the selection appear throughout the image, they will become part of the new selection.

Using Live Marquee

The Live Marquee feature is available for all five bitmap selection tools. By default, it is active (selected) in the Properties panel. Live Marquee gives you immediate control over the edge of your bitmap selection after you draw it. You can choose Hard for an aliased, hard-edged selection; Anti-alias for a softer, slightly blended selection edge; or Feather for a very soft blend. When you choose Feather, you set the amount of feathering you want. This amount will gradually blend any effect applied to the bitmap selection on both the inner and outer edges of the selection.

Protecting original art

Think back to our web page design from Lesson 3. Most websites have more than one page, and in this lesson, you're being tasked with cleaning up a few more images for the website, as well as showing off your creative flair. The bitmap selection tools, filters, and even the Commands menu will come into play.

Applying a bitmap filter to a bitmap selection permanently changes the pixels in an image, however, so take a moment to protect your assets. When you plan to apply permanent changes to a bitmap object, you should always work with a duplicate of the image so that the original is not damaged. In this exercise, you'll use keyboard commands to create that duplicate.

1 Choose File > Open, and browse to the Lesson04 folder.

2 Select bigsky.jpg, and then click Open.

   Notice how bright and pale the sky is; that's what you'll be working on shortly.

3 Select the Pointer tool, and click on the image to make it active.

4 Press Ctrl+Shift+D (Windows) or Command+Shift+D (Mac) to create a clone of the image. You now have two identical bitmap images in the Layers panel. You can also access this command from the Edit menu (Edit > Clone).

5 In the Layers panel, double-click the bottom bitmap image name, and change it to **Original**.

6 **Lock the original image.**

7 Double-click the top image, and rename it **Retouching**.

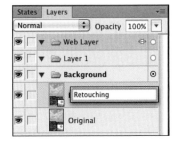

Clone or Duplicate?
What's the dif, dude?

Accessed from the Edit menu or keyboard shortcuts, the Clone and Duplicate commands accomplish the same basic task: create a copy of an object. Their difference is one of positioning. The Clone command creates a copy with exactly the same X and Y coordinates, much like dragging an object to the new/duplicate bitmap icon in the Layers panel.

The Duplicate command also creates an exact copy, but offsets the new copy by a few pixels from the location of the original, making it easier to differentiate between the two or to select either image right on the canvas.

Selecting and modifying with the Magic Wand tool

The original image is safe. In this section's exercises, you'll use a variety of selection tools and techniques to modify specific parts of two images. The Magic Wand tool will play a big role in making these selections. You will also adjust the selection with the Live Marquee and apply bitmap filters to improve the scene, and in the case of one image, completely change the look of the photograph.

Creating and adjusting the selection

First, create the selection using the Magic Wand tool.

1 Select the Magic Wand tool (✎) from the Tools panel.

2 Move the cursor over the cloud portion of the image, and click once. As illustrated here, a selection appears, but areas are missing from the selection.

3 In the Properties panel, make sure Live Marquee is enabled and then change the Tolerance setting to 100.

4 Press the Tab key to apply the change. The entire sky is now selected.

5 Zoom in to the horizon, and notice that Fireworks also selected some edge pixels from the hills. The changes you are about to make will have a detrimental effect on the image if this is not corrected.

6 Choose Select > Smooth Marquee, and set the value to 1 pixel. This will have a very subtle result, but it will smooth out the bottom edge of the selection a bit without altering the other selection edges.

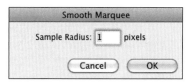

7 Tap the Up arrow key once, to shift the selection 1 pixel higher. The selection edge now sits at the horizon rather than in the hills.

8 From the Select menu, choose Feather and set a value of 4 pixels. Feathering blends the pixels on either side of a selection edge, making for a smoother, more natural result.

A value of 4 pixels means that the edge will be blended 2 pixels on either side of the selection. It's not a lot, but you are dealing with a fairly low-resolution image. On higher-resolution images, this value would probably need to be higher.

9   Zoom back to 100%.

Applying bitmap filters

You will apply two permanent bitmap filters to the sky to *punch it up*. When working with bitmap selections, you must use bitmap filters instead of Live Filters. You may even notice that there is no option in the Properties panel to apply a Live Filter when a bitmap selection is active. Live Filters work at the *object level* only, which means that you cannot apply them to selected regions.

1   To see how our alteration blends with the rest of the photo, choose View > Edges (or press Ctrl+H on Windows or Option+F9 on Mac). This hides the selection from view but still lets you perform actions on it, such as applying filters.

▶ **Tip:** On a Mac laptop you also have to hold down the fn key when using the F keyboard commands.

2   Choose Filters > Adjust Color > Levels.

3   Set the Midtone (Gamma) input value to **0.7**. You can do this by typing into the Input box or dragging the middle slider.

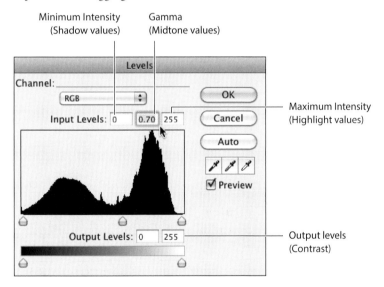

4   Toggle Preview off and on again repeatedly to see how the cloud definition has changed, and then click OK to apply the filter.

One more filter needs to be added, to increase the saturation of the sky.

5   Choose Filters > Adjust Color > Hue/Saturation.

6 Change the Saturation value to 15. Any higher, and things start looking a bit strange.

7 Toggle the Preview option off and then on so you can see the difference, then click OK.

Saving a Fireworks PNG file

The file you opened was a JPG file, but since opening it, you have created a duplicate bitmap object. So saving the file at this point presents a couple of choices. Fireworks recognizes that this altered image has properties that are not supported in a flat JPEG file, so you will see a dialog box asking you for a decision about which type of file you'd like to save.

If you choose to save the file as a JPG, it will be flattened to a single layer and you should rename it so you don't overwrite the original image. If you choose the option Save Fireworks PNG, the file retains its editability (both bitmaps are retained) and Fireworks automatically appends **.fw.png** to the file name. The .fw is not mandatory, but it's a great, simple way to differentiate between Fireworks PNG files and standard, flat PNG files.

1 Choose File > Save.

2 Click the Save Fireworks PNG button and accept the default name.

3 Close the file.

Using the Magic Wand tool with keyboard modifiers

Because the Magic Wand tool selects based on contiguous pixel color, areas you want included may not always become part of your original selection. Changing the Tolerance setting helps, but might not get you as accurate a selection as you want without some trial and error. Another alternative is to use modifier keys to add to the selection.

In this exercise, you are going to use the Magic Wand in conjunction with the Shift key to select multiple areas. You will also learn how to save a bitmap selection, and invert—or reverse—the selection.

1 Choose File > Open, and browse to the Lesson04 folder.

2 Select sand_river1.jpg, and then click Open.

This image is fairly flat, or low in contrast and saturation. The maple leaves in the foreground are a dull red instead of a vibrant reddish-orange. That's one of the changes you will make. While this file is open, you will also desaturate the background of the scene to further enhance the leaves and create a more artistic result.

3　Select the Zoom tool, and draw a box around the leaves. This zooms you right into the area you will be working on.

4　Select the Pointer tool, and click the image to make it active.

5　Press Ctrl+Shift+D (Windows) or Command+Shift+D (Mac) to create a clone of the image, and rename this duplicate **Retouching** in the Layers panel.

▶ **Tip:** You might want to change the name of the original image to Original.

6　Select the Magic Wand tool from the Tools panel.

7　In the Properties panel, set the Tolerance to **40**.

8　You hid selections from view in the last exercise, and this setting is sticky. Choose View > Edges (or press Ctrl+H on Windows or Option+F9 on Mac) to restore the visibility of the selection edge.

9　Move the cursor to the middle of the top leaf, and click once. A selection appears. The section is also called a marquee due to the apparent blinking and shifting of the visible selection edge. The not-so-technical term is *the marching ants*.

Your first selection may be a little different, depending on exactly where the Magic Wand was when you clicked the mouse. Regardless, you see that there are areas not yet selected by the Magic Wand. No worries; you'll be adding to the current selection next.

10　Hold down the Shift key, and click elsewhere on the red leaves, where there is no selection.

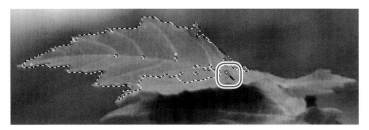

Note: The modifier keys—Alt (Windows), Option (Mac), and Shift (both)—work with the Rubber Stamp, Lasso, Marquee, and Oval Marquee tools.

11 Continue this process of Shift-clicking until you have the leaves selected. You may need to spend a bit of time on this, experimenting with tolerance settings.

If you create a particularly complex selection, such as the one you've just done, it's a really good idea to save your efforts as an alpha channel in order to reuse the selection at a later time. See the sidebar "Saving and restoring bitmap selections." (Your file is currently a perfect fit for this.)

Saving and restoring bitmap selections

Once you've created a complex selection, you can save it, giving you the option to deselect it, work on other parts of the image, and come back to that selection later. These functions are available regardless of the selection tool you've used in the first place. To save a selection, you first need to have an active bitmap selection.

1   Choose Select > Save Bitmap Selection.

2   In the Save Selection dialog box, change the name to **leaves**. Leave all other settings as they are.

3   Click OK.

Once a selection is saved, you can then call it up any time you need it during your session. If you save the file as a Fireworks PNG file, the selection remains with the file and can be restored even after the file has been closed and reopened.

4   Press Ctrl+D (Windows) or Command+Shift+A (Mac) to deselect the bitmap selections on the canvas (so that you can see how to restore it).

5   Choose Select > Restore Bitmap Selection.

6   Click OK. The selection reappears on the canvas.

Note: If you have more than one saved selection, you can choose the correct one from the Selection menu in the Restore Selection dialog box.

Note: Creating the leaf selection took some time, so it's wise to save the selection as you did with the previous document (choose Select > Save Bitmap Selection).

Oh no! I selected too much!

Sometimes the Magic Wand selects areas that you don't want as part of the selection. Welcome to the fine art of bitmap selections! Usually, you do not have to start over. You can first try undoing the last step (Ctrl+Z/Command+Z) and making the selection again at a lower tolerance.

If that is not successful, use the Lasso tool to *subtract* from the selection. Subtracting from a selection is a common action when making complex bitmap selections:

1   Zoom in to the area by pressing Ctrl++ (Windows) or Command++ (Mac).

2   Holding the Alt (Windows) or Option (Mac) key, click the area you wish to remove from the selection.

Remember, the Shift key *adds* to a selection. The Alt or Option key *subtracts* from the selection.

Adding saturation

It's finally time to make those leaves pop, using yet another bitmap filter.

1   Hide the selection by choose View > Edges.

2   Choose Filters > Adjust Color > Hue/Saturation.

3   Set the Saturation value to 70. Yes, pretty extreme, but those are pretty dull leaves!

4   Click OK.

Before Saturation adjustment

After Saturation adjustment

5   Save the file. Again, Fireworks prompts you about the format.

Note: If you had chosen File > Save As, Fireworks would assume you want to save the file as a JPEG. There's a warning message in the Save As dialog box; pay attention to it! Some people don't notice the warning and later reopen the file only to learn the edits have been flattened and the original unaltered image has been lost. Make sure you click on the Save As Type options and choose the format you prefer.

6 Choose Fireworks PNG and accept the default file name when the Save dialog box appears.

	Save	
	Save As: sand_river1.fw.png	

◀ ▶	🔲 lesson04	🔍

	Name	▲	Date Modified
▼ DEVICES		bigsky_final.fw.png	12-02-05
🖥 Macinto...		bigsky.jpg	12-02-05
💿 iDisk		sand_river1_final.fw.png	12-02-05
▼ SHARED		sand_river1.jpg	12-02-05
🖥 belkin n+		trash_sign_final.fw.png	12-02-24
▼ PLACES		trash_sign.fw.png	12-02-24
🖥 Desktop		trash_sign.jpg	07-08-11
Adobe E...			
Pictures			
Adobe Fl...			

☑ **Add Filename Extension**

New Folder Cancel Save

Desaturating the background

To make the leaves jump off the page even more, you will use the bitmap selection and the Command menu to convert the background to black and white.

Note: If you don't see the selection appear, make sure that the marquee is not hidden by selecting View > Edges.

1 Choose View > Edges to bring back the selection you hid in the last exercise. You're doing this only to see how the selection changes on screen. Although this step is not required to complete the effect, you'll be able to see right away if the selection has been removed. If you accidentally removed the selection, use Selection > Restore bitmap selection to bring it back.

2 Show the entire image by pressing Ctrl+0 (Windows) or Command+0 (Mac).

3 Choose Select > Select Inverse. This reverses the selection, so now the leaves are protected and the background can be edited.

4 Hide the selection again.

5 Choose Commands > Creative > Convert to Grayscale. Remember, this is a permanent change at the pixel level, not an editable Live Filter effect.

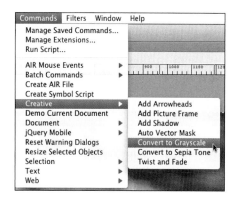

6 Now, hide the retouch object from the Layers panel, so you can see the original image again. I think you'll agree, this image has come a long way!

7 Make the retouched object visible again, and save the file.

Converting a selection to a path

In Fireworks, you can easily convert bitmap selections to vector paths. Paths can be easier to edit than bitmap selections, in part because you aren't as likely to delete an entire path by accident. If you are adjusting a bitmap selection and forget to use the Shift and Alt (Windows) or Option (Mac) modifier keys, you can easily delete the entire selection. By converting a selection to a path, you eliminate this danger. To edit the shape of a path, you can use the Subselection tool (🖈) to drag individual control points in the path. Path objects are also scalable, unlike bitmap objects.

In this exercise, you will work with another image.

1 Choose File > Open and locate the trash_sign.jpg file in the Lesson4 folder.

2 Select the Magic Wand, set its tolerance to 32, and click on the stick figure on the sign.

3 Hold down the Shift key and click on the circle.

4 Choose Select > Convert Marquee to Path.

The selection is removed, and in its place is a new path object, filled with the last attributes used for vector objects. Depending on how much you've been experimenting in Fireworks, the fill and stroke of your path may be very different from what is seen in the example figure.

5 Select the Pointer tool, if it's not already selected.

6 In the Properties panel, set the fill to white, and if necessary, set the stroke color to No Fill.

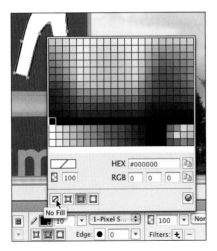

7 In the Layers panel, rename the path to **figure**.

8 Select the Magic Wand again, and click on the waste bin shape.

9 Convert this selection to a path as well (Select > Convert Marquee to Path). Note that the bin takes on the fill and stroke properties of the stick figure.

10 Rename this object to **bin**.

Repurposing paths

You will need each cube as a separate path, but rather than making selections for each cube, you will use the Marquee tool to draw a perfect square and then clone the shape.

1 Zoom in to the three cubes that are falling into the waste bin.

2 Select the Marquee tool.

3 Position the cursor at the upper-left corner of the bottom cube.

4 Hold down the Shift key and drag down to the bottom right corner of the cube. A 60-pixel square should do the job.

5 Choose Select > Convert Marquee to Path.

6 Select the Pointer tool.

7 Hold down the Alt or Option key and drag the path up toward the next cube.

8 Repeat step 7 for the third and final cube. You should now have three vector squares.

9 With the top cube still active, select Modify > Transform > Numeric Transform.

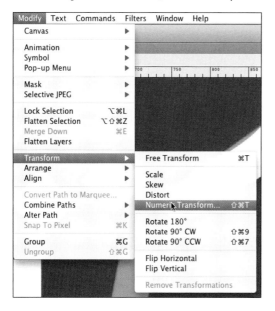

10 Change the transform option from Scale to Rotate.

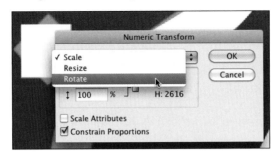

11 Set the angle to 45 degrees, and click OK.

12 Repeat steps 9 through 11 with the middle cube.

13 Use the Pointer tool and the arrow keys to reposition the rotated cubes if necessary.

14 Rename the cube shapes to **red**, **green**, and **blue**, from top to bottom.

15 Select each cube using the Pointer tool, and from the Properties change the fill to the appropriate color, based on the object names.

16 Double-click the Layer 1 name and change it to **vectors**.

17 Move all the new paths to this layer. The fastest way, you might remember, is to select the objects in the Layers panel, then drag the proxy icon from the background layer to the vector layer.

18 Save the file as a Fireworks PNG file.

You will learn much more about working with paths in Lesson 5.

Review questions

1 What is the difference between selecting objects and making bitmap selections?

2 What are the five bitmap selection tools in Fireworks, and what are their functions?

3 What does the Tolerance setting do when you're using the Magic Wand tool?

4 What are the two keyboard modifiers you can use in conjunction with the bitmap selection tools?

5 How do you create a clone of a bitmap image? Why would you do this?

Review answers

1 When you click on an object in the Layers panel or use the Pointer tool to click an object on the canvas, you are selecting (or activating) the entire object, allowing you to move, copy, edit, or cut that object from the design, without affecting anything else on the canvas. A bitmap selection differs from this in that you are selecting a specific part of a bitmap image rather than the entire object. Once you've made a selection, you can copy or edit only the area within the selection border. The bitmap selection tools cannot be used on vector objects.

2 The Fireworks selection tools are the Marquee and Oval Marquee tools, the Lasso and Polygon Lasso tools, and, finally, the Magic Wand tool.

Typically, you use the Marquee or Oval Marquee tool to select regularly shaped areas, and the Lasso or Polygon Lasso tool to select irregular areas. You use the Magic Wand tool to select pixels based on color.

3 The Magic Wand tool selects contiguous pixels of the same color range based on the tolerance setting in the Properties panel. You can increase the tool's sensitivity by changing the Tolerance setting in the Properties panel to a higher value.

4 The Shift key is one of the keyboard modifiers you can use with bitmap selection tools, and the Alt (Windows) or Option (Mac) key is the other. Both of these modifiers work with the Rubber Stamp and freehand Lasso tools, as well as the rectangular and elliptical marquees. Holding down the Shift key lets you add to an existing selection. To subtract from a selection, hold down Alt (Windows) or Option (Mac).

While drawing the initial selection, holding down the Shift key constrains the marquee tools to symmetrical objects (squares and circles) and the Polygon Lasso tool segments to 45-degree increments.

5 To clone a bitmap image (or any other object), press Ctrl+Shift+D (Windows) or Command+Shift+D (Mac), or choose Edit > Clone to create a clone of the image. Creating a clone of your original image lets you edit and retouch a copy without damaging the original.

5 WORKING WITH VECTOR GRAPHICS

Lesson overview

You can draw almost any shape in Fireworks by using vectors. In this lesson, you'll work on vector graphics for both the Near North website project from Lesson 3 and the Local mobile app you were introduced to in Lesson 2. You will also use the Properties panel and Subselection tool to modify vectors you've created. In this lesson, you'll learn how to do the following:

- Draw simple vector shapes

- Identify the differences between vector and bitmap images

- Use the Compound Shape tool

- Create paths with the Pen and Line tools

- Edit paths with the Pen and Subselection tools

- Create a custom shape

- Use Auto Shapes

- Customize the fill and stroke of a vector shape

 This lesson takes approximately 90 minutes to complete. Copy the Lesson05 folder into the Lessons folder that you created on your hard drive for these projects (or create it now, if you haven't already done so). As you work on this lesson, you won't preserve the start files. If you need to restore the start files, copy them from the *Adobe Fireworks C65 Classroom in a Book* CD.

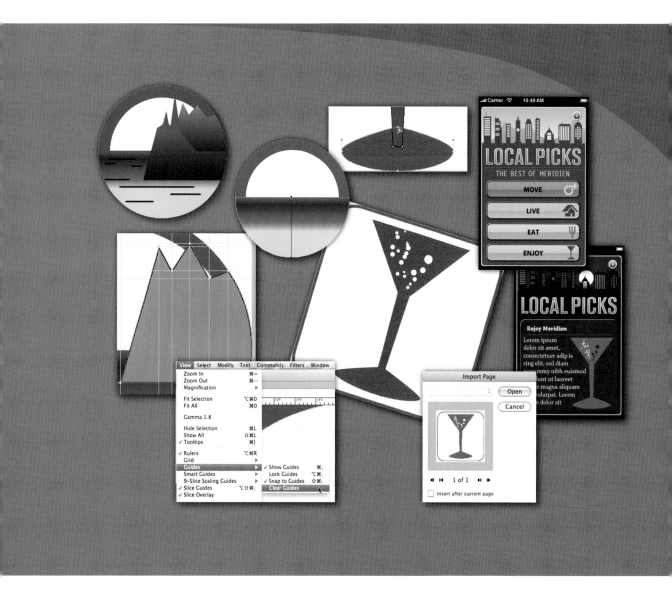

Vectors are a powerful component of Fireworks, giving you the flexibility to create unique custom shapes or call on the many prebuilt vectors that are part of Fireworks.

Understanding vectors

Computer drawings that use mathematical equations to draw lines and fills onscreen are known as vectors. A *vector* is simply the path between two defined points on the screen, with properties such as color and thickness applied to the path.

Fireworks comes with a range of prebuilt vector shapes, most of which are found in their very own section of the Tools panel. The Shapes panel also contains a series of special vector-based Auto Shapes that you can use and customize.

The most commonly used vector tools are the Text, Shape, and Pen tools.

Vector shapes are often used as masks for bitmap objects, too.

With a bit of practice, you'll be creating your own custom vector shapes and masks before you know it. For now, start off simply by re-creating a logo for the Near North website.

Bitmap and vector graphics: What's the difference?

The intrinsic ability of Fireworks to move back and forth between vectors and bitmaps—and even combine both graphic types—makes it a powerful creative tool. But it's important to understand the differences between these two types of graphics, so you know which to use in any situation.

Bitmap graphics (also referred to as raster graphics) are made of a specific number of pixels "mapped" to a grid. Each pixel has a specific location and color value. The greater the number of pixels, the higher the resolution of the image and the larger the file size. If you resize a bitmap image, you are either adding pixels to or taking pixels away from the image, and this will affect image quality and file size. The initial number of pixels in a bitmap image is set at the time of capture.

Vector graphics are mathematical equations describing the distance and angle between two points. You can also specify additional information, such as the color and thickness of the line (stroke) and the contents of the path (fill). Unlike bitmaps, vectors can be resized up or down with no detrimental impact to the vector shape itself.

One example of the differences between vector and bitmap is this: A photograph can accurately depict a physical scene in a single image layer, but its resolution is a fixed size. Scaling the image impacts image quality because as you scale an image, you're basically asking the software to generate pixels that didn't exist in the original.

On the other hand, producing similar "photo-like" realism in a vector illustration could require hundreds and hundreds of vector shapes stacked on each other. But you could scale this image as often as you like with no reduction in image quality.

This is not to suggest that bitmaps are better than vectors, or vice versa; both of these main graphic types are integral to visual communication.

Basic vector drawing techniques

The Tools panel contains several basic vector shapes, including the Line tool, the Ellipse tool, the Polygon tool, and the Rectangle tool, with which you worked in previous lessons. To create one of these shapes, select the appropriate tool, and then click and drag on the canvas. You can then scale, skew, and distort shapes using the Transform tools in the Tools panel, as well as use the Properties panel to change the fill and stroke and even add a texture for a more realistic look.

Paths, shapes, and composite paths

Much like basic geometry, a **path** is simply a line that starts in one place and ends in another. It has a minimum of two *control points* (or *anchors*) that define those starting and ending points. Adding additional anchor points to the path allows changes in direction or even curvature of the path.

When a path has more than two anchors, the distance between any two points is often referred to as a **path segment**. Paths are created with the Pen or Line tools.

A **shape** is a closed path, meaning that its start point joins with its end point to *close* the path. In the context of Fireworks, the term "shape" usually refers to a prebuilt, closed vector path that can be drawn easily with a vector tool, such as rectangles, ellipses, and polygons.

A **composite path** is the result of merging two or more shapes or paths into a single path.

In the example below, the rectangles on the left are standard rectangle shapes. On the right, those two paths (shapes are paths, remember) were combined using a command called *Punch*; the smaller rectangle merged with the larger rectangle by punching a hole, making the background gradient colors visible.

Two separate rectangles   Composite path created by combining paths

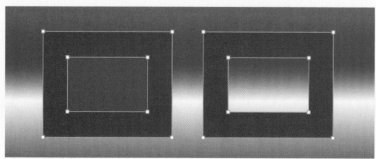

In this first exercise, you will add two ellipses to a brand-new document to begin the logo. In the next, you will cut out, or *punch*, a hole to turn the ellipses into a single hollow ring. Finally, you will add a water effect to the logo. Remember that at any time, you can refer to the final version of the logo, logo.fw.png.

1   Choose File > New.

2   In the New Document dialog, set Width and Height to **400** pixels each, Resolution to **72**ppi, and a canvas color of white.

New Document		
Canvas Size:	625.00 K	
Width:	400	Pixels	W: 400
Height:	400	Pixels	H: 400
Resolution:	72	Pixels/Inch	
Canvas Color		
⦿ White		
○ Transparent		
○ Custom:		
Templates...	Cancel	OK

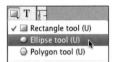

3   Choose the Ellipse tool from the vector tools.

4   Set the fill type to solid, using the appropriate fill-type icon in the Properties panel, and set the color to **#0000FF**.

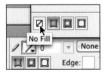

5   While pressing the Shift key, draw the cursor from the top-left corner of the canvas to the bottom right. The final circle should be as large as the canvas, 400 x 400 pixels, centered vertically and horizontally within the canvas.

6   Make sure there is no color applied to the stroke. If there is a stroke color, choose No Fill from the color picker.

7   Create a Clone of this ellipse by pressing Ctrl+Shift+D (Windows) or Command+Shift+D (Mac). Cloning places the new ellipse in exactly the same X, Y location as the original. You will be using this cloned ellipse to punch a hole through the original ellipse, creating a hollow ring shape.

8 Constrain the Proportions in the Properties panel, and set a width of **350** pixels for the new circle.

9 Press the Tab key to proportionately resize the ellipse.

10 The smaller ellipse needs to be evenly centered on top of the larger ellipse in order to get the intended result. To align the smaller ellipse to the center of the canvas, open the Align panel and select the Relative To Canvas option.

11 Click the Align horizontal center and Align vertical center icons.

Punching a vector shape

The smaller ellipse will be used to punch a perfectly centered, round opening in the larger ellipse, creating the ring shape.

1 Select the Pointer tool and then drag the cursor over both ellipses to select them.

2 Select Modify > Combine Paths > Punch.

You now have a ring. Because two shapes have been altered and in a way merged together, the end result is no longer an ellipse shape but a new path called a *composite path*.

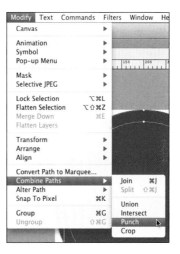

3 In the Layers panel, rename this new composite path to **ring**.

4 Rename the Layer to ring, and lock the layer.

6 Save the file as logo_working.fw.png.

Adding the water

The water effect is created by using a half circle, a custom gradient fill and some lines to give the water a bit of texture.

For the first stage of the logo's water effect you'll draw an ellipse, then use the Knife tool to cut it in half.

1 Create a new Layer by clicking the New/Duplicate Layer icon in the Properties panel.

2 Name this new layer **water**.

3 Select the Ellipse tool.

4 While pressing the Shift key, draw the cursor from the top-left corner of the canvas to the bottom right. You should end up with an ellipse that is 400 x 400 pixels in size, centered vertically and horizontally on the canvas.

5 Zoom to 200%.

6 Select the Knife ( ) tool from the vector tools.

Note: If things don't appear to be working as expected, save your work and restart Fireworks.

7 Place your cursor (which turns into a knife icon) over the left-center control point for the ellipse.

8 While holding down the Shift key, drag straight across to the left past the center-right control point, and then release the mouse.

As you can see in the Layers panel, you just split the ellipse into two half circles.

9 Click off the canvas to deselect all the objects.

10 Select the upper half circle in the Layers panel and delete it.

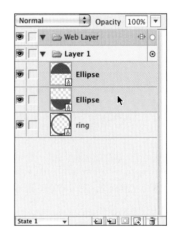

Cutting the path with the Knife tool created a half circle, but the path is technically *open*, which can cause issues. For example, if you wanted to add a stroke to this path, the stroke would only follow the actual path of the half circle. The straight edge across the top would not be stroked. Next, you will close the path.

11 Choose the Subselection tool.

12 Click on the left-center anchor point to select it. The white anchor turns blue.

13 Hold down the Shift key and click on the right-center anchor point.

14 Open the Path panel (Window > Path).

15 From the Edit Points section, choose Join Points.

16 Rename this object to **water**.

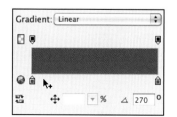

Creating a custom gradient

To create the look of water, you will change the solid fill to a custom gradient.

1 With the half circle still selected, change the fill type from Solid to Gradient.

2 Click the Fill Color box to launch the Gradient Editor.

3 Select the first color stop (colored box under the gradient bar) at the left edge of the gradient bar. The Location Of Stop field should read 0.

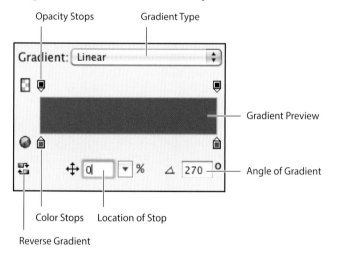

▶ **Tip:** The Location Of Stop field is measured in percentage, from 0 (starting point of gradient ramp) to 100 (ending point). You do not need to have a color stop at the 0 and 100 markers, but you must have at least two color stops to make up any gradient.

● **Note:** If the colors in your gradient ramp don't match the figures shown here, don't worry; just select the color swatches to change the colors.

4 Place your cursor to the right of the first color stop. A black arrow and plus sign (+) icon appear. This is the *new color stop* cursor.

5 Click the mouse. A new color stop appears. Its location also displays.

6 In the Location Of Stop field, set the value to **12**.

7 Click on the new color stop to launch the color picker.

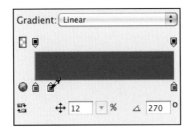

8 Type a hex value of **#12006F** into the HEX field, and then press the Enter key.

> ▶ **Tip:** If you accidentally add a color stop, simply drag it away from the gradient preview to remove it.

9 Add another color stop, and set its location to 36.

10 Change the color of this stop to **#3333FF**, and press the Enter key.

11 Select the final color stop at the right edge, and change its location value to **56**.

12 Set the color of this stop to **#66CCFF**.

You should now have four colors in your custom gradient.

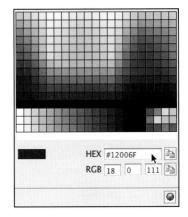

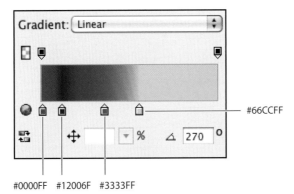

13 Tap the Enter key to close the Gradient Editor.

14 Select the Pointer tool if necessary, and then click on the "water" object.

A black control arm appears on the shape. This "arm" controls the location, direction, angle, and length of the gradient fill. The arm has a circle control point at one end and a square control point at the other. The circle controls the position/starting point for the gradient; the square controls the angle and length. By default, the linear gradient runs from top to bottom, the full height of the object.

The custom gradient looks OK, but you might notice it isn't very smooth or continuous. You can smooth the appearance of linear gradients (such as this one) or radial gradients by using the Gradient Dither option.

15 In the Properties panel, click the Gradient Dither button ( ).

The "water" looks a little smoother now.

16 Save the file.

Adding water lines

To add a bit of texture to the water, you will use the Line tool to draw a few horizontal lines of varying length.

As mentioned earlier, a line is the most basic of paths. It consists of an origin point and an end point. Point A to Point B—basic geometry. The stroke properties you set in the Properties panel determine the look of the line (thickness, texture, color) between those two points.

Study the finished version of the logo (logo_finished.fw.png). You need to draw several lines of varying length and position on the water shape.

1 Deselect all objects and then select the Line tool ( ), and in the Properties panel, set black for the stroke color, set Tip Size to **4**, and choose Pencil > 1-Pixel Soft for Stroke Category.

2 To draw a line, click and hold the mouse to set the origin point of the line.

3 Drag the cursor to a different location on the canvas, and release the mouse button.

Congratulations, you've just drawn a line! To maintain perfectly straight lines, hold down the Shift key as you draw each line. Make sure you release the mouse button before you release the Shift key.

4 Continue this process of drawing lines, comparing your work to the finished art. The exact lengths do not need to match the final sample, but all the lines should be horizontal.

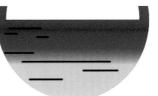

5 Save the file when you are done.

● **Note:** New CS6 options in the Gradient Editor include the Location Of Stop and Gradient Angle fields. These two settings give you pixel-level control over the starting point of a gradient color (location) and the ability to numerically set the angle of the gradient.

● **Note:** The Line tool is the vector equivalent of the bitmap Pencil tool. Instead of drawing bitmap lines that get rasterized into the nearest bitmap layer though, the lines created by the Line tool remain as individual vector paths, making them easy to edit and reposition. The Line tool creates a single path and has attributes for the stroke only. There are no Fill attributes applied to a path.

Understanding paths and the Pen tool

The next phase of the logo project is to add the mountainscape. You will be creating these shapes using the Pen tool. A very powerful vector tool, the Pen tool lets you create custom shapes and paths by drawing with the mouse or a stylus. You can also use it to edit existing shapes by adding anchor points. Unlike the Pencil bitmap tool, with which you basically just click and drag to draw a bitmap line, using the Pen tool involves clicking the mouse to set a straight line between two *anchor points* (a place where the path can change direction) or clicking and dragging to create a curved section of a path. Every time you want to change the direction of a path, you move the mouse to the desired position and then click to set an anchor point. Before you try to move mountains, try some practice work.

1 Create a new document that is 500 x 500 pixels.

2 Set the Canvas color to white if it isn't already, and click OK.

3 Select the Pen tool (✎).

4 Make sure a stroke color has been applied, so you'll be able to see and select the finished path later. Black is fine.

5 Click once near the left side of the canvas and release the mouse to create the first anchor point.

6 Move your cursor near the middle of the canvas. A line follows your cursor.

7 Click again to set another anchor point. A blue line (the actual path segment) appears, connecting the two points. Depending on the thickness of your stroke, you may also see the stroke itself. With a thin stroke like this, you won't really see the stroke until after the path is deselected.

8 Move the cursor to the right side of the canvas.

9 This time, instead of just clicking the mouse, hold down the mouse button and *drag*. This pulls out curve control arms for that section of the path, so that you can change the path segment from a straight line to a curve. As you drag the mouse, you're pulling the curve arms and the curve increases.

10 When you have drawn a curve to your satisfaction, release the mouse button. As you move the cursor to add more anchor points, Fireworks continues to display the path outline in blue.

To end a path, you have to disengage the Pen tool, otherwise the path just keeps following the pen cursor all over the canvas. To disengage the tool either:

* Close the path (create a shape) by clicking the original starting anchor point.

* Double-click the last anchor point to create an open path.

▶ **Tip:** If you see a crosshair cursor icon instead of the Pen icon, check to see if your Caps Lock key is active.

Other vector tools

This lesson won't use all the vector tools that Fireworks has, so here is a breakdown of the other tools available and what they do:

* **Vector Path tool** (🖌): Draws paths in a more organic manner. You'll get the best results with Vector Path tool using a stylus and drawing tablet, due to the precise control and varying degrees of pressure that a tablet allows, but you can also use a mouse to draw these independent paths. Think of the Vector Path tool as a freehand version of the Pen tool or the vector equivalent of the brush tool.

* **Redraw Path tool** (🖋): Gives you another way to edit a vector shape or path without having to use the Pen and Subselection tools. Like the Vector Path tool, you use this tool in a freehand manner. Unlike the Vector Path tool, its primary use is to edit an existing, active path by connecting the active path to a segment drawn with the Redraw Path tool, changing the original path's shape. The trick with this tool is that it must begin by intersecting part of an active path or vector shape.

* **Freeform tool** (🖋): Lets you bend and reshape vectors interactively instead of altering anchor points. You use this tool to push or pull any part of a path, and Fireworks adds, moves, or deletes points along the path as you change the vector object's shape.

* **Reshape Area tool** (🖉): Pulls the area of all selected paths within the outer circle of the reshape-area pointer. Think of it as a smudge tool for vectors, but instead of smearing pixels, it alters a path's shape.

* **Path Scrubbers** (🖑) (🖑): Alter the heaviness of the stroke, which is applied to the path, either adding to or subtracting from the stroke, depending on which version of the tool you use. They affect the stroke only in the areas you paint over with the tool. This can give the stroke a bit more of a hand-drawn look.

Anchor point basics

Anchor points have two states: straight and curved. You can convert a straight point to a curved point by using the Pen tool to click and drag out the curve control arms, also known as Bezier control arms.

To convert a curved anchor to a straight point, just click on it once with the Pen tool. Click a second time to delete the anchor point entirely.

If you want to delete a straight anchor point, select it with the Subselection tool, and press the Delete key.

Editing paths

Creating paths and shapes is empowering (and fun!), but it's only half the battle. Knowing how to edit vectors—that is, being able to customize them—is equally important.

Adding points with the Pen tool

You can add anchor points to an existing path using the Pen tool. Try it with the path from the previous exercise.

Note: If you add a point to a curved segment, it is automatically a curved anchor point.

1 Make sure the path is active by selecting it with the Pointer tool.

2 Select the Pen tool.

3 Position the cursor on the straight segment of the path; note the plus sign (+) that appears next to the Pen tool's cursor. Click once to add a new anchor point. The length of the path doesn't increase; you've just added a new point where you can change the path's change direction with the Subselection tool or the path segment's curvature using the Pen tool.

Note: The exception to adding points to a path is if you are working with rectangle shapes. These must be ungrouped before you can add additional anchor points to them.

4 To disengage the Pen tool, double-click the last control point in the path. This frees up the tool to draw a new, separate path.

Editing paths with the Subselection tool

After creating a path, you can use the Subselection tool ( ) to select and alter the location of individual anchor points, thus changing the shape of the path. The Subselection tool works similarly to the Direct Selection tool in Photoshop or Illustrator.

1 Select the Subselection tool from the Tools panel.

2 Move the tool to the middle anchor point of the first practice path you created with the Pen tool. If the vector is no longer active (highlighted in blue), click anywhere on the path to activate it.

3 Click and drag the middle anchor point lower on the canvas. The path redraws when you release the mouse.

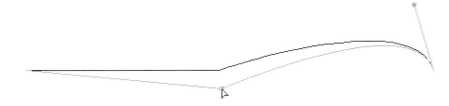

Feel free to practice more with the Pen tool, but there is no need to save this practice file (unless you really like what you created, of course). You're going to make use of the Pen tool in the next exercise.

Making mountains out of vectors

The Near North logo has some symbolic mountains on the right side of the shape. You will create that mountain range with the Pen tool.

To help you with this first foray into creating a custom shape, you will set up some guides first.

Adding guides

Guides are great tools for aligning and precisely placing or drawing objects on the canvas. By default, the Pen tool automatically snaps to the nearest guide. To help draw the mountains, you will put several guides in place prior to using the Pen tool.

1 Switch back to the logo image by clicking on its tab.

2 Make sure that the Rulers and Tooltips are enabled (View > Rulers, View > Tooltips).

3 Select the Pointer tool.

4 Move your cursor over the left ruler.

Note: To use the Subselection tool on Auto Shapes or on vectors created by the Rectangle tool, you must first ungroup them by choosing Modify > Ungroup or pressing Ctrl+Shift+G (Windows) or Command+Shift+G (Mac). They will lose their unique characteristics: Auto Shapes will lose their yellow control handles, and you will no longer be able to change the corner radius of a rectangle from within the Properties panel.

Note: Many designs include objects to visually "contain" other objects such as text and graphics. Think back to the website mock-up from Lesson 3, where you used rectangles to define the sidebar and main content areas. When standard shapes aren't enough, you can turn to the Pen tool to create your own custom vector shapes or paths.

Note: Text is also a vector, but you're focusing on shapes and paths in this lesson.

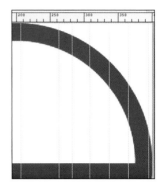

5 Click and drag toward the canvas. You will see a vertical guide appear. You will also see a tooltip appear beside the guide, with an X value.

6 When the tooltip displays x:206, let go of the mouse. The guide drops at that location.

▶ **Tip:** If you want a higher degree of accuracy, double-click on the guide and then set the location numerically.

7 Place six more vertical guides at these X values: 263, 282, 308, 337, 365, and 395.

8 From the top ruler, drag down five guides at the following Y locations: 48, 53, 87, 98, and 246.

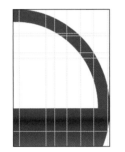

▶ **Tip:** If you find the guides getting in the way, you can hide them temporarily by pressing Ctrl+; (Windows) or Command+; (Mac), or by choosing View > Guides > Show Guides. You can clear the guides completely by choosing View > Guides > Clear Guides.

Drawing a custom vector shape using guides

This array of lines may seem confusing at first, but because you're new to working with paths, and you want a fairly accurate reproduction of our original logo, the guides will be very handy.

1 Create a new layer and call it **mountains**.

2 Choose View > Guides, and make sure that Snap To Guides is selected.

3 Select the Pen tool from the Tools panel.

4 In the Properties panel, choose Black for the stroke color, set Tip Size to 1, and choose Pencil > 1-Pixel Soft for Stroke Category.

5 Set the fill color to **#4D8E3B**, a medium green color.

Now, these next steps might sound a little confusing as they describe cursor positions, so be sure to check out the figures that go along with these steps. It really is easier than it sounds!

6 Place the cursor where the left-most and bottommost guides intersect and click once to set the origin point.

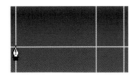

7 Move the cursor up to the intersection of the next vertical guide to the right and the second-lowest horizontal guide.

8 Click the mouse to set a new anchor point.

9 Move the cursor down and to the right, where the third vertical guide intersects with the third lowest horizontal guide.

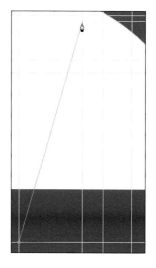

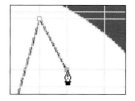

10 Click the cursor again to set a new anchor point.

11 Move the cursor up and to the right, where the topmost horizontal guide intersects with the next vertical guide, and click the mouse again.

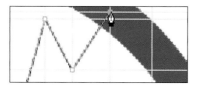

12 Move the cursor down and to the right, where the fourth lowest guide intersects with the third from the right guide, and then click the mouse.

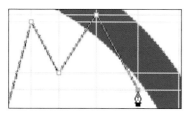

13 Move the cursor up and to the right, where the third lowest guide intersects with the second-from-the-right vertical guide, then click to set the anchor point.

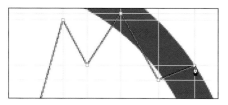

14 Move the cursor down to where the right-most vertical guide intersects with the bottommost horizontal guide, then click and drag the cursor to create a curved path.

15 Drag the curve control arms far enough down and to the right that the curve of the mountain matches the curve of the outer edge of the blue ring of the logo. Release the mouse button. Don't worry if you're a few pixels off; this can be fixed by editing the point later on.

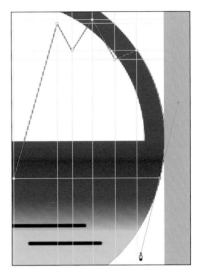

Once you are happy with the curve, you need to change the path back to a straight line.

16 Bring the cursor back to the anchor point you just created and click on the anchor *once*. This changes the path back to a straight line for the final segment of the path.

17 Move your cursor over to the original anchor point. When you see the close-path cursor, click the mouse a final time.

The path closes and fills with the solid green color you set back in step 5.

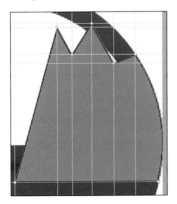

18 You've done a lot of work here! Save your file before you go any further.

Extra credit

All right, you've learned how to create custom gradient fills, and the basics of working with the Pen tool. The logo still needs a gradient fill added to your first mountain range and, based on the finished version, also needs another set of mountains in the foreground.

Study the finished file and see how well you do at adding a new custom gradient as well as creating another set of mountains using the Pen tool. Remember, you can unlock the objects in the finished file to learn more about their properties.

Creating an icon

There's been a request to add some iconography to the navigation buttons for the Local mobile application mock-up and to include that icon in the summary page for each category. You've been charged with creating a martini glass icon for the Enjoy button and for the Enjoy summary page of the mock-up.

You will use the Compound Shape tool for everything except some of the bubbles. You'll use another trick to create most of those.

Found in the Properties panel, the Compound Shape tool lets you temporarily group vector shapes together, making it easier to create complex vector shapes from simpler vector objects. You can subselect vectors that are grouped this way and edit them as individual objects, or you can use the Pointer tool to reposition the entire group at once. When you are happy with the work, you can combine the group into a single compound path.

The Compound Shape tool consists of six controls: Normal, Add/Union, Subtract/Punch, Intersect, Crop, and Combine. Normal is the default setting; each drawn shape is a single independent object. When you draw a vector shape such as a rectangle, ellipse, or polygon, or use the Pen tool, you can use the other controls to group shapes together in different ways.

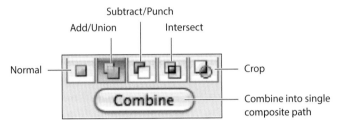

Before you begin adding shapes, take a moment to prepare your canvas:

1 Create a new document that is 500 x 500 pixels.

2 Set the canvas to white.

3 Make sure that Smart Guides and Tooltips are still active (View > Smart Guides > Show Smart Guides, View > Tooltips).

4 Make sure the Properties panel is expanded so you can see the Compound Shape tool at the right side of the panel.

Adding the shapes

Glassblowers may be able to create stemware in one piece, but you'll assemble your martini glass from three distinct shapes: the bowl, the stem, and the base. Each uses a slightly different vector technique, but they are all combined together using the Compound Shape tool.

The bowl

To create the bowl of the glass, you'll use the Polygon tool to draw a triangle.

1 Select the Polygon tool.

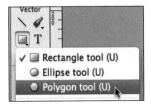

2 Set the fill color to red and the stroke color to No Fill.

3 In the Properties panel, make sure the shape is set to polygon, the sides to **3**, and the angle left at Automatic.

4 Draw the triangle, aiming for a horizontal width of 250 pixels. The actual drawing is a little tricky because as you draw, the triangle rotates as well. Try to get the top part of the triangle as horizontal as possible, but don't stress too much on this detail. You can use the Subselection tool later to tidy things up. This will be the bowl of the glass.

5 Reposition the triangle so that it's centered left to right. Smart Guides will help with this.

6 Choose the Scale tool.

7 Hold down the Alt (Option) key and drag the left- or right-center control handle until you have a satisfactory width for the bowl of the glass.

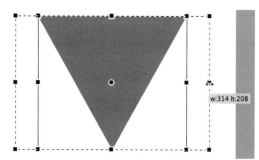

> **Tip:** If you can't seem to get the top of the bowl perfectly straight, drag a horizontal guide down from the top ruler so that it lines up with the top of the bowl. Zoom in on the anchor point and drag the point to the guide. You may need to do the same thing to the opposite anchor point to get a razor-sharp line.

8 Press Enter to commit the change.

9 If you need to straighten the top edge of the triangle, choose the Subselection tool and click on the control point you want to change. Use the arrow keys to alter the control point location one pixel at a time.

The stem

Adding the stem is next on the list. You'll use the Compound Shape and Rectangle tools this time.

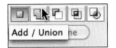

1 In the Properties panel, select the Add/Union icon of the Compound Shape tool. As you mouse over each icon, Fireworks will display a tooltip to tell you what the icon represents.

2 Select the Rectangle tool and draw the stem for the glass. The stem should overlap the bottom of the triangle and be relatively narrow (around 40 pixels).

3 Select the Pointer tool, and then click on either shape; you'll see that both shapes become selected. Now you can move them as a single object with the Pointer tool.

4 Choose the Subselection tool, and click on the rectangle.

All four points for the rectangle become highlighted in blue. The bowl of the glass has black control-point outlines. The blue indicates the subselected object.

5 To taper the bottom of the stem, the rectangle must first be ungrouped, so press Ctrl+Shift+G (Windows) or Command+Shift+G (Mac) to make the corner points editable. Alternatively, you can use the Skew tool to narrow the bottom of the rectangle.

6 Bring the bottom corners toward the center by about 10 pixels, either by using the Subselection tool and dragging the bottom control points, or by selecting the Skew tool, and holding down the Option/Alt key while dragging either bottom corner point.

The base

Finally, you'll add the base: an ellipse joined to the glass with Add/Union.

1 Select the entire object with the Pointer tool, and make sure the Add/Union icon is still selected in the Compound Shape tool.

2 Select the Ellipse tool, and draw an oval to act as the base of the glass.

3 Use the Subselection tool to reposition the oval so it is centered left to right.

Next, you need to alter the base of the glass so it has a more cone-like appearance.

4 Select the Pen tool, and click once on the top control point for the ellipse. This converts the point from a curved point to a straight point, which makes your cone.

5 Hold down the Shift key and press the up arrow once or twice to enhance the profile of the cone. If necessary, select Modify > Canvas > Fit Canvas to make the canvas extend to contain the entire object.

The main compound shape is finished.

● **Note:** Remember to name your objects appropriately as you build your design. When the main compound shape is finished, name it martini glass.

● **Note:** When the main compound shape is done, don't forget to save your hard work. Use the file name martini_icon.fw.png.

A fizzy Cosmo, please

To add some fizz to the glass, you'll try a couple of different techniques. The first one relies on the Compound Shape tool again, and while it takes a little longer to do, the bubbles are more controllable.

Method 1: Punching circles

Remember the steps you did for punching out the ring in the logo artwork? Not too complex, but imagine having to do it *over and over again* like you might for a bunch of bubbles. The Compound Shape tool makes short work of punching holes in vectors, *and* they remain editable after the fact.

1 Select the Ellipse tool from the Vector toolset in the Tools panel.

2 Press the Shift key while drawing a small circle, somewhere in the bowl of the glass.

3 Select the Subselection tool and click the circle, which will be filled with the same color as the glass.

4 Click the Subtract/Punch icon in the Compound Shape tool. This punches the circle through the main shape, showing the white canvas.

The cool part about this is the flexibility of punching in a compound shape. Normally, this process alone takes several steps, and the result is permanent. Not so with the Compound Shape tool.

5 With the Subselection tool still active, click and drag the ellipse. See how easy it is to reposition the punch effect?

Adding more bubbles

Now, one bubble just isn't enough—obviously. Rather than draw more, however, you can duplicate the existing one.

1 With the bubble selected, press Ctrl+Shift+D (Command+Shift+D) to clone it.

2 Use the arrow keys or the Subselection tool to reposition the bubble. Create a few more and position them as you like. Note that the punch effect remains for each ellipse.

3 Clone and reposition a few more bubbles.

Now, with all these bubbles scattered about, it's unlikely they'd all be the same size, right? Right.

4 Select any of the ellipses using the Subselection tool.

5 In the Properties panel, constrain the proportions by clicking on the hollow square between the width and height.

6 Type a new width and press tab. The selected ellipse changes in size uniformly.

7 Select another ellipse. Note that the constrain proportions lock remains. This setting is not object-based. It's a global setting for the document.

8 Continue in this manner, resizing the bubbles on the right side of the glass, until you have something you like or it matches the example file.

Method 2: Using a Custom Stroke (optional)

If you want more randomness (or just a faster way to create a bunch of bubbles), you can draw a path and apply a custom stroke. This option should *not* become part of the compound shape though; the Compound Shape tool requires shapes (closed paths), and it will force your path to become a shape if you attempt to include the path.

1 Click away from the martini glass, off canvas, to ensure nothing is selected.

2 Choose the Vector Path tool.

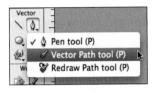

3 Set the stroke style to Unnatural > Paint Splatter.

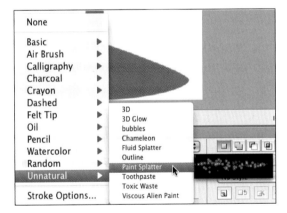

4 Choose white for the stroke color, set the size to **15**, and set Edge to **1**.

5 Choose the Edit Stroke button.

6 Increase the Spacing to 101%, set the Edge Effect to None, and then click OK.

7 Click the Save Custom Stroke icon in the Properties panel to save this as a custom stroke, and call it **Bubbles**.

8 Now use the Vector Path tool to draw a curved "S" path on top of the martini glass. Instant bubbles! This is a pretty random effect, so don't expect the bubbles to exactly follow the contour of the path.

9 Save your work.

If you feel the bubbles are still too clustered, choose Modify > Alter Path > Simplify and set an amount of 10. This will reduce the number of bubbles and spread them out.

The first time doing this did take a few steps, but now you have a *custom stroke* that you can use anytime you want.

Working with Auto Shapes

Auto Shapes are vector art that have additional diamond-shaped control points that let you alter visual properties, such as corner roundness, corner shape, or the number of points in a star. Behind the scenes, JavaScript logic redraws the shape based on your changes to the control points. Most of these control points also have tooltips that describe how they affect the Auto Shape. You will now add an Auto Shape to surround the martini glass.

1 Choose the Rounded Rectangle tool from the Vector section of the Tools panel (click and hold the Rectangle tool to see the other tools available).

2 Hold down the Shift key and drag out a square that is 550 x 550 pixels.

Yes, this is larger than the canvas. When you release the mouse, you'll see the yellow diamonds in each corner. You might also see that the shape takes on the properties of the last vector, which can make for a pretty busy-looking design, with all those bubbles floating about.

3 In the Properties panel, choose Fit Canvas. The canvas expands to hold all the artwork.

When you alter the canvas in this way, Fireworks automatically (and perhaps annoyingly) selects all the artwork on the canvas.

▶ **Tip:** Dragging layers up and down in the Layers panel moves them away or toward the front of the canvas, respectively. You can also choose Modify > Arrange, and then choose one of the four options to alter the stacking order of selected objects: Bring to Front, Bring Forward, Send Backward, and Send to Back. If you use this feature frequently, memorizing the keyboard shortcuts (Ctrl+Up/Down arrow for Windows, or Command+Up/Down arrow for Mac) will be a great time-saver.

4   Select the Pointer tool, and click away from the canvas so that nothing is selected.

5   Reselect the rounded rectangle.

6   Change the fill color to No Fill and set the stroke color to the same red as the martini glass. Do this by moving the cursor over the glass after you invoke the color picker.

7   Change Stroke Category to Felt Tip > Dark Marker.

8   Set the stroke size to **10** and the Edge to **0**.

9   In the Layers panel, rename the new shape **border**, and adjust the stacking order so that the border is below the martini glass.

10 Use the Pointer tool and Smart Guides to reposition the glass so it is centered under on the canvas.

11 Drag any one of the four corner control handles to alter the corner radius of the rectangle.

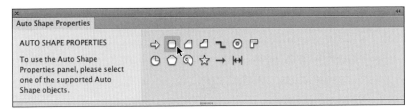

● **Note:** To use the Subselection tool on Auto Shapes or on vectors created by the Rectangle tool, you must first ungroup them by choosing Modify > Ungroup or pressing Ctrl+Shift+G (Windows) or Command+Shift+G (Mac). They will lose their unique characteristics: Auto Shapes will lose their yellow control handles, and you will no longer be able to change the corner radius of a rectangle from within the Properties panel.

Alternatively, you can open the Auto Shapes Properties panel (Window > Auto Shapes Properties) and numerically adjust the radius by choosing the Rounded Rectangle icon. Just make sure the Auto Shape is selected before opening the Auto Shapes Properties panel; otherwise, you will end up creating a new shape.

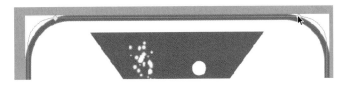

With the border created, this icon could also visually work as a button if desired.

12 Save and close the file.

Next, you will import the martini glass file into a mobile app prototype.

Importing and resizing a vector object

The martini glass is larger than necessary for the mobile app, but it was easier to create the icon at this size rather than very small. And, because you were working with vectors, scaling larger or smaller has no real impact on the overall image quality. You'll import the icon now into the mobile app mock-up and then scale it to fit the design.

1   Open localpicks_320x480_icons.fw.png.

2   Select the HomeDay page, and locate the **icons** subfolder. Note that this subfolder has been added to the Main buttons folder, which is shared across multiple pages. So, any objects added to the subfolder are also shared to the same pages.

3   Select the icons subfolder.

4   Choose File > Import, browse to your completed martini glass and click Open. Because this is a Fireworks PNG file, you will get the Preview window first. Just make sure Insert After Current Page is *not* enabled, and click Open.

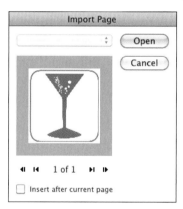

5   Place the Import cursor near the top-right edge of the Enjoy button, drag to the bottom edge of the button, and then release the button.

6   The style of the other icons doesn't include the border you created earlier, so locate the border in the Layers panel and delete it. If you created the second batch of bubbles, using the custom stroke, you can delete them as well, as they're a bit small to be recognizable.

7 Check the size of the martini glass in the Properties panel. If it's taller than 37 pixels, enable the Constrain Proportions box, change the height to **37**, and press the Tab key.

8 Set the X and Y position to **258** and **414**, respectively. It should fit inside the button and not hang out at the top or bottom.

9 Save the file.

● **Note:** When importing images in Fireworks on the Mac, you may have to click once on the canvas to make it active, then click a second time to import the image.

This has been a big lesson, but vectors are a large part of the creative toolset in Fireworks, and it's important that you get comfortable with the tools. Although we did not work with the Auto Shapes panel, we recommend you have a look at the panel and check out the prebuilt vector shapes that are included with Fireworks.

Review questions

1 What is one of the main differences between bitmaps and vectors when scaling is applied?

2 What command flows text with a path shape, and where is it located in the menus?

3 What are Auto Shapes, and where can you find them?

4 How do you edit the control points of a regular vector path or shape once it has been drawn?

5 What is the Pen tool used for?

6 What does the Compound Shape tool do?

Review answers

1 Vector images do not degrade in quality when they are resized smaller or larger, and bitmap images do.

2 The command to flow text within a vector shape can be found at Text > Attach in Path. Both a vector shape and the text must be selected on the canvas before this command will work. The text and the vector shape remain editable after this command has been invoked.

3 Auto Shapes are objects that include additional diamond-shaped control points that let you alter visual properties, such as corner roundness. Dragging a control point alters the associated visual property. Most control points have tooltips that describe how they affect the Auto Shape, too. Basic Auto Shape drawing tools are found in the Tools panel; more complex ones are found in the Shapes panel.

4 To edit the control points of an existing vector object, select the Subselection tool, click on a control point, and drag the control point to reposition the paths connected to it.

5 The Pen tool lets you create custom shapes and paths by drawing with the mouse or a stylus. It also allows you to add anchor points to existing paths. Using the Pen tool involves clicking the mouse to set a straight line between two anchor points (a place where the path can change direction) or clicking and dragging to create a curved section of a path. Every time you want to change the direction of a path, you move the mouse to the desired position and then click to set another anchor point.

6 The Compound Shape tool lets you create complex vector shapes by temporarily grouping other, simpler shapes together, while maintaining the ability to edit each individual shape. You can quickly and easily experiment with various vector effects such as punching or intersecting, without having to walk through a series of destructive steps.

6 MASKING

Lesson overview

Masking, combined with strokes, live filters, and gradient fills, is a key technique for creating and editing imagery without permanently affecting images. Fireworks lets you work with both bitmap and vector masks easily and seamlessly. In this lesson, you'll learn how to do the following:

- Create a bitmap mask from a selection

- Edit a bitmap mask using the Brush tool

- Create a vector mask from a vector shape

- Edit the vector mask and change its properties using the Properties panel

- Use the Auto Vector Mask command

 This lesson takes approximately 90 minutes to complete. Copy the Lesson06 folder into the Lessons folder that you created on your hard drive for these projects (or create it now, if you haven't already done so). As you work on this lesson, you won't preserve the start files. If you need to restore the start files, copy them from the *Adobe Fireworks CS6 Classroom in a Book* CD.

Masking opens up a world of creative options and adds flexibility to your designs because you are not permanently deleting pixels—you're merely hiding them from view.

About the project

Note: All photographs in this and other lessons featuring the the fictitious Near North website were created by Jim Babbage and are free to use for personal or educational use.

In this lesson, you will work with masks to create a new banner image for the Near North Adventures website. Along the way, you'll have a chance to brush up on importing images and using the Pen and Subselection tools.

Before you get into that, however, you need to understand the differences between the two types of masks and to take a look at the finished artwork to give you an idea of where you're going.

1 Open the near_north_banner_final.fw.png file from the Lesson06 folder.

   In this file, masks have been used on the inset images. In many cases, the mask fill has been changed to a gradient to provide a more realistic fade into the background.

   If you check out the Layers panel, you will see that beside each bitmap thumbnail is another thumbnail, representing the mask. You can switch between editing the mask and the image by clicking on the appropriate thumbnail.

   The chain link icon between the two thumbnails indicates that the two objects are linked. This is important to note; when an object and mask are linked, both objects will scale together and move as one object.

   You can unlink the objects by clicking on the icon, letting you scale or move each object independently of the other.

2 Close this file, or keep it open for reference as you progress through the lesson.

About masks

In a nutshell, masks hide or show parts of an object or image. At their simplest, masks are a nondestructive way of cropping objects in your design, without permanently deleting anything. A mask can be edited or discarded at any time. You can also permanently apply a mask, flattening it to the image being masked. There are two basic kinds of mask: bitmap and vector.

Bitmap masks

Bitmap masks hide bitmap image data using a pixel-based mask. You can create bitmap masks using other bitmap images, selections, or the Brush tool (✐).

Bitmap selections

To create a selection for a mask, you can use any of the bitmap selection tools (Marquee, Oval, Lasso, Polygon Lasso, or even the Magic Wand). Decide on the type of edge you want for the selection (Hard, Anti-alias, or Feather) using the Live Marquee settings in the Properties panel. Then, just draw your selection. Bitmap selections can create masks for other bitmaps only.

Brush tool

Using the Brush tool, you can easily create or edit the mask live on the canvas, just by painting. Black hides, white reveals, and shades of gray produce semitransparency. (We'll remind you of this important basic concept later in the lesson.) If you set your brush color to a shade of gray, the pixels you paint over will be semitransparent.

Tip: You can use the grayscale values of one image to mask another. Simply select two bitmap objects that are in the same physical location, and choose Modify > Mask > Group as mask. The topmost image is converted to grayscale, and those values determine what is visible in the bottom image. The darker tones in a photo used as a mask will hide areas on the image being masked. Lighter tones will reveal parts of the masked image.

Creating a bitmap mask with the Brush tool

Creating a bitmap mask can be as easy as clicking on the Add Mask icon in the Layers panel and painting with the Brush tool.

Original image

Beginning to paint a bitmap mask using the Brush tool and black for the brush color

The final masked image

Vector masks

Vector masking is one of the most powerful features in Fireworks. Like bitmap masks, vector masks are a nondestructive way of cropping, but unlike bitmap masks, vector masks can be applied to vectors, bitmaps, groups, or graphic symbols.

Compared to bitmap masks, vector masks tend to have a higher degree of control and accuracy, because you use a path, not a brush, to create them. It's easy to change the fill or stroke of a vector mask. Generating the same type of effect with a bitmap mask can be more time-consuming.

Vector masks use one of two modes: Path Outline or Grayscale Appearance. You can change the mode in the Properties panel.

Mask: ⦿ Path outline
○ Grayscale appearance

In Path Outline mode, the vector mask acts like a cookie cutter, using the shape of the path to act as the mask.

In Grayscale Appearance mode, any bitmap information in the vector fill gets converted to a grayscale alpha channel. Grayscale Appearance uses the pixel values of the vector's fill, its stroke, *and* the vector shape itself to create the mask. If your vector mask has a range of tones in it, such as a gradient fill, the image will be hidden or revealed based on those tones. Just like with bitmap masks, black hides, white reveals, and shades of gray produce semitransparency, as in this example, where a linear gradient has been used to fill the vector shape.

The convenient Auto Vector Mask command works in this way as well. You'll try that out later in the lesson.

You can easily apply a shape as a mask, whether you drew a vector shape using a shape tool or used the Pen tool to create a custom shape.

Designing the banner

The banner you build in this lesson has many elements to it: imported assets, masks, gradients, text, layers, and so on. It will give you good practice with bitmap and vector masks, as well as reinforce some of the techniques you learned in previous lessons.

Creating the document

Start by creating the new, basic document to hold all your further work.

1 Choose File > New.

2 In the New Document dialog box, set the dimensions to **960** pixels wide by **120** pixels high.

3 In the Layers panel, change the default layer name to **background**.

4 Create two more empty layers, and call them **text** and **collage**. The text layer should be at the top of the layer stack.

5 Lock the text and collage layers.

6 Save the file as **near_north_banner.fw.png**.

Adding the background

The background for the final banner is not just a flat color; it's a photograph, and you will add it now.

1 Make sure the background layer is selected.

2 Choose File > Import, and browse for the bluesky.jpg file.

3 Place the Import cursor at the bottom-left corner of the canvas, and drag to the right edge of the canvas. The imported image will be taller than you need, but that's OK. It gives you some flexibility on what section of the image to use.

   The finished banner uses the bottom portion of the sky image; however, feel free to reposition the image vertically and pick an area pleasing to you to use as the background.

▶ **Tip:** On the Mac, you may have to click once to bring the canvas back into focus, then click a second time to import the image.

4 Lock the background layer.

Creating the collage

You're ready to import the five scenic images that will act as the collage. You will import all five images before applying any masking. This workflow is not mandatory, but because most of the masks will blend visually with each other, it will help as you apply the masks to each image.

1 Unlock the collage layer by clicking the lock icon beside the layer name.

2 Choose File > Import.

3 Open the loon.jpg file in the Lesson06 folder.

4 When the import icon appears, position the cursor outside the left edge of the canvas. Drag until the width is approximately 410 pixels. Remember, tooltips do not appear when you are scaling an imported image, so keep an eye on the Properties panel.

5 In the Properties panel, set the X and Y coordinates for the photo to **−183** and **−68** pixels, respectively. This places the loon itself near the left.

6 In the Layers panel, rename the object **loon**.

7 Choose File > Import, locate the highfalls.jpg file.

8 Drag the import icon until the width is approximately 215 pixels, then release the mouse.

9 In the Properties panel, set the X and Y coordinates to **141** and **−18** pixels, respectively.

10 In the Layers panel, rename the object **waterfall**.

11 Import the joe_kayak.jpg file.

12 Release the mouse when the width reaches approximately 330 pixels. Set its X and Y coordinates to **237** and **−42** pixels, respectively.

13 In the Layers panel, rename the object **kayak**.

14 Import the final two images: white_river.jpg and tracks.jpg.

15 The white river image should be imported to a width of 214 pixels with a location of X: **495** and Y: **−8**

16 The train tracks shot should be set to a width of 104 and a location of X: **665**, Y: **−22**.

At the moment, things aren't looking too great. But all that is about to change, as you apply a variety of different masking techniques to create a polished banner graphic.

▶ **Tip:** Remember, importing files into an open document saves you the time of opening, copying, and pasting one image into another.

Using the Auto Vector Mask for quick fades

You'll do more complicated masking shortly, but for the loon, the Auto Vector Mask is just the feature to use. It not only creates a mask quickly, but lets you preview the effect. This command can be used on vector or bitmap objects.

1 Hide all the images except for the loon and the background image.

2 Select the loon in the Layers panel or on the Canvas.

3 Choose Commands > Creative > Auto Vector Mask. A dialog box appears.

4 Choose the horizontal linear gradient, solid to transparent.

5 Move the dialog box so it is not covering the loon and you can see the effect previewed on the canvas.

● **Note:** The green squares indicate the four corners of the mask. The Auto Vector mask uses a rectangle shape for the mask, and because this is a special shape, you don't see the bounding box on all four sides. If you create a mask manually with the Pen tool or Ellipse tool, or ungroup the rectangle shape, you will see an outline of the vector shape when the mask is selected.

6 Click the Apply button.

This command creates a vector mask that covers the entire dimensions of the original image, regardless of how much of the image is visible on the canvas. As you can see, the fade effect is starting too early, as a sizeable part of this photo is not on the canvas.

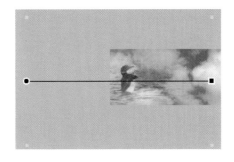

7 Select the Pointer tool.

8 Drag the round control handle so that it is centered on the loon. You might need to zoom out to see the controls.

▶ **Tip:** Thanks to the Live Preview of the Auto Vector Mask effects, not only can you see the result of your choice before you apply it, the Properties panel also shows you what type of gradient is being used to create the effect.

9 Drag the square handle to the left so that it terminates the fade just inside the right edge of the image.

The photo now blends seamlessly with the background image. You'll apply a different Auto Vector Mask to the waterfall.

10 Lock the loon image, and make the waterfall image visible again.

11 Choose Commands > Creative > Auto Vector Mask again.

12 Select the Ellipse shape gradient, and click Apply.

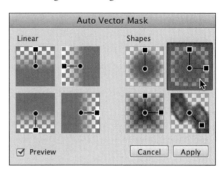

13 Use the Pointer tool to adjust the length of the two control arms. The vertical control arm should end just before the top of the image; the horizontal control arm should be dragged to the left until there is no obvious hard edge on either side of the photo.

▶ **Tip:** Once a mask has been added, you can reposition the image being masked by dragging the small blue control icon (⬚) in the middle of the image. This icon is visible when the image object, rather than the mask, is active.

14 Activate the Gradient Editor by clicking on the Fill box in the Properties panel.

15 Select the White color stop, and change its location to **33%**.

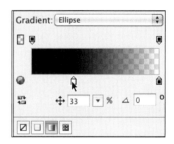

16 Press the Enter key to lock in the change. The center part of the waterfall is now much more solid.

17 Save the file.

Creating and editing masks

You've now come quite a long way with the banner, and a lot of the assets are in place. You will use custom masks to hide most of those backgrounds and blend the other images into the collage.

Creating a vector mask

The Auto Vector Mask is very handy if you want to quickly mask an entire object, but often having more control over the size and shape of the mask is very important. You'll create a simple custom mask in this next exercise.

1 Make the Kayak image visible again.

Comparing the completed version with your working version, you can see that the kayak shot in the finished file is showing much less area.

2 Select the Rectangle tool from the Tools panel.

3 In the Properties panel, change the edge from Anti-alias to Feather, with a value of 20.

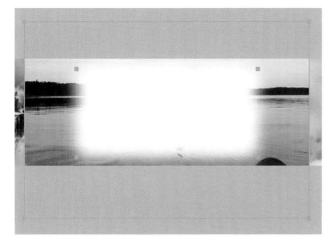

4 Select the Solid Fill icon, and set the Fill color to White.

5 Draw a small rectangle on top of the kayak photo. The size should be 210 x 99 pixels. You'll adjust the location shortly; for now, just make sure that the rectangle is roughly centered over the kayak photo.

6 Select the Pointer tool.

7 Hold down the Shift key and select the kayak photo to select both objects.

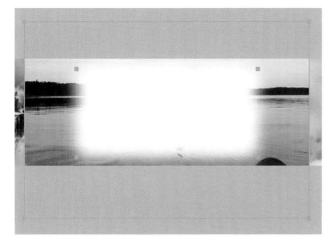

8 Choose Modify > Mask > Group As Mask.

The rectangle now masks the photo and gently fades out to the background on all four sides. The feathered edges of the white fill create a soft blend. The small blue handle in the center of the masked image allows you to reposition the image *within* the mask, by dragging with the Pointer tool. As with our other two images, you will see the mask thumbnail beside the image thumbnail in the Properties panel.

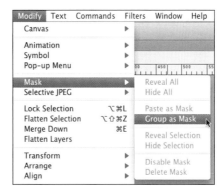

Changing vector mask attributes

Although the rectangle is nice, you will kick things up a bit by using the Skew tool to alter the shape of the rectangle into a parallelogram. You will also ensure the mask is in the correct location. To do these things, you must break the link between the mask and the photo.

1 In the Layers panel, click the chain link icon between the kayak and the mask. While remaining grouped, the two objects are now independent in terms of position, size, and shape.

2 Click the mask thumbnail in the Layers panel to select it.

Notice that the mask object has a green highlight around it in the Layers panel. Additionally, the mask icon appears beside the object name. This indicates that the mask—and not the image—is active.

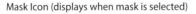

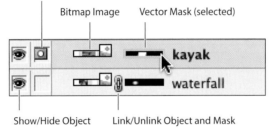

3 In the Tools panel, choose the Skew tool, which is found within the Scale toolset.

A bounding box appears around the mask.

If you see a much larger bounding box extending beyond the height of the design, it means you probably selected the photo rather than the mask. Just hit the Esc key, select the mask in the Layers panel and then re-select the Skew tool.

4 Move your cursor to any of the top control handles of the bounding box.

5 Keeping an eye on the dimensions in the Properties panel, drag a control handle to the right. You want the width to end up at 235 pixels, so just drag a little, release the mouse, and check the width. If you need to drag more, go ahead

and do so. If you overshot the width, drag the other way. When the size is right, press the Enter key to lock in the change.

6 Use the Pointer tool or the arrow keys to reposition the mask (not the photo), so that things are fairly balanced on both sides. In the example, the final location is X: 298, Y: 11.

7 Enable the link between the image and the mask, lock the object, and then save your work.

Editing a vector mask

When a vector mask is made active from the Layers panel, you can use the Properties panel to change the Fill Category and Edge settings, as well as those of the stroke (category, size, and edge).

You edit the vector shape itself by choosing the Subselection tool and repositioning the vector control points, just as you would with a regular vector shape. You can even add points by using the Pen tool.

If you have used the Rectangle tool, Fireworks will prompt you to ungroup the shape before using the Subselection tool. Ungrouping the shape discards any special properties that shape may have had.

For more information on editing vectors, refer to Lesson 5.

Adding Live Filters to a masked image

Although this chapter is all about masking, it doesn't mean we have to limit ourselves to just masking. The white river image is a color image, but you will use a command to convert it to a black-and-white image, and a Live Filter to further improve the tonality of the image. These effects can be applied before or after you add the mask, so you will mask the image first.

1 Make the white river image visible from the Layers panel.

2 Select the Rectangle tool again.

3 Set the color to White if necessary, and change the edge to a feathered value of **10** pixels.

4 Draw a rectangle that is 200 x 99 pixels, but before releasing the mouse, tap the Up arrow key ten times to instantly round off the corners of the rectangle.

5 Use the Pointer tool to center the shape over the image.

6 Hold down the Shift key and select the image. Now both the rectangle and the photo are selected.

7 Choose Modify > Mask > Group as Mask.

8 Choose Commands > Creative > Convert to Grayscale. In the Filters list of the Properties panel the Hue/Saturation Live Filter appears.

9 Click the plus sign (+) above the Filters list, and choose Adjust Color > Levels.

10 In the Input Levels fields, set the Minimum Intensity (Shadows) to **13**, Gamma (Midtones) to **1.13**, and Maximum Intensity (Highlights) to **246**. Click OK.

This filter adjusts the overall tonal range for a more pleasing effect.

Creating a bitmap mask

A bitmap mask can give you a more natural, organic-looking mask than you might be able to create with a vector shape, especially when you draw the selection freehand with the Lasso tool.

1 Make the Tracks image visible.

2 Select the Lasso tool ().

3 Make sure the Lasso edge is set to Feather with a value of 10. The Live Marquee can remain selected.

4 Zoom in on the tracks image, and draw a loose selection around the tracks themselves, emulating the S-curve of the railway. Precision is not necessary because the selection will be feathered anyway.

5 Click the Add Mask button at the bottom of the Layers panel. The background disappears from around the tracks.

Editing a bitmap mask

It is important that the mask remain active while you are performing these next steps. If at any time the mask is deselected, just click on it in the Layers panel.

Take a look at the mask. The color black has replaced the nonselected area of the image. Remember that the color black, when painted on a bitmap mask object, hides pixels. White, on the other hand, reveals pixels. You will adjust the mask as needed using the Brush tool.

1 Zoom in to 200%.

2 Select the Brush tool.

3 Press the D key to set the brush color to black (the default color).

4 Make sure the Stroke Category is set to Soft Rounded. (If necessary, choose Basic > Soft Rounded from the Stroke Category pop-up menu.)

5 Change the Tip Size value to **20** pixels and Edge to **100** pixels. The Texture value should be 0%.

6 Paint over any additional areas of the background that you want to hide. Apply this technique *outside* the visible area of the image, painting inwards. If you start inside the mask, you'll be hiding parts of the image that should remain visible. Do this in a subtle manner, just bumping the edge of the brush against the contour of the mask. If you overdo it, not to worry.

7 Press the X key to switch the brush color to white.

Note: If you didn't make any mistakes while creating the selection, you can still test this technique by painting over part of the background. The area under the brush reappears when you paint with white, and disappears when you paint with black.

8 Find an area that was masked by accident or that you feel needs to be more visible. It may just be a subjective question of rounding the edges of the mask. You may find it necessary to set a smaller brush size. Paint from *within* the visible area, outwards. The mistakenly hidden pixels are revealed.

If you end up revealing areas you don't want, switch back to black and paint over those areas.

You now have a pretty good-looking banner, but no indication of the website! In the next lesson, you'll add the website name and a tagline while learning how to use the Text tools.

Changing colors quickly

When working with bitmap masks, you may want to switch from black to white to gray to customize the mask. To do so quickly, use these shortcuts:

- Press the B key to switch to the Brush tool.
- Press the D key to set the color boxes to their default colors (black for stroke, white for fill).
- Press the X key to toggle the current colors between stroke and fill.

Review questions

1 What are the primary differences between bitmap masks and vector masks?

2 How do you use the Auto Vector Mask?

3 How do you create a vector mask?

4 How do you create a bitmap mask?

5 How do you edit a bitmap mask?

Review answers

1 Bitmap masks are made using selections or the Brush tool. Using the Brush tool, you can easily edit the mask live on the canvas. Bitmap masks can be applied only to other bitmaps. Vector masks tend to have a higher degree of control and accuracy because you use a path, not a brush, to create them. It's easy to change the fill or stroke of a vector mask. Generating the same type of effect with a bitmap mask can be more time-consuming. Vector masks can be applied to bitmap or vector objects.

2 The Auto Vector Mask can be applied to bitmap or vector objects. Select the object on the canvas, and then choose Commands > Creative > Auto Vector Mask. Choose the type of mask from the dialog box, and then click Apply.

3 To create a vector mask, draw a vector shape, then hold down Shift and select the object to be masked. Choose Modify > Mask > Group as Mask. You can select the mask in the Layers panel, and change its fill, edge, and stroke properties. You can also use the Pen tool or Subselection tool to edit its shape.

4 You create a bitmap mask in one of two ways:

   • Draw a bitmap selection, select the object you want to mask from the Layers panel, and click the Add Mask button in the Layers panel.

   • Select the object you want to mask from the Layers panel, and click the Add Mask button in the Layers panel. Select the Brush tool, setting the brush color to black, and then paint on the canvas. As long as the mask object is selected, painting with black will hide pixels from view.

5 To edit a bitmap mask, select the Brush tool then select the mask object in the Layers panel. Select a suitable brush size, stroke category, and edge softness. On the canvas, paint over the area of the mask you want to change. Use a black stroke color to hide more of the visible image, or a white stroke color to show more of the masked image.

7 WORKING WITH TEXT

Lesson overview

Working with type can be a fun and creative part of your design. Fireworks includes many text-formatting features normally found in desktop publishing applications, such as kerning, spacing, color, leading, and baseline shift. You can edit text any time—even after you apply Live Filter effects. Because Fireworks CS6 uses the same text engine as Photoshop and Illustrator, you can move or copy text between these applications easily. In this lesson, you'll learn how to do the following:

- Create both fixed-width and auto-sizing text blocks

- Import text from a .txt file

- Edit text properties

- Use commands to alter text

- Scale, rotate, and distort text

- Attach text to a path

- Flow text within a vector shape

 This lesson takes approximately 60 minutes to complete. Copy the Lesson07 folder into the Lessons folder that you created on your hard drive for these projects (or create it now, if you haven't already done so). As you work on this lesson, you won't preserve the start files. If you need to restore the start files, copy them from the *Adobe Fireworks CS6 Classroom in a Book CD.*

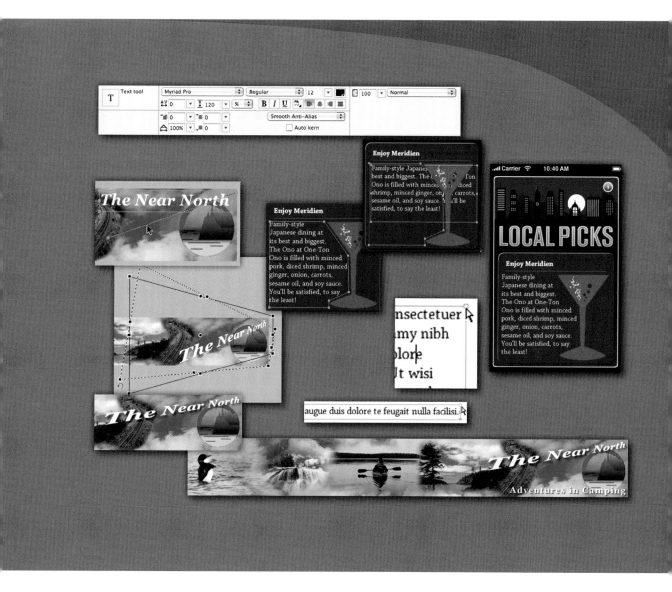

You don't need to settle for dull text. Fireworks includes text-formatting features that help you get the look you want. You can make your text pop off the page with Live Filters, masks, and strokes, or even make a block of text flow within a custom vector shape.

Text basics

Typography is a big part of web design, especially now that most modern web browsers support nonstandard fonts using CSS and a font service like TypeKit or Font Squirrel. Even if you're not mocking up a website design, you might be designing a banner ad or creating a prototype for a tablet or smartphone app. No matter the circumstance, Fireworks CS6 offers a variety of tools to help you get the look you want.

Text in Fireworks always appears inside a *text block* (a rectangle with handles). Text blocks can be either auto-sizing or fixed width.

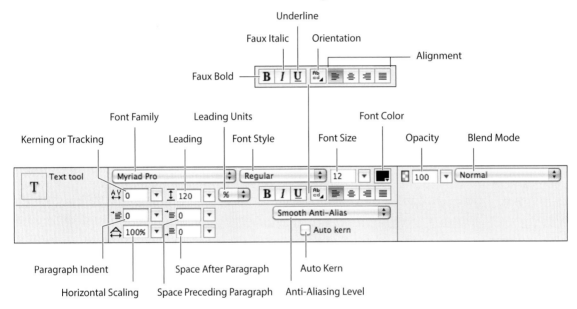

Auto-sizing and fixed-width text blocks

When you click on the canvas with the Text tool and just start typing, Fireworks creates an *auto-sizing* text block, which expands horizontally as you type. Auto-sizing text blocks expand vertically only when you press the Return or Enter key. The block automatically shrinks when you remove text. Auto-sizing text blocks typically get used for short single lines of text, such as titles or headings.

augue duis dolore te feugait nulla facilisi.

Auto-Sizing Text Handle Indicator

Fixed-width text blocks allow you to control the width of wrapped text. As you add more text, the box expands vertically, rather than horizontally. Fixed-width text blocks are created when you drag to draw a text block using the Text tool.

More often then not, you'll use fixed-width text blocks with paragraphs or columns of text, generally for mock-up purposes.

nsectetuer ┌─── Fixed-Width Text Handle Indicator
my nibh
)lore
Jt wisi

When the Text tool is active within a text block, a hollow square or hollow circle appears in the upper-right corner of the text block. The circle indicates an auto-sizing text block; the square indicates a fixed-width text block.

Double-click the hollow control point to change a text block from a fixed-width block to an auto-sizing block, or vice versa.

Adding the banner heading and tagline

The Near North website has a pretty good-looking banner. The artwork is already in place, including a newly added logo (you can thank us later); you just need to add some text elements: a heading and a tagline. For the heading, you will make use of the default, auto-sizing text block.

1   In Fireworks, choose File > Open, browse to the Lesson07 folder, and open the near_north_banner.fw.png file.

2   Unlock the text layer.

3   Select the Text tool.

4   Select the following settings in the Properties panel:

   Font Family: **Georgia**

   Font Style: **Bold Italic**
   (do not use the faux B
   or I icons)

   Font Size: **26**

   Color: **White**

   Tracking or Kerning: **30**

   Anti-aliasing: **Crisp Anti-Alias**

5   Move the cursor to the remaining sky area at the right of the banner.

6   Type **The Near North**.

● **Note:** Fireworks remembers the most recent fonts used by the Text tool, even after you've shut down and restarted your computer. They appear at the top of the font family list. You can change the number of recent fonts displayed by editing the Type preferences.

Attaching text to a path

Attaching text *to* a path lets you put text on an angle or even follow a curve. You will do this now.

1   With the Pen tool, click to set a starting point, about one-third of the way up from the bottom of the tracks image.

2   Bring the cursor near the upper-right corner of the banner and click again to set an end point. (We've hidden the text in this figure so it's easier for you to see the path.) The color of the stroke is not important.

3   Double-click on the end point to disengage the Pen tool.

4   In the Properties panel set the Width, Height, X, and Y values as indicated in the figure to the left.

5   Select the Pointer tool.

6   Hold down the Shift key, and select the heading. Both the path and the heading should now be selected.

Note: If you have more text than can fit inside a vector shape (or on a vector path), Fireworks hides the extra text and displays the Text Overflow indicator (■). In order to see the extra text, you must either increase the size of the vector, or reduce the size of the text.

7   Choose Text > Attach To Path. The text follows the angle of the path (and remains editable).

With the text on an angle, the vertical angle of the text is not visually appealing. This is easy enough to fix.

8   With the text object still selected, choose Text > Orientation > Skew Vertical. The vertical elements of the text are now perfectly straight.

Adding more depth to text

Another way to change the angle of text and add more depth is to use the Skew tool and Distort tools. You will use these to make the text larger at the beginning of the heading and then taper off as the heading reaches the top corner of the banner. This is not an exact science. Although the goal here is to get something similar to the final sample, don't worry if your version isn't an exact match. Hey, you may even like your version better!

1 Select the Skew tool (hidden beneath the Scale tool) from the Tools panel.

2 Move the cursor over the upper-left control handle of the selected block of text.

3 Click and drag the cursor upward until you roughly match the angle in the figure below.

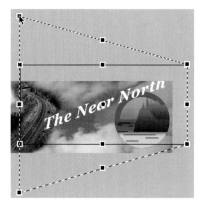

4 Release the mouse, and then select the upper-right handle.

5 Drag the cursor down until you match the angle of the figure below.

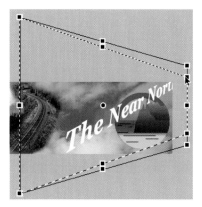

These transformations may shift the text out of the canvas on the right side. You can reposition the text even while making edits like this.

6 Move the cursor within the text area. The cursor changes to a move cursor (four arrow heads).

7 Drag the text block so it is visible on the canvas.

8 Press the Enter or Return key to lock in the changes.

9 Switch to the Distort tool (also part of the Scale toolset). Unlike the Skew tool, the Distort tool lets you move any one of the eight control handles independently. There's more freedom of movement, hence more opportunity to distort the object.

10 Drag the left-middle control handle farther to the left by at least 100 pixels, and press Return or Enter.

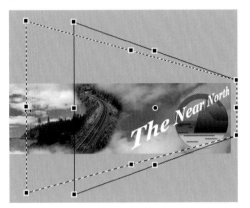

Note: Remember, you are dealing with text, which is essentially a vector. You can distort the text over and over, and it will still maintain its quality. Also remember that the text is still live; at any time, you could use the Text tool to edit the text itself.

Based on the final sample, your version may not be running at the same overall angle, because the various distortions you added can affect the angle of the original path. You can rotate an object while any of the scaling tools are active by moving your cursor slightly away from any of the four corner handles. The cursor changes to a rotate icon, and you can spin the object as much or as little as you want.

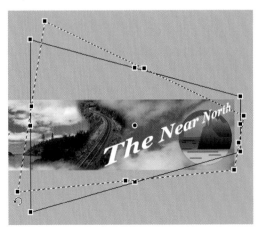

Adding a drop shadow

For a bit more separation from the background, you will add a drop shadow to the heading.

1 Select the Pointer tool.

2 In the Properties panel, add a new Live Filter by clicking on the plus (+) sign; choose Shadow and Glow > Drop Shadow.

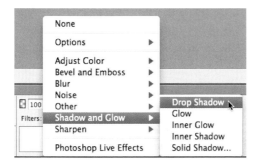

3 When the Drop Shadow properties dialog box appears, accept the default settings by tapping the Return key. The shadow appears.

4 Use the Pointer tool to reposition the text block to what you feel best suits your banner. Feel free to further distort the text if you like.

5 Save your work.

Adding the tagline

The tagline helps to set the mood for the website. It's brief and smaller in size than the site name.

1 Make sure the website name is not selected, by clicking off the canvas with the Pointer tool.

2 Select the Text tool.

3 Make the following settings in the Properties panel:

Font Family: **Georgia**

Font Style: **Bold Italic**

Font Size: **18**

Color: **#D6D6D6**

Kerning/Tracking: **110**

Anti-aliasing: **Strong Anti-Alias**

4 Move the cursor near the bottom of the banner.

5 Type **Adventures in Camping**.

6 In the Properties panel, add a new Live Filter by clicking the plus (+) sign; choose Shadow and Glow > Drop Shadow.

7 When the Drop Shadow properties dialog box appears, change the settings to:

Distance: **4**

Opacity **80%**

Softness: **3**

This adds more contrast to the smaller text, making it easier to read.

8 Press the Enter key to lock in the new settings.

9 Use the Pointer tool to reposition the text block to X: 698, Y: 94.

10 Save the file—you're done!

● **Note:** As of this writing, you may experience text issues when opening a file created in versions of Fireworks earlier than CS4. Text must be updated when opening a legacy file to minimize issues.

About anti-aliasing

Text anti-aliasing controls how the edges of the text blend into the background so that text—large or small—is cleaner, more readable, and more pleasing to the eye. Fireworks examines the color values at the edges of text objects and the background they are on. It blends the pixels at the edges based on your anti-alias settings in the Properties panel.

By default, Fireworks applies smooth anti-aliasing to text. Small font sizes, however, tend to be easier to read when anti-aliasing is removed or at least reduced. This is why you changed the anti-aliasing settings to Crisp Anti-Alias earlier. Anti-aliasing settings apply to all characters in a given text block.

Fireworks provides four preset anti-aliasing levels and a custom setting from the Properties panel:

- **No Anti-Alias:** Disables text smoothing completely. Text is not blended, and anything but horizontal or vertical lines are noticeably jagged. Although not ideal for large text, it can actually make text at small sizes (8 points or less) easier to read. At large font sizes, the text tends to look poorer in quality.

- **Crisp Anti-Alias:** Displays a hard transition between the edges of the text and the background. Some blending occurs, but text still appears sharp.

- **Strong Anti-Alias:** Creates an abrupt transition between the text edges and the background, preserving the shapes of the text characters and enhancing detailed areas of the characters. Text appears almost bold in comparison to Crisp Anti-Alias.

- **Smooth Anti-Alias:** Creates a soft blend between the edges of the text and the background, and is the default for text pasted into Fireworks.

- **Custom Anti-Alias:** Applies the settings you specify with the following options:

    - **Oversampling:** Sets the amount of detail used for creating the transition between the text edges and the background.

    - **Sharpness:** Sets the smoothness of the transition between the text edges and the background.

    - **Strength:** Sets how much the text edges blend into the background.

Typography terms

To help you get the most out of the Text tools, you need to be familiar with some basic typography terms:

- **Auto Kerning:** Adjusts the space between letters based on character pairs. There is strong kerning (more space) between the letters V and A, for example, and no kerning between the letters S and T. You can enable Auto Kerning in the Properties panel.

- **Kerning** or **Tracking:** Tracking adds equal amounts of space between all selected characters. Fireworks combines manual kerning and tracking settings into one field. If you select a string of text and enter a value in the field, you are adjusting the space equally between multiple characters (tracking). If you place your cursor between two characters, you can adjust the gap between the two letters adjacent to the cursor (kerning).

- **Leading:** Controls the amount of vertical spacing between lines of type and is also known as line spacing. The word "leading" comes from the lead strips that were put between lines of type on a printing press to fill available space on the page.

- **Horizontal Scaling:** Adjusts the width of each selected character or characters within a selected text box.

- **Baseline Shift:** Controls how closely text sits above or below its natural baseline. For example, superscript text sits above the baseline. If there is no baseline shift, the text sits on the baseline. To adjust baseline shift, select the actual text (not the text box) and input a value into the Baseline Shift field in the Properties panel.

- **Paragraph Indent:** Sets the amount of indent for the first line in the paragraph.

- **Paragraph Spacing:** Sets the amount of spacing before and after a paragraph in a selected text block. Any value set here is respected by all paragraphs within a text block.

Note: This file contains real text, so depending on your operating system and the fonts available, Fireworks may display a message that the fonts are not available and prompt you to either replace the font or maintain its appearance. For this exercise, simply choose Maintain Appearance. The fonts will not change unless you attempt to edit the text using that missing font.

Flowing text around an object

In Fireworks, rather than having rectangular blocks of text, you can contour a text block to a custom shape by using a vector path or shape. This mimics the type of effect you can create in programs such as Adobe InDesign, where text can wrap around photographs and other objects.

You will do this in the next couple of exercises, adding text to the Enjoy page of the Local mobile prototype, creating a custom shape using the Pen tool, and then using a Text command to make the text appear to flow around the martini glass.

1   Open the localpicks_320x480_wrap.fw.png file.

2 Select the Enjoy page from the Pages panel.

A block of text needs to be added to this page, and it must follow the left contour of the martini glass.

3 In the Layers panel, select the text layer.

4 Choose File > Import, and locate the one_ton_text.txt file. Yes, a text file.

The Import icon appears on the canvas.

5 Position the Import icon near the left side, below the dividing line for the heading, and click to import the text.

The text appears, and Fireworks uses the default font settings for imported text: a fixed-width text block, set to Myriad Pro, Regular, 12 point, Black.

6 The text block type (fixed-width) is fine, but change the font settings as follows:

Font Family: **Chaparral Pro**

Font Style: **Regular**

Font Size: **16**

Color: **White**

Creating the custom path

Much like you did in Lesson 6, you'll be using the Pen tool to create a custom shape, but this time your shape will follow the left contour of the martini glass.

1 Hide the newly imported text.

2 Select the Pen tool.

3 Place the Pen cursor near the top-left edge of the glass, and click the mouse to set your origin point.

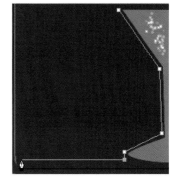

4 Move your mouse down, following the angle of the glass. Where the bowl of the glass changes to the stem, click the mouse again to set a new anchor point and change direction.

5 Continue moving the mouse and clicking to set anchor points for a custom outline on the left side of the glass.

▶ **Tip:** Another way to add temporary placement text is to use Commands > Text > Lorem Ipsum. This command automatically places a paragraph of text on the canvas, using the current font properties.

● **Note:** If you don't have Chaparral Pro, choose a similar font such as Georgia, Regular, at 15 points.

6 When you get to the bottom of the glass, set an anchor point, move the cursor near the bottom-left edge of the container, and click again. (If you hold the Shift key while dragging out to the left, you get a perfectly straight line.)

7 Move the cursor up, and click again to set an anchor point just below the header's dividing line.

8 Finally, bring the cursor back to where you started, and when the cursor changes to the close path cursor, click again to complete the path.

Your path may get filled with a color. This won't affect what you'll be doing next, but if you find it distracting, click the No Fill icon in the Properties panel.

9 If you need to tweak your shape (straightening a top or bottom path segment, for example), use the Subselection tool to select individual anchor points, then tap the arrow keys to reposition the anchor.

Wrapping text in a path

Here's where the magic happens. Both objects need to be selected in order for the text wrapping to work.

1 In the Layers panel, make the description text visible again.

2 Hold down the Ctrl key (Windows) or the Command key (Mac) and then click on the path you just created.

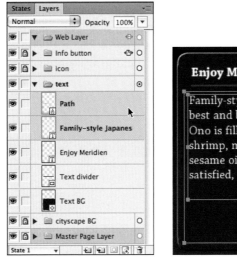

3 With both objects selected, choose Text >
Attach In Path.

The two objects are grouped, and the text reflows
within the confines of the shape!

The appearance of custom-flowed text within the finished page gives the mock-up
that extra bit of polish.

Don't forget to save your hard work!

Editing text

Text in a path can still be edited, as it is still real text. Simply double-click in the text area to enter standard text-editing mode. Likewise, the path is also editable; just choose the Subselection tool, click on an anchor point, and you can start changing the shape of the path. If you make significant changes, the text will reflow to fit within the edited shape.

1   Select the Pointer or Text tool, and triple-click anywhere within the paragraph.

    The entire paragraph is quickly selected.

2   In the Properties panel, set the Tracking or Kerning value to **20** to make the text a little more readable.

Note: When you edit a text block, each change during that edit session is considered a separate step, making it easy to undo individual changes.

3   Save your work.

Review questions

1   What are the two types of text blocks you can create, and how do you create them and switch between them?

2   What is anti-aliasing?

3   How do you flow text within a path?

4   How can you quickly select a single paragraph in a text block?

5   What typographic attributes can you control using the Properties panel, and how do these elements affect text?

Review answers

1 You can create auto-sizing and fixed-width text blocks. Auto-sizing text blocks are created by default when you select the Text tool, click the canvas, and begin typing. Auto-sizing text blocks expand in width as you add more text. Fixed-width text blocks are created by dragging out with the Text tool on the canvas before typing. Fixed-width text blocks allow you to control the width of wrapped text. As you add more text, the box expands downward. To switch between the two text block types, make sure you are in an active text block, with the text tool selected. Then double-click the hollow circle (auto-sizing) or hollow square (fixed-width) control handle in the upper-right corner of the text bounding box.

2 Text anti-aliasing controls how the edges of the text blend into the background so that large text is cleaner, more readable, and more pleasing to the eye.

3 Draw a vector shape using the vector shape tools or the Pen tool. Select both the vector shape and the text, and then choose Text > Attach In Path. Once text is attached in a path, it still remains editable. (Note: If you create a shape with one of the Auto Shape tools, you will first have to ungroup the shape before you can attach the text within it. Select the Auto Shape, and then choose Modify > Ungroup to do this.)

4 You can quickly select a single paragraph in a text block by triple-clicking anywhere inside the paragraph.

5 Kerning, Tracking, Leading, Horizontal Scaling, Baseline Shift, Paragraph Indent, and Paragraph Spacing can all be controlled from the Properties panel:

- Auto-Kerning adjusts the space between letters based on character pairs. You can turn Auto Kerning on or off in the Properties panel.

- Manual Kerning or Tracking adds equal amounts of space between all selected characters, or the space between two, nonselected characters.

- Leading, also known as line spacing, is the amount of vertical spacing between lines of type.

- Horizontal Scaling adjusts the width of each selected character or characters within a selected text box.

- Baseline Shift controls how closely text sits above or below its natural baseline. To adjust Baseline Shift, select the actual text (not the text box) and input a value into the Baseline Shift field in the Properties panel.

- Paragraph Indent sets the amount of indent for the first line in the paragraph.

- Paragraph Spacing (two settings) sets the amount of spacing before a paragraph (preceding) and after a paragraph in a selected text block.

8 USING STYLES AND THE STYLES PANEL

Lesson overview

A powerful but often overlooked feature of Fireworks is the Styles panel. Working with styles can improve productivity, because you can apply a series of preset effects for text, vectors, and, to some extent, even bitmap images. You can then save that same series as a style and use it as often as you want without having to rebuild—or match—the complex effect from scratch. In this lesson, you'll learn how to do the following:

- Apply prebuilt styles
- Edit styles
- Update styles applied to objects
- Create custom styles
- Export and share styles

 This lesson takes approximately 45 minutes to complete. Copy the Lesson08 folder into the Lessons folder that you created on your hard drive for these projects (or create it now, if you haven't already done so). As you work on this lesson, you won't preserve the start files. If you need to restore the start files, copy them from the *Adobe Fireworks CS6 Classroom in a Book* CD.

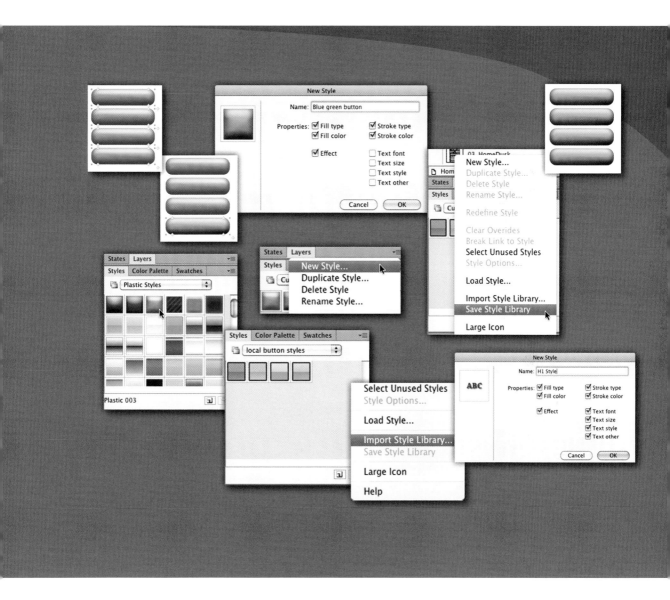

Styles can speed up your design workflow
and allow for the use of consistent effects
on team-based projects.

What are styles?

Styles are to Fireworks what Cascading Style Sheets (CSS) are to HTML, or what styles are to a Word document: a way to quickly, reliably, and consistently apply specific effects to an object. How can styles help? Imagine you need to create icons or buttons with a consistent look and feel for a CSS sprite sheet or to test out text styling for CSS style sheets. Now imagine a ten-page application mock-up where the button effects need to be changed on *all* pages. Fireworks can save you time in all these scenarios. When you use styles, you can make changes to the styles of one object on one page, then cascade those changes through the entire mock-up.

● **Note:** For more advice on working with CSS sprite sheets, see Lesson 10.

Styles are an editable collection of Live Filters and other object properties that you can quickly apply to a selected object. Fireworks ships with a large collection of prebuilt styles (presets), found in the Styles panel. Think of those presets as a launching point toward creating your own custom special effects.

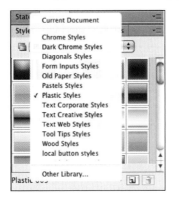

Font properties, fills, strokes, and Live Filters (effects) can all be saved as part of a style.

You will take a look at how to create and work with styles in the upcoming exercises.

Applying style presets

Before working with styles in the example files, you should take some time to familiarize yourself with the Styles panel and how to apply styles.

1 Choose File > New, and create a new document that is 500 x 500 pixels, with a white canvas color.

2 Select the Rounded rectangle tool from the vector toolset of the Toolbar.

3 Draw a rectangle that is 200 pixels wide by 50 pixels high.

4 Open the Styles panel (Window > Styles, if you don't see the Styles panel tab).

The default panel display is Current Document. If no styles have been applied, this view will be empty.

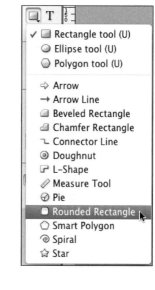

Tip: If you don't get the dimensions you want when drawing the rectangle, open the Auto Shapes Properties panel (Window > Auto Shapes Properties) and set the dimensions and corner radius you prefer. Do not use the W and H values in the Properties panel, as doing so can actually distort the corner radius.

5 Click the Current Document drop-down list to see the several categories of styles available.

6 Choose the Plastic Styles library.

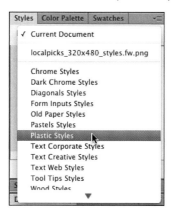

7 In the top row of styles, select the third style from the left (Plastic 003). Note that in the bottom-left corner of the Styles panel, Fireworks displays the name of the style that your cursor is hovering over.

8 Take a look in the Filters section of the Properties panel and note that automatically, several Live Filters have been applied to achieve the matte blue effect.

If you don't like the blue, don't worry: Changing the look of the button is as simple as clicking on a new style.

9 Choose Plastic 004, the style just to the right of the blue style you chose earlier.

10 Try out a couple other styles, but when you are done experimenting (it can be a little addictive) make sure to reselect Plastic 003.

11 From the drop-down list, switch to Current Document. Every style you tried is listed in the Current Document window, even if it is not in use. If you do a lot of testing, this can make for a crowded panel of undesired styles, but Fireworks can help you clean things up quickly.

12 From the Styles panel options menu, choose Select Unused Styles. All styles not in use in the document get highlighted.

13 Click on the trash can icon in the Styles panel. Fireworks will prompt you to confirm you want to delete the selected styles. Click OK. You are only deleting the styles from the current document, *not* from the Plastic Styles library.

Editing styles

Remember, preset styles are a starting point for creating your own custom styles. You might find a style that is *almost* what you want, but not quite. Maybe you want a drop shadow applied, or an inner glow, or even just a minor change to the fill color. Editing a style and then applying that change to all objects using the style is a real time-saver, and it is what you will do next.

1   Use the Edit > Duplicate or Edit > Clone command to create a copy.

2   Press Ctrl+Y (Windows) or Command+Y (Mac) twice to create two more buttons.

3   Press Ctrl+A (Windows) or Command+A (Mac) to select all the buttons.

4   Open the Align panel, and choose the Align Left Edge icon.

5   In the Space field of the Align panel, type a value of **10**.

6   Click the Space Evenly Horizontally icon. You now have a perfectly aligned button bar!

7   Select a single button and in the Properties panel, click the Fill box. Then change the main fill color to a value of **#73FF73**.

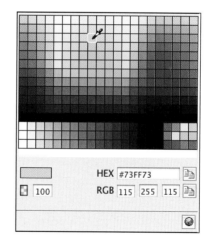

This doesn't change all the blue hues in the button; many of the Live Filters applied to this style also have blue as their main color. Often, some of the most dramatic effects of a style are created using Live Filters. Feel free to see what each filter does for the style by toggling the Enable/Disable icon next to each filter name in the Properties panel. For the purposes of this exercise though, changing the fill color is enough.

Updating styles applied to objects

Notice that the only object to change was the selected button. Because all the buttons are using the same style, however, you can quickly update the other objects in a couple different ways.

Method 1: Redefining a style

This method is very quick and will update all objects in an open document using the current modified style.

1　Click the Redefine Style icon in the Properties panel, just below the document style drop-down list.

Immediately, Fireworks updates the other three buttons, applying the changes to this document's version of the Plastic 003 style.

For quick changes, this method works just fine, but the updates to the style are not permanently part of the preset plastic style. For permanence, you can save a new custom style.

Method 2: Saving a new style

When you make changes to a style that you may want to use again, it's a good idea to save the updated style with a new name. This way you can make the style name more relevant and easy to reuse because the style is no longer linked to the preset.

1　Select any of the buttons.

2　In the Styles Panel options menu, choose New Style.

3　Name the style **Blue green button**, and click OK.

4　Select all the buttons and in the Styles panel, click the newly created style. You won't see a change in the look of the buttons, but if you check the Properties panel, you will see that the Blue green button style has been applied.

5　Remove the now unused Plastic 003 style.

Creating custom styles from scratch

Method 2 is also the way to create a style from your own, homegrown effects. For example, maybe you styled some text to represent the CSS styling for a web page heading, an H1, for example.

	New Style	
	Name: H1 Style	
ABC	Properties: ☑ Fill type	☑ Stroke type
	☑ Fill color	☑ Stroke color
	☑ Effect	☑ Text font
		☑ Text size
		☑ Text style
		☑ Text other
	Cancel OK	

With the text selected, simply follow the steps in Method 2 to create a text style that you can quickly apply to other text blocks in your design.

Exporting and sharing styles

Creating styles can certainly speed up *your* workflow, but these styles are *document-specific* to the current file, on your hard drive. This means that if you open another document or create a new document, these new styles usually won't be available in the Styles panel. Likewise, if you work as part of a design team, the other team members won't have access to your customized styles without opening the original document themselves.

So what happens if you or your coworkers want to use these great new styles in *other* documents?

The answer is to create a custom style library. Just like the preset style libraries, a custom style library is available to any document, new or old, unlike the Current Document styles. With a custom style library, you can share the styles you create with the entire team. This further improves design consistency for any team-based project.

Note: If you have multiple documents open, you can select styles from other files, if they have any styles as part of the document structure. This is the one exception to document styles not being available to other files.

You will learn how to export, share, and access a style library in the final exercises of this lesson.

1 Open the localpicks_320x480_styles.fw.png file from the Lesson08 folder.

2 If necessary, open the Styles panel.

3 Choose the Current Document view.

This document already contains four styles, each one representing a different button style for the main navigation.

4 From the Styles panel options, choose Save Style Library.

Fireworks automatically opens a save box, targeting the Fireworks styles folder. If you plan on making your new styles available to any Fireworks document on your computer, you must save the library in this folder.

5 Name the library **local button styles**, and click Save.

In the Styles panel, the local button styles library is now the active library. In the custom styles folder, Fireworks has saved a special file with an *.stl* extension.

Sharing styles

To share these styles with others, you could drill down into your computer's hard drive to locate the new library, but honestly, it's faster and easier just to save the library again, this time pointing to your desktop.

1 From the Styles panel options, choose Save Style Library.

2 When the Save dialog box appears, browse to your desktop.

3 Name the library **local button styles** if necessary, and click Save.

Fireworks creates a new STL file containing the new styles on your desktop. To share this library, simply email it or place it on a file-sharing site, such as the Adobe Creative Cloud, DropBox, or Box.com.

Importing a style library

What if you receive an STL file from a teammate and you wish to use it for a current or new design? Doing so is pretty straightforward. We've included a sample STL file in the Lesson08 folder for you to work with.

1 From the Styles panel options, choose Import Style Library.

2 Browse to the Lesson08 folder, and select the sample button styles.stl file.

3 Click Open.

The library is now imported and available for any document at any time.

> ✓ Current Document
>
> buttons.fw.png
> localpicks_320x480_styles.fw.png
>
> Chrome Styles
> Dark Chrome Styles
> Diagonals Styles
> Form Inputs Styles
> Old Paper Styles
> Pastels Styles
> Plastic Styles
> Text Corporate Styles
> Text Creative Styles
> Text Web Styles
> Tool Tips Styles
> Wood Styles
> local button styles
> sample button styles
>
> Other Library...

Styles galore!

You're not limited to the style libraries that come with Fireworks. A quick Google search for **fireworks style libraries** yields hundreds of results. The wider Fireworks design community is a friendly place filled with skilled professionals who love to share with others.

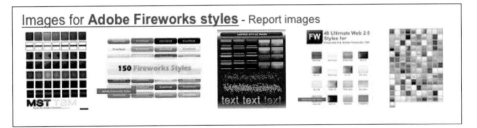

Loading Styles for a current document

There may be times when you only want a new style library associated with a specific file. If so, follow these steps:

1   Select Load Style from the Styles panel options menu.

2   Select a style library (*.stl) to load to the current document. The styles loaded are available to the current document.

Review questions

1 How do you apply prebuilt styles?

2 How do you edit applied styles?

3 How do you update an edited style that is applied to multiple objects?

4 How do you create custom styles?

5 How do you export and share styles?

Review answers

1 You apply prebuilt (or preset) styles by first selecting an object. Then you open the Styles panel, and click on the drop-down list to choose a style library. Once you have a library selected, simply click a style in the panel to apply it to the selected object.

2 You use the Properties panel to edit styles applied to objects. Select the object that has a style applied to it, and then change the various attributes in the Properties panel to alter the look of the style. Don't forget that very often the most dramatic aspects of a style are created using Live Filters. It's important that you inspect the filter properties to see what each filter is doing to the style. To view filter properties, select one of the applied filters in the Properties panel and click on the (*i*) icon next to the filter name. You can also toggle the Enable/Disable icon to see what effect each filter has on the style.

3 To update a style that has been edited at the object level, click the Redefine Style icon in the Properties panel. This will update the style in the Current Document styles window and force the edits to be applied to any objects that are using the existing style.

   Alternatively, you can save the edited style as a custom style. This breaks the link to the original preset style, but gives you a unique style. You can then give the new style a more relevant name and edit it further without affecting objects that use the original style.

4 You create a custom style by applying properties (fill, stroke, filters, font attributes) to an object, then choosing New Style from the Styles panel options menu.

5 To export styles for sharing with others, choose Save Style Library from the Styles panel options. If you save the new styles to the custom styles folder of Fireworks, the library is available to all documents, new or existing, from the style library list in the Styles panel. If you plan to share this library with others, you can either browse to the .stl file's location within Fireworks or simply resave the styles to a more accessible location such as your desktop. Then it's just a matter of emailing the file, or uploading it to a file-sharing site.

9 USING SYMBOLS

Lesson overview

One of the great productivity tools in Fireworks, symbols have been around since the beginning of the application. Symbols can contain multiple objects within a single asset while still giving you quick access to editing those objects. They are a great option for reusing common graphical elements, such as logos and buttons, in a design. Symbols can contain text, vectors, and bitmaps, each with its own Live Filter attributes.

In this lesson, you'll learn how to do the following:

- Add symbols from the Common Library

- Add symbols from the Document Library

- Create and edit a graphic symbol

- Create and edit a button symbol

- Save a symbol to the Common Library

- Preview rollover effects

 This lesson takes approximately 60 minutes to complete. Copy the Lesson09 folder into the Lessons folder that you created on your hard drive for these projects (or create it now, if you haven't already done so). As you work on this lesson, you won't preserve the start files. If you need to restore the start files, copy them from the *Adobe Fireworks CS6 Classroom in a Book* CD.

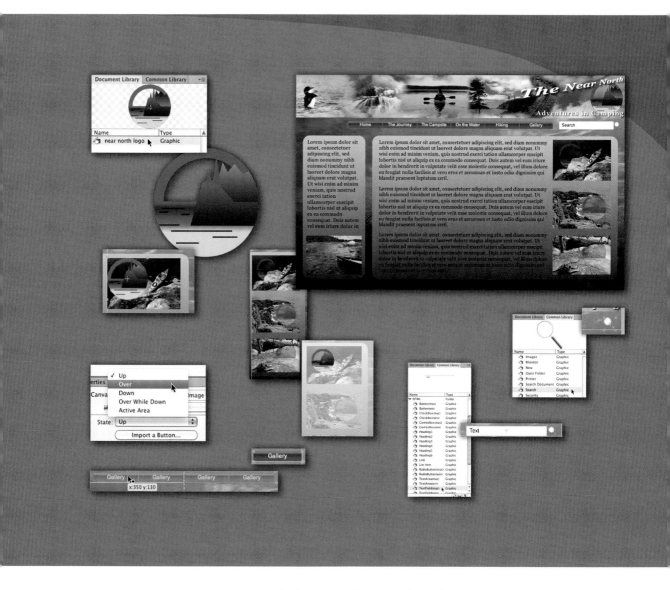

Symbols are great to reuse and share for common
graphical elements, such as logos or buttons.

What are symbols?

A symbol is a master version of a graphic or of a collection of graphics objects. It can include vectors, bitmaps, and even text. A symbol is essentially a self-contained document within a document. You have all the editing capabilities at your fingertips that you would have for a complete design, but all the assets of the symbol itself are kept together. You can access symbols from two panels: the Document Library panel and the Common Library panel. Symbols in the Document Library are available to the currently open document only. Symbols in the Common Library are available to any document.

When you place a symbol on the canvas, you're actually placing a linked copy of the symbol, which is known as an *instance*. When you edit the original symbol object, the linked instances on the canvas automatically change to reflect the edited symbol.

You can also edit any symbol instance on the canvas, changing size, color, or opacity, or adding Live Filters, without altering the original symbol. For example, you might have a fairly large image of a company logo. If you convert that image into a symbol, you can simply drag an instance onto the canvas and scale it down without affecting the quality or size of the original large version.

Another advantage to symbols is increased productivity. Instead of having to locate the original file each time you need a logo, you can turn it into a symbol and make it quickly available from the Document Library panel. This is a big advantage if you regularly reuse objects.

Although you can build your own symbols, Fireworks also comes with a wealth of predesigned symbols that you can use as part of your designs or for jump-starting your own creative talents. These prebuilt symbols are found in the Common Library, organized into folders.

Three main types of symbols are available within Fireworks: graphic, button, and animation symbols. There is also an enhanced graphic symbol type referred to as a *component symbol.* In this lesson, you will be creating and editing a graphic symbol and a button symbol.

You'll be working with the Near North website mock-up again in this exercise, turning the logo into a graphic symbol and button symbols for navigation, as well as also creating what we call a "hi-res symbol." Rather than a specific symbol type, the hi-res symbol is more a workaround that can help with potential bitmap scaling issues.

Graphic symbols

A graphic symbol is a commonly used asset in Fireworks. It is a static, single-state symbol that can be used over and over again throughout a document (or in multiple documents as well, depending on how you set it up). Use a graphic symbol if you do not require built-in animation or multiple states.

Creating graphic symbols

In this exercise, you will convert a simple logo graphic into a graphic symbol.

1 Open the file called nn_webpage.fw.png.

2 Make sure rulers and tooltips are active (View > Rulers and View > Tooltips).

3 In the Layers panel, unlock the header layer and expand the layer.

4 Select the logo: 11 objects group.

5 Choose Modify > Symbol > Convert To Symbol.

6 Name the symbol **near north logo**.

7 Make sure Type is set to Graphic, and leave the options deselected.

8 Click OK.

In the Layers panel, note that in the bottom-right corner of the thumbnail, a new icon appears, indicating the logo is now a graphic symbol. On the canvas, you will notice a faint blue plus sign (+) in the middle of the graphic. This indicates that the graphic is a copy—or instance—of the symbol.

9 Click on the header-layer title to select all the objects in the header layer, including the symbol.

10 Choose Modify > Symbol > Convert To Symbol, and name the symbol **near north banner**.

11 Make sure Type is set to Graphic, leave the options deselected, and click OK.

12 Lock the header layer so nothing is accidentally selected.

You now have two symbols (one nested within another). You might be wondering why you didn't create one symbol in the first place. The reason is that you need access to the logo symbol separately from the banner.

Adding a graphic symbol to a document

It's all well and good to *create* a symbol, but far better to make use of it. You will use this new symbol to create watermarks for the photos on this page.

1 Open the Document Library panel. The new symbol is displayed here. You can drag the logo symbol onto the canvas as many times as you want, changing the size, opacity, and location of each instance without affecting the symbol itself.

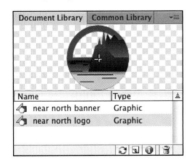

2 Unlock and select the Content layer to make it active.

Saving to the Common Library

The Convert To Symbol dialog box contains a tempting option: Save To Common Library. The advantage to selecting this option is that the new symbol becomes available to *any* document you work on, not just the current document. This advantage, however, comes with a somewhat unexpected side effect: When you create a new symbol, saving it to the Common Library in this manner also removes the object from the canvas! You need to locate the newly created symbol in the Custom Symbol folder of the Common Library panel and insert it back into your document.

A better choice is to leave this option off, and simply click OK to save the symbol to the Document Library. You can always add a symbol to the Common Library after it has been created; for details, see the section "The universal Common Library."

3 Drag the logo symbol onto the canvas, and position it in the upper-left corner of the kayak photo. You will convert this instance to a watermark using the Properties panel.

4 In the Properties panel, lock the proportions of the instance and set the new width to **70** pixels.

5 Tab to the Height field, and the image scales proportionately. Notice that the instance within the banner image does not change.

6 Set the Opacity of the instance to **40%**.

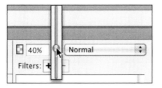

7 While holding down the Alt or Option Key, drag the instance down to the next photo. Let the Smart Guides help you align the instance copy in the second photo, or move it elsewhere on the photo.

We think the watermark should be obvious, but not cover up important details of the photo, so in our finished file, we've placed the watermark to the right on the second and third images.

8 Repeat Step 7 for the third photo.

Now the feature images have been watermarked.

9 Save your work.

A vector symbol is still a vector

The symbol creation process does not change the properties of vector objects. You can drag this symbol on the canvas and resize it 10 times larger (or more), and it will not lose any image quality. If anything, it probably looks better.

The same is true if your symbol is made of bitmaps. Fireworks still treats the objects as bitmaps. Bitmaps are resolution dependent, and scaling them larger than their original size will cause a breakdown in image quality. To counter this problem, we use a special technique that we like to call the "hi-res symbol." You'll learn more about it later in this chapter.

The universal Common Library

When you create a symbol without adding it to the Common Library, it is linked only to the document where it was created. If you open or create another document, you won't see your newly created symbol in the Document Library. After you have gone to all the trouble of creating those symbols, you may want them available for use in other designs, without having to first open a file, copy the instance on the canvas, and then paste it into a new document. This is where the Common Library comes to the rescue. The Common Library makes symbols easily accessible for any design.

● **Note:** Once a symbol has been copied from the Common Library, it becomes part of that file's Document Library. Dragging the symbol a second time from the Common Library will prompt a warning message from Fireworks stating that one or more library items already exist in the document.

1   In the Document Library panel, select the near north logo symbol.

2   Choose Save To Common Library from the Document Library options menu.

A Save As dialog box (or Save dialog box on the Mac) opens, and points to the Custom Symbols folder, where all user-created custom symbols are located by default. This folder displays automatically in the Common Library panel, so it's a good idea to save your new symbol there.

There is a specific structure to symbol file names, starting with the symbol name and appended with the symbol type (graphic, animation, or button), preceded by a period.

● **Note:** The Common Library does not become populated with symbols until a document—even a new, empty one— is open in Fireworks.

```
New Symbol...
Duplicate
Delete

Edit Symbol
Properties...

9-slice scaling guides
Lock 9-slice scaling guides

Save to Common Library...

Select Unused Items
Update...
Play

Import Symbols...
Export Symbols...

Help
```

3   Click Save.

Editing graphic symbols

As you have seen, some attributes (size, opacity, blending mode, and Live Filters) can be applied to individual instances on the canvas. Changes to a selected instance do not affect other instances on the canvas. Editing the symbol, however, changes properties in all instances of the symbol.

In this exercise, you're going to make a small edit to the logo symbol.

1 Using the Pointer tool, double-click on any of the watermark instances.

Everything but the instance fades slightly, and a breadcrumb bar appears above the document window. You are now in a symbol-editing mode called Edit In Place (a feature that has been available in Adobe Flash for quite some time). You can also enter this mode by choosing Modify > Symbol > Edit In Place. The breadcrumb trail tells you how far you have drilled down into a symbol. Changes made to a symbol in this mode are instantly reflected in all the linked instances on the canvas.

You can exit in-place editing and switch back to the main design by clicking on the top-level breadcrumb (Page 1) or by double-clicking anywhere on the canvas except the active symbol.

2 Select the Subselection tool.

Remember that originally, the logo was a group of 11 objects. Turning the logo into a symbol has not changed this. So you need the Subselection tool to access one vector element in the group.

3 Select the background mountain.

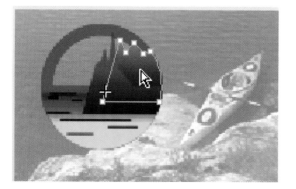

4 In the Properties panel, click on the Fill color box to open the Gradient Editor.

5 Reverse the direction of the gradient fill by clicking on the Reverse Gradients icon.

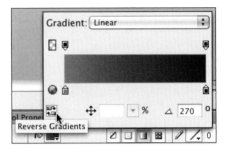

All logo instances on the canvas change to the new gradient fill, including the logo that is part of the banner symbol.

6 Click on Page 1 of the breadcrumb trail to return to the main design.

7 Save the file.

Isolation mode

Another option for editing symbols is referred to as *isolation mode*. This is the default mode for any symbol to which the 9-Slice Scaling Guides option has been applied. You can access isolation mode for any symbol, though, by choosing Modify > Symbol > Edit Symbol. The symbol remains on the canvas, but all other objects are hidden from view. If you have a full design, this mode may make it easier for you to edit aspects of symbols without any distractions.

Adding prebuilt symbols from the Common Library

The Common Library holds a wealth of prebuilt symbols you can use for your designs or as a starting point for your own symbols. To familiarize yourself with this useful feature, you will add a mock-up of a search box using two prebuilt symbols. But first, you need to add some breathing room for the search field.

1 In the Layers panel, click on the content layer name to select everything in the content layer.

2 Hold down the Shift key and tap the Down arrow three times. This opens up some space for the search field and for the site navigation.

3 Create a new layer in the Layers panel, and call it **navigation**.

4 Drag this layer to the top of the layer stack, if necessary.

5 Make sure the new layer is selected.

6 Open the Common Library panel (Window > Common Library), and scroll until you see the Web & Application folder.

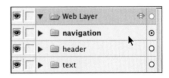

7 Double-click the folder icon (Windows) or click the disclosure triangle (Mac) to open the folder.

8 Locate the Search symbol, and drag the symbol—either the graphic itself or its name—onto the canvas.

The instance of a magnifying glass is fairly large and needs to be resized.

9 Lock the Proportions in the Properties panel, and set the width to **20** pixels.

10 Tab to the next field, and the instance updates on the canvas.

11 With the Pointer tool, reposition the magnifying glass to X: 930, Y: 130.

Adding a component symbol

A component symbol has a higher level of function-ality than a graphic, button, or animation symbol, because JavaScript controls some of its properties. You don't need to know JavaScript to take advan-tage of these properties though; you can make all the available changes using the Symbol Properties panel. By default, Fireworks displays the Symbol Properties panel as a tab beside the main Proper-ties panel. You'll first add the new symbol, then make some changes to it.

1 In the Common Library panel, locate the HTML category, expand it, and select the TextField(mac) or TextField(win) symbol.

2 Drag this symbol to the left of the search icon.

3 In the Properties panel, deselect Constrain proportions and set the width to **160**.

4 Reposition the text field as needed. Our final settings were X: 768, Y: 127.

5. Open the Symbol Properties panel by clicking on its tab (or choose Window > Symbol Properties).

While the panel may have been logically grouped with the Properties panel, it generally has more information than is visible at the default height of the panel.

6. Move your cursor to the divider between the Properties panel group and the document window. When the cursor changes to a double-headed arrow, drag upwards until you see all the properties for the symbol.

Name	Value
Text	Text
Color	000000
Font	Arial – Helvetica – sans-serif
Size	12
Style	normal
Weight	normal
Type	Text

For the text field symbol, you can change a variety of properties such as the field label and many font attributes, including family, color, style, and size. You will adjust the field label. Note there are two columns: Name and Value. You can edit the values but not the names.

7. The very first name/value pair controls the label for the text field. Select the word "Text" in the Value column.

8. Replace Text with **Search**, and press the Enter/Return key. The text field updates with the new label.

Name	Value
Text	Search

You now have a mock-up of a search bar.

9. Save the file.

Button symbols

Button symbols serve a specific purpose: making the various button states for navigation buttons. This could be mouseover events on a desktop screen or even tap events for mobile devices, although that second option requires a little creative thinking.

Button symbols are an efficient way of generating up to four visible states for a button (Up, Over, Down, and Over While Down) and adding a hyperlink to that button. Almost any graphic or text object can become a button. After you create a single button symbol, you can reuse it again and again for navigation. Each instance of a button symbol can also have its own custom text label, URL, and target without breaking the two-way symbol-instance relationship.

A button instance is self-contained. The slice object, graphic elements, and states are kept together, so if you move the Up state of a button on the main canvas, the other states and the button slice move with it.

When you export a button using the HTML And Images option, Fireworks generates the JavaScript necessary to display the rollover effect in a web browser. In Adobe Dreamweaver, you can easily insert JavaScript and HTML code from Fireworks into your web pages or into any HTML file. It's recommended, though, that you use the HTML And Images export only for prototyping a site design, not for a final website.

More and more, the HTML And Images workflow is being overlooked in favor of just a straight image export workflow, where the graphics are later coded into the CSS as background images, with HTML text being used directly in the web-page document. Where the HTML And Images export still shines, though, is in creating realistic prototypes.

Creating button symbols

You can create a button from any object, but usually the button starts out as a vector shape or a bitmap object.

1 Make sure the nn_webpage.fw.png file is still open.

2 Still on the navigation layer, select the Rectangle tool and draw a rectangle that is 100 pixels wide by 20 pixels high.

3 Use the Pointer tool or the Properties panel to position the rectangle at X: 650 and Y: 130.

4 Open the Styles panel, choose Plastic Styles from the Styles list, and then choose the style Plastic 099 to give the rectangle a deep, blue style.

5 Choose Modify > Symbol > Convert To Symbol.

6 Name the symbol **navButton**.

7 Change Type to **Button**, and click OK.

You're now back on the main canvas. Fireworks automatically adds a green slice to a button symbol, because button symbols are mainly used for rollover effects, and a slice allows for both image optimization and image swapping to other button states.

To maintain a good-quality gradient, you will set the export options for this file to PNG 24.

8   Open the Optimize panel and, if necessary, choose PNG 24 from the Export File Format list. PNG 24 will do a better job of maintaining crisp text than the JPEG format for a mock-up, and even though PNG files will be larger in file size than JPEGs, the small size of these buttons should not add too much weight to a final page.

Editing a button symbol

At first, a button symbol (like a graphic symbol) only has one state. Buttons also need text labels. The slice created by Fireworks tries to include all visual properties of the button, some of which are not easy to see. You will add text to the button, and add another state.

1   Double-click the button slice. All objects other than the button are grayed out.

2   Select the Text tool.

3   Make the following settings in the Properties panel:

Font Family: **Arial**

Font Style: **Regular**

Font Size: **12**

Fill Category: **Solid**

Color: **White**

Text Alignment: **Center Alignment**

Anti-aliasing: **Strong Anti-Alias**

4 Click right on top of the rectangle, and type **Gallery.**

5 Select the Pointer tool, and drag over both the rectangle and the text block to select them.

6 Open the Align panel, and click the Align Horizontal Center and Align Vertical Center icons to position the text within the rectangle.

7 Click away from the button using the Pointer tool to get ready to create a rollover state.

8 In the Properties panel, choose Over from the State menu. The button disappears.

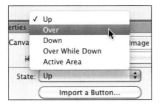

Note: If you need a refresher on the concepts of pages or states, refer back to Lesson 2.

Note: For production sites, most designers tend to create the rollover effect using CSS and background images, rather than JavaScript and inline images. Button symbols, however, can't be beat for creating interactive HTML prototypes.

9 Click the Copy Up Graphic button. This adds a duplicate of the Up state to the Over state.

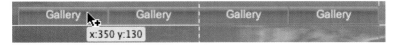

10 Select the rectangle using the Pointer tool.

11 Open the Gradient Editor, and choose Reverse Gradients.

12 Click the Page 1 breadcrumb to go back to the main canvas.

Adding more buttons

Most sites need more than a single navigation button, so you will add a few more.

1 Make sure the Pointer tool is selected and the button slice is active.

2 Hold down the Alt (Windows) or Option (Mac) key, and use the Pointer tool to drag the button to the left, until it snaps to the right edge of the original button. (Remember, holding down Alt/Option creates a copy of the selected object.) Let the Smart Guides help you position the new button directly next to the first button.

> **Tip:** The expectation with button symbols is that you will be creating one or more graphical navigation buttons, with different visual appearances to reflect the state of the button. So it is important to determine what the longest string of button text will be, in order to set a font size that will allow the various button-text strings to fit comfortably within the button shape.

3 Select both buttons, and then repeat step 2 twice. You have six buttons.

All six buttons currently have the same text labels. That's not much help!

4 Select the leftmost button. The word "Gallery" appears in the text box in the Properties panel.

5 Change the text to **Home**, and press Enter or Return.

The button text updates.

6 Select the second button, change the button text to **The Journey**, and press Enter or Return.

7 Select the third button, and change the text to **The Campsite**.

8 Change the text for the fourth button to **On the Water** and the fifth button to **Hiking**.

Take this time to rename the slices as well. For organization's sake, take the time to adjust the layer hierarchy to match the nav bar's visual order.

9 Click on the Home button, and in the Properties panel, change the button name to **button_home**.

10 Click on the Journey button, and change the button name to **button_journey**.

11 Click on the Campsite button, and change the button name to **button_campsite**.

12 On the subsequent two buttons, change the names to **button_water**, **button_hiking**, respectively.

Testing rollovers

Now it's time to test the rollovers.

1 Click the Hide Slices And Hotspots icon (▣) in the Tools panel.

2 Click the Preview button at the top of the document window.

3 Move your mouse over the six buttons. On each one, the gradient reverses when you mouse over it.

4 Switch back to Original view.

▶ **Tip:** Using a consistent prefix for each slice name (such as "button_" in this exercise) makes it easier to find groups of similar graphics in Windows Explorer, the Mac Finder, or even in Dreamweaver's Files panel, as this is the name Fireworks will use when you export the graphics.

● **Note:** The red lines you see appearing as you add button symbols are Slice Guides. This is Fireworks telling you how it will slice or cut up the design if it is exported as HTML And Images, or if images are exported using the slices. They're not very important at the moment, so if you find them distracting, you can turn them off in the View menu: View > Slice Guides.

Animation symbols

Animation symbols let you quickly generate various types of state-based (frame-based, in older versions of Fireworks) animation, including movement, visibility, opacity, and size. Because animations require multiple states in a document, they are best created on their own—either in a new document or on a separate page of an existing document—rather than as part of a complete web-page design. This eliminates the potential for exporting unwanted images from other parts of the design.

Onion skinning

Animation symbols are a bit different from just having objects in different states. The animation direction and distance is controlled by dragging the animation path in State 1. Normally, you see only the objects that are part of a selected state. However, you can use a feature called *onion skinning* to see as many states as you like. Onion skinning allows you to see states that occur before and after the currently selected state.

Export options

Animation symbols can be exported as either Animated GIFs or rasterized SWF files. Animated GIFs don't have a lot of features when it comes to animation, which is why you won't see a lot of fancy special options for animation in Fireworks. (If you are interested in creating complex animations for the Web, investigate Adobe Edge.)

Altering animation settings

Although you can use the playback controls to watch the animation, they do not emulate the true speed of the animation. For this, you will have to preview the animation in a web browser or in the Preview window.

The speed at which the animation runs is referred to as *state delay*, and by default, each state in an animation remains visible for 7/100 of a second. Increasing this value (to 20/100s, for example) will slow the animation; conversely, decreasing the value will speed up the animation. You can change the state delay for any individually selected state, or you can select a series of states and alter the delay for all of them.

To learn more about creating GIF animations, be sure to check out the Fireworks help files.

Creating a "hi-res" symbol

Remember that if your symbol contains bitmaps, image quality will degrade if you scale the symbol larger than the original bitmap. There is a cool workaround for this, however, using a method we call "hi-res symbols." In a nutshell, you create the symbol using a high-resolution bitmap, an image much larger than you would ever need in the screen-based design. We'll walk you through this process for the background image of the web page.

Destructive scaling

Scaling a bitmap permanently alters pixels, either by removing them when you scale smaller or adding them when you scale larger. You'll run a little experiment here so you can see firsthand what happens when you scale bitmap images.

1   Lock and hide all layers except the background layer.

2   You may also want to hide the Slice Guides created by the button symbols. Choose View > Slice Guides to hide them.

3   Unlock the background layer, and select the background image.

    You're about to do something destructive, but it's to prove a point. More importantly, it's reversible.

4   Select the Scale tool.

5   Drag from the bottom-right corner of the image up to the left until the photo is only about 150 pixels wide. The exact width is not important.

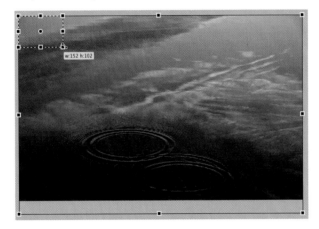

6   Tap the Enter or Return key to commit to the scaling. The image looks fine at this size, but if you change your mind and rescale the image larger again…well, let's have a look.

7 Select the Scale tool again, and resize the image so it fills the width of the design or close to it.

Without even committing to the new size, you can already see how poor the image looks. This is because scaling an image is normally a destructive process; pixel data is thrown away. And it is not brought back simply by making the image larger again.

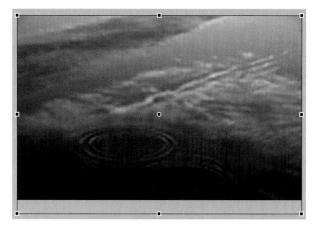

8 Tap the Esc key to cancel the scaling, then press Ctrl+Z (Windows) or Command+Z (Mac) to undo the original downsizing.

Note that the image has a Levels Live Filter applied to it.

9 Press Ctrl+C (Windows) or Command+C (Mac) to copy the image for the next phase of the project.

Ready for the magic?

Some scaling magic that is. You're going to create that hi-res symbol now.

1 Choose File > Import, locate the web_background_lrg.jpg file, and open the file.

2 When the import cursor appears, just click on the canvas to import the image at its original dimensions of 2000 x 1339 pixels.

3 Select Modify > Symbol > Convert to Symbol.

4 Name the symbol **background image**, set the type to **Graphic**, and click OK.

The instance on the canvas is still very large.

5 Zoom out to at least 25% so you can see the bounding area of the image.

6 Select the Scale tool, and scale the image down so the width fits the page design. Tap Enter or Return to lock in the changes.

7 Zoom back in to 100%

8 In the Layers panel, hide the original image.

9 Make the new instance active, and select the Scale tool again.

10 Downsize the image to about 150 pixels. Again, pixel accuracy is not important; just remember to scale by dragging one of the *corner* control handles, not the middle ones.

w:151 h:101

Note: Using the high-resolution technique will also increase the file size of the Fireworks PNG file. Take care not to use this technique too often in a document as Fireworks performance may degrade.

11 Tap Enter or Return to commit to the new size.

Remember the ugly, blurry mess you created by rescaling the small image in the last exercise? See what happens this time you rescale.

12 Select the Scale tool one more time, and upsize the image until its width matches the canvas width again. The image will extend outside of the canvas a little, but that's fine; the aspect ratio of the page design and the photo are different. Don't forget to press Enter or Return to commit the change.

Note that there is *no* change in image quality this time. It's like you never scaled the image in the first place! Fireworks is scaling the instance based on the *original* resolution of the symbol, which is 2000 pixels wide. In order to see any breakdown in image quality, you would have to enlarge this image past that 2000-pixel limit.

This technique can be very handy in the early design stages, when you're not sure how large or small bitmap images need to be for a particular design. It can save a lot of undoing of steps or searching for the original file again and again.

One last piece of magic

You've learned how surprisingly easy it is to maintain consistent effects across multiple images or to replicate effects accurately. You've worked with styles and symbols, and now here's one last trick. A little while back, you copied the original low-res image. Now you're going to use that low-res copy to set the color effects on the larger image.

1 Select Edit > Paste Attributes. The Levels Live Filter is automatically applied to the instance.

2 Make the other layers visible again, and unlock the main content layer.

3 Save the file.

Completing the design

For a finishing touch on your mock-up, you will add some placement text to the sidebar and main content areas.

1 In the Layers panel, unlock and select the text layer.

2 Select the Text tool.

3 In the Properties panel, choose a conservative serif font (the example uses Georgia) and make the following changes:

Font Style: **Regular**

Font Size: **14** (This may need some adjustment, depending on your font.)

Kerning/Tracking: **10**

Text Alignment: **Left Aligned**

Color: **Black**

4 Select Commands > Text > Lorem Ipsum to add a paragraph of placement text.

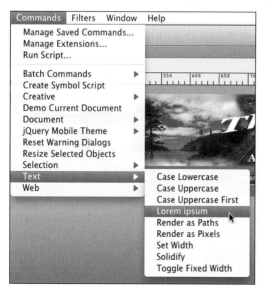

5 Use the Pointer tool to drag the paragraph on top of the sidebar. Let the Smart Guides help you align the left edge of the text block with the kayak photo.

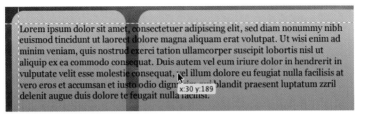

6 Drag the right-middle control handle to the left until the text block snaps to align with the kayak.

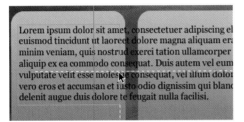

The text block resizes, and there is obviously too much text for the sidebar.

7 Double-click within the text block to enter text-editing mode, select the overlapping text at the bottom of the sidebar and delete it.

8 Triple-click on the text to select the entire paragraph.

9 Hold the Ctrl key (Command for Mac), and press the right arrow key twice to increase the kerning by another 10%.

10 If necessary, edit the text further so that it doesn't overlap the photo.

11 Repeat Step 4 to add another paragraph, and align it beside the first image in the main content area. Use the Pointer tool to resize the width of the block to 500 pixels.

Lorem ipsum dolor sit amet, consectetuer adipiscing elit, sed diam nonummy nibh euismod tincidunt ut laoreet dolore magna aliquam erat volutpat. Ut wisi enim ad minim veniam, quis nostrud exerci tation ullamcorper suscipit lobortis nisl ut aliquip ex ea commodo consequat. Duis autem vel eum iriure dolor in hendrerit in vulputate velit esse molestie consequat, vel illum dolore eu feugiat nulla facilisis at vero eros et accumsan et iusto odio dignissim qui blandit praesent luptatum zzril.

12 Delete any extra text that runs lower than the kayak photo's bottom edge.

13 Holding down the Option or Alt key, use the Pointer tool to drag a copy of the paragraph and align it with the second photo.

14 Repeat Step 13 to create a paragraph of text to align with the third photo.

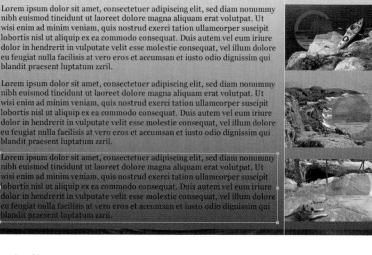

15 Save the file.

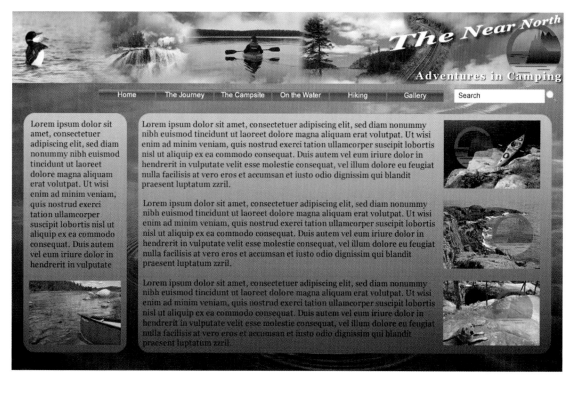

Review questions

1 What are the three main types of symbols?

2 What objects can be included in a symbol?

3 How do you create a graphic symbol?

4 How do you create a button symbol?

5 What is the importance of the Common Library?

Review answers

1 The three main types of symbols are graphic symbols, button symbols, and animation symbols.

2 A symbol can include vector, bitmap, or text objects. You can even include other symbols in a symbol, which is referred to as nesting symbols.

3 To create a graphic symbol, select the objects you wish to be part of the symbol, and then choose Modify > Symbol > Convert To Symbol. Name the symbol in the Convert To Symbol dialog box, and set Type to Graphic. Based on your requirements for this symbol, you can choose to select the Enable 9-Slice Scaling and Save To Common Library options.

4 You can create a button symbol by selecting an object and choosing Modify > Symbol > Convert To Symbol, and then choosing Button as the symbol type. The real strength in button symbols comes from the fact you can create up to four states for a symbol. You create the various states by first opening the button symbol into symbol-editing mode (double-clicking on the symbol). With no artwork selected, you can choose from four states in the Properties panel. Adding new artwork to each state is as simple as clicking the Copy Up (Over, Down) button. Edit each state as you see fit.

5 The Common Library contains a large number of prebuilt graphic, button, animation, and component symbols that you can easily drag and drop into your design. You can also save your own custom symbols to the Common Library, so they can be used in any of your documents.

10 OPTIMIZING FOR THE WEB AND MOBILE

Lesson overview

Fireworks has its roots in web graphics so is no stranger to optimization—that balancing act of quality versus file size. Proper optimization minimizes quality loss while reducing file size, thus cutting download times for images. In previous lessons, you learned the basics of working with graphics in Fireworks. Now you'll combine those skills with some new tools to optimize assets for web pages, and for web-page creation itself. In this lesson, you'll learn how to do the following:

- Export a single image to a web-ready format

- Determine the optimal web format for a sliced graphic

- Use the Optimize panel and Preview views to optimize images

- Slice up graphics in a web-page mock-up using the Slice tool

- Export a single-page HTML prototype

- Export a CSS sprite sheet

- Extract CSS properties from vector artwork

 This lesson takes approximately 90 minutes to complete. Copy the Lesson10 folder into the Lessons folder that you created on your hard drive for these projects (or create it now, if you haven't already done so). As you work on this lesson, you won't preserve the start files. If you need to restore the start files, copy them from the *Adobe Fireworks CS6 Classroom in a Book* CD.

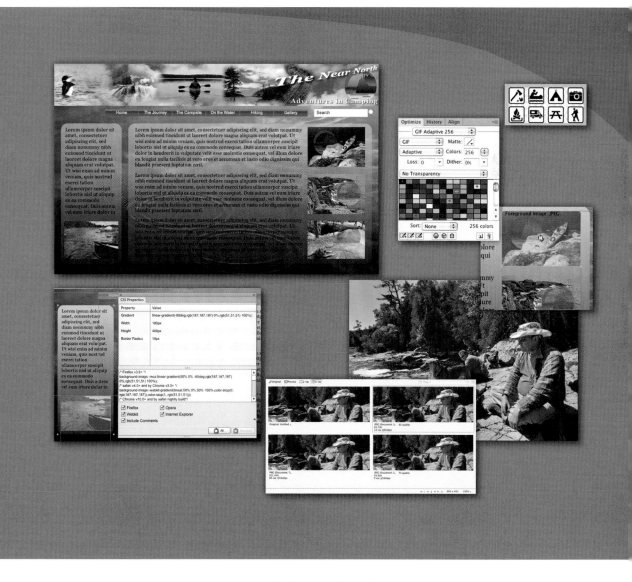

Fireworks does many things, but at its roots it is a web graphics application—be it for creating mock-ups, editing screen-resolution images, exporting graphics for use in Adobe Edge or mobile applications, or optimizing and exporting images to CSS and HTML.

Optimization basics

Why optimize images for the Web and mobile applications? Simply put, not every-one has the luxury of a high-speed Internet connection, where web pages down-load at lightning speed. Optimizing images reduces the size of files, decreasing the amount of time it takes for a user to download them, regardless of the available bandwidth (connection speed). The effective *page weight* (combined file sizes of all assets of a web page, including the page itself) is reduced. Files take up less room on the web server and reduce the bandwidth required for downloading. Also keep in mind, it's a mobile world out there; tablet devices and smartphones can easily chew up costly bandwidth fees when downloading websites.

Optimizing graphics ensures they possess the right balance of color, file compres-sion, and quality. You are trying to get the smallest possible file size (for quick download) while maintaining acceptable quality. Optimizing graphics in Fireworks involves two basic and important components:

- Choosing the best file format for your various graphics
- Setting format-specific options, such as color depth or the quality level

Web-graphic formats

To a degree, the file format you choose is a subjective decision, but here are some definitions and general guidelines:

- **JPEG (Joint Photographers Expert Group)**: For photographic images, JPEG format gives you photorealistic (24-bit) color, and you can control the quality and compression of the file. Higher quality means less compression, which in turn means a larger file size. JPEG is also a *lossy* format, meaning that each time a JPEG file is saved, more of the original image data is discarded. If you require the JPEG format, try to edit files in a lossless format such as PNG, TIFF, or PSD, and then save or export the final file as a JPEG. (JPEG format is also used when a composition includes gradients, shadows, or glows.)

- **GIF (Graphic Interchange Format)**: GIF images are limited to 256 colors (8 bits), but these colors are customizable. GIF files are best for images with solid color, such as logos, line art, or text-based graphics. This format supports transparency settings (indexed transparency) that can give your image the impression of floating over the top of another image or colored background. GIF supports frame-based animation for creating simple web-graphic anima-tions (Animated GIF or GIF 89a). For complex or large web, animations, consider using Adobe Edge instead.

- **PNG (Portable Network Graphic)**: The PNG format tries to give you the best of both worlds: You can choose from among 32-bit, 24-bit, and 8-bit PNG output. A 32-bit PNG allows for 24-bit photorealistic color with 8-bit *alpha transparency,* so you can get more realistic drop shadows or glows around an image or even make the image appear semitransparent on the web page. The image will blend seamlessly with the background color of the web page. A 24-bit PNG is mildly compressed and lossless, meaning that no image data is discarded when the file is saved. However, you cannot control the compression or quality as you can with JPEG files. The file size is what it is. An 8-bit PNG is much like a GIF, but it does not support frame-based animation. PNG 8 also supports both indexed and alpha transparency. Often, you will get smaller file sizes by exporting as PNG 8 rather than GIF. It's definitely worth testing.

Note: Fireworks uses a modified version of the PNG format as its native file format, giving you a great deal of flexibility for editing files. This modified format contains information about layers, states, and effects, and as a result, it produces a much larger file size than a standard flattened PNG file. For this reason, avoid using a native Fireworks PNG format as part of the real web page, even though the browser will render it. If you want to use the PNG format for web graphics, export an 8-bit, 24-bit, or 32-bit PNG file. PNG 32 is a 24-bit PNG file with 8 bits added for alpha transparency.

Saving versus exporting

Fireworks makes a distinction between the terms "saving" and "exporting."

In general, *exporting* a file results in a flattened bitmap image; the final file has no layers, vectors, or other unique editable objects. Exporting a file also uses the information in the Optimize panel to control the exported file format, quality, and color depth. Optionally, you can include an HTML page when exporting. The one exception to the flattened image rule is the Export As Adobe PDF option. You will learn more about this export workflow in Lessons 11 and 13.

Saving a file (File > Save) saves the file back in original format, unless features not supported by that format have been added. For example, a JPEG file is a flat file; it doesn't support additional objects, layers, or editable effects. So if you add these types of features to an open JPEG file, upon saving, Fireworks displays a warning message about losing the editable features, and asks if you really want to save the file back as a JPEG or would you rather save it as a Fireworks PNG file. Saving a file bypasses the Optimize panel settings and uses the default settings inherent in the file.

Choosing Save As (File > Save As) offers a wider variety of formats and allows you to customize the Optimize panel's settings as well. You can save in flattened formats such as JPEG, BMP, and GIF; SWF or multilayered Adobe Fireworks PNG files; Adobe Photoshop PSD files; or even Adobe Illustrator AI files (AI version 8 only). By clicking the Options button in the Save As dialog box, you can reach the Optimize panel settings for adjustment.

Other options, such as the ability to maintain XMP metadata, are available for certain file types when you save them; however, XMP data is not maintained when you export a file.

Alpha versus indexed transparency

There are two types of transparency for bitmap graphics: alpha and indexed.

With *indexed transparency*, every color in the color table is given a transparency designation. This value can either be 0 (transparent) or 1 (opaque). There are no intermediate opacities; the color is either displayed or it is not, so indexed transparency is incapable of displaying high-quality drop-shadow or glow effects.

With *alpha transparency*, each color in a graphic has an alpha channel value, indicating how transparent it is. When you see the color space RGBA (very common in CSS3-based effects), the color is defined by the red, green, and blue (RGB) channels. The alpha (A) value defines the opacity for that color. The value can run from 0 (transparent) *through* to 1 (opaque). So, you could have a value of .5 for example, which represents 50% opacity. Values closer to 0 are more transparent, and values closer to 1 are more opaque. This allows for very realistic drop shadows and glows, as well as gradients that blend seamlessly with the background behind them, whether that background is a solid color, pattern, or even a photograph.

About the Optimize panel

By default, the Optimize panel is located in the topmost panel group. If you don't see it, choose Window > Optimize to bring it to the front. In the Optimize panel, you choose the graphic file format you would like to use when exporting a single image file, a selected image slice, or a group of slices. Each slice in a design can have completely different optimization settings; this gives you a high level of control over a web page's weight.

When an image or part of a web design has no slices, you can use only one optimi-zation setting for those areas. An image with one or more slices can have different optimization settings for each slice and another optimization setting that applies to any unsliced areas. Any changes you make to the optimization settings in either the Properties or the Optimize panels applies to the currently selected slice or slices. If no slices are selected, the optimization setting applies to all the unsliced areas.

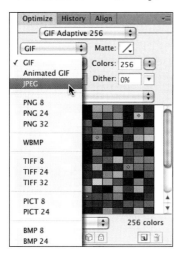

The Optimize panel is context sensitive. As you change export formats, the panel displays options for that specific format. For example, when you choose JPEG, the Optimize panel displays options only for Matte color, Quality, Selective Quality, and Smoothing.

For GIF, Animated GIF, and PNG 8 formats, you can change Matte color, Indexed Palette type, number of colors, Loss, Dither, and Transparency options.

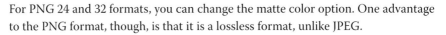

For PNG 24 and 32 formats, you can change the matte color option. One advantage to the PNG format, though, is that it is a lossless format, unlike JPEG.

● **Note:** Understand that, to a degree, optimization is a subjective choice, especially when you're dealing with small changes in quality or file size. If you're designing a site for an intranet, you have a little more leeway with your decisions about file size and quality.

The Optimize panel options menu contains several features and actions not available in the panel itself, such as the ability to interlace GIF files or to select Progressive JPEG. The panel menu also gives you quick access to the Export Wizard and the Optimize To Size command.

What is matte color?

Matte color—available in all the export formats—is the color Fireworks uses on all areas of the canvas not covered by an object. Changing the canvas color of the document updates the matte color to match, but you can also change the matte color independently in the Matte Color field without affecting the original canvas color. This feature is helpful when you need to export the same graphic for use on a variety of web-page background colors. Matte color is also used when you export a GIF or flat PNG file with a transparent background. Set the Matte color to match your web-page background color for a more seamless blend in transparent areas.

Optimizing a single-image file

You will start by optimizing a single image destined for use in the Near North website. You will learn about several fundamental features of the Fireworks export process by altering image quality, format, and compression.

Working with previews

The Preview mode is an essential tool for determining optimization settings.

1 Open the sand_river.tif file from the Lesson10 folder.

2 Choose Window > Optimize to open the Optimize panel, if it isn't visible in the panel dock.

3 Set the Zoom level to 100% by pressing Command+1 (Mac) or Ctrl+1 (Windows).

   At the top-left of the document window, notice the four view options: Original, Preview, 2-Up, and 4-Up. The default view is Original, which is your editing view. The other three views let you preview your design in different formats, based on the settings in the Optimize panel.

4 Click the Preview button.

   This view is similar to the Original view, but it applies the settings from the Optimize panel. You cannot edit or select individual objects while in this view.

5 In the Optimize panel, choose GIF Adaptive 256 from the Saved Settings pop-up menu.

6 Zoom in to 200%, and study the face of the man in the foreground. Note how his face seems to be made up of blotches of solid color. Likewise, the blue sky in the upper-left corner has lost its smooth, continuous tone. Rough concentric circles of solid color have replaced it.

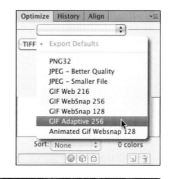

   GIF files can display up to 256 color values only and, as a result, don't do a good job of rendering many color photos.

7 Look at the bottom-left corner of the document window. The status bar displays information about the export file. Here it reads "175.16K 28 sec @56kbps GIF (Document)." (These file

Note: When using GIF or PNG 8, you can apply dithering to an image to emulate missing hues. The pattern created by the dithering helps give the impression of continuous tone, but you pay for it through increased file size.

sizes may differ slightly on your system.) This file information area, also visible in Original view, tells you the file size and the download time of the image based on the optimization setting and an admittedly very slow dial-up connection.

175.16K 28 sec @56kbps GIF (Document)

8 In the Optimize panel, choose JPEG – Better Quality from the Saved Settings pop-up menu. Recall that JPEG is usually a much better option for exporting an image with gradients and a wide color range.

The colors and tones smooth out dramatically. Equally—if not more— important is the updated information in the status bar of the document window: "83.79K 13 sec @ 56 kbps." The image quality has improved, and the file size has decreased by over 50%.

83.79K 13 sec @56kbps JPEG (Document)

9 Select the 2-Up view. The document window splits into two panes. On the left, Fireworks displays the Original view; on the right, the current optimization settings for the image. The 2-Up view is helpful when comparing differences in quality between the original design and an optimized version.

Tip: On a MacBook Pro, in addition to pressing the space bar, you have to press down on the trackpad in order to pan.

10 With the Pointer tool, click on the right pane. A border appears around that window, indicating it is the active window.

11 Hold down the spacebar, and when the cursor changes to a hand, drag the image so you can see most of the hiking group. Note that panning the image occurs in both windows.

Original: Untitled ▾

JPEG (Document, f▾   80 quality
83.79K
13 sec @56kbps

12 In the Optimize panel, change the Quality setting to **50**%. You can change the value by typing it and pressing the Tab key (or Enter or Return) or by dragging the slider. (When you type the value, there is a slight delay before the preview updates with the new quality setting.)

The file size decreases to approximately 34.21K. But it's becoming obvious that the image is degrading. This is the fine line we've been talking about: creating the balance between acceptable image quality and small file size. 34K is pretty small for such a large image, but image quality is in pretty rough shape.

▶ **Tip:** You can also set basic web-optimization settings for a slice using the Properties panel, but the Optimize panel gives you much more control. The Optimize panel also contains non-web formats such as TIFF and BMP, in case your designs— or elements of it—are destined for other uses or mediums.

Choosing optimization settings

Comparing the potential exported image to the original is important, but there are subtle changes in the Optimize panel that can make a big difference to the final exported file. You'll now experiment with the other preview options.

1 Zoom back out to 100%. Even at this 1:1 magnification, the artifacts are still somewhat visible and may be unacceptable to you or a client.

2 Click the 4-Up button. The document window is now split into four previews, with the Original view remaining in the top-left corner.

3 Set the upper-right compression to **80**.

4 Select the bottom-right preview, and change the Quality setting to **70**.

5 Select the bottom-left preview, and change the File format to **PNG 24**.

You can now compare different quality/compression/format previews to the Original view. By comparing these versions of the same file, you can quickly determine the best combination of file size and image quality.

6 Zoom in to 150%, and compare the PNG 24 preview to the original. There is no discernible difference between them; however, the file size of the PNG 24 export is over 500K—far too large for a single image on a web page!

7　Compare the two JPEG versions against the original image. Bearing in mind that neither will be quite as good as the original, try to determine which of them is most suitable. The 80% quality looks good, but it's almost 84K. The 70% quality, clocking in at almost 60K is pretty good, and at 100% magnification, the JPEG artifacts are not very noticeable. But that 70% quality option is still a large file size.

If only there was a way to retain more quality in specific areas and to more highly compress areas without important detail. Oh, wait—you're using Fireworks! There is a way, and it's called Selective Quality.

Optimizing with Selective Quality

Selective Quality is one of those unsung heroes in Adobe Fireworks. By using bitmap selections, you can *mask* specific areas with important detail in a photo and set a higher-quality (lower compression) value for those areas.

1　Switch back to Original view.

2　Select the Lasso tool.

3　In the Properties panel, change the Edge setting for the lasso to Feather, and set the value to **10**.

4 Draw a rough selection around the hikers.

5 Hold down the Shift key, and draw a rough selection around the blue sky in the upper-left corner of the photo.

High JPEG compression is known to overly compress areas of solid color, like a blue sky, or even solid-colored text. You're going to keep the sky looking good. Even though it doesn't have any important detail, the JPEG artifacts will be very obvious and will impact the overall quality of the photo.

6 Select Modify > Selective JPEG > Save Selection As JPEG Mask.

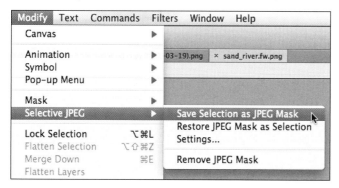

7 The selection disappears, replaced by a translucent pink overlay. This is the JPEG mask.

8 Switch to the 2-Up view, and select the right pane, if necessary.

In the preview, the mask is hidden, but you will still see the mask in the Original view.

9 From the Export File Format list, choose JPEG if it is not already selected.

10 Set the Quality to **40** and Selective Quality to **70**.

Note the updated file size of approximately 43K. You have a smaller file and the only areas being heavily compressed are areas without important detail.

11 Just to prove that Selective Quality is helping, try this: Change the main Quality setting to **5**. The difference should be very obvious. Reset the main Quality to **40**.

Exporting the file

The final step is to export the TIFF file as a JPEG file.

1 Choose File > Export.

2 Browse to the Lesson10 folder.

3 Change the filename to **sand_river.jpg**.

4 Choose Images Only from the Export menu, if it is not already chosen.

5 Leave the Include Areas Without Slices and Current Page Only options selected.

6 Click Save (Windows) or Export (Mac).

7 When you return to the canvas, save the file as a Fireworks PNG file so that the settings you made in the Optimize panel remain with it as well as the JPEG mask, and then close the file.

About the web tools

To produce compositions in Fireworks that make their way into an HTML prototype web page, you need to be familiar with the available web tools.

You'll find a number of web-related tools in the Tools panel:

- The three hotspot tools let you draw rectangular, circular, or polygonal shapes over portions of your image. When exported with HTML, hotspots link to other web pages or trigger other events on a web page, such as a remote rollover.

- The Slice tool (image) and the Polygon Slice tool (image) let you cut a larger image into smaller pieces or select which parts of a web-page prototype will be exported as graphics for a web page.

- The Hide Slices and Hotspots button (image) hides slices and hotspots.

- The Show Slices and Hotspots button (image) makes slices and hotspots visible.

Creating and optimizing slices

A *slice* is a portion of an image or design that you intend to export as a unique graphic. When exported as HTML And Images, individual slices can include interactivity such as image rollovers, hyperlinks, and remote rollovers, but this workflow is suitable for interactive prototypes only, not final web pages. Slices are always added to the Web layer of a Fireworks document.

New in Fireworks CS6 is the ability to export sliced graphics as a single graphic file, referred to as a *sprite sheet*. A sprite sheet can then be used in conjunction with CSS to show or hide different portions of the file through the use of the `background-position` property. Icons, buttons, logos, background images— all the window dressing of a web page—can be added to a sprite sheet.

With the exception of a sprite sheet, each web slice has its own optimization settings. Without slices, your image or design has only one optimization setting applied to it, as in the first exercise in this lesson.

In this section, you'll learn several ways to create slices, as well as how to optimize the slices for various types of graphics, to name the slices, to create a sprite sheet, and to extract CSS properties from a vector object. Later, Lesson 12 will look at more of the interactive features and dig more deeply into a multi-page prototype.

Which Slice tool do you choose?

You can choose from two Slice tool styles: rectangle or polygon. Because web pages are essentially laid out in a grid format, you will most often use the standard (rectangular) Slice tool.

The Polygon Slice tool can be useful if you want a nonrectangular area to be interactive, but this tool uses a combination of HTML tables and hotspots as well as slices (the resulting exported file consists of rectangular slices in a table and a polygon hotspot).

You can't have true polygon-shaped images, just like you can't have elliptical-shaped images on a web page. Like it or not, everything ends up as a rectangle, because HTML uses *only* width and height for an image in a web page. If you use a lot of polygon slices, your HTML code can become quite complex and require more CPU processing time, thus slowing down the browsing experience.

Creating slices manually with the Slice tool

You will use the standard Slice tool to cut up a web-page mock-up. Accurate slicing is important. If you are going to create manual slices, be sure to zoom to at least 150% or 200% to ensure your slice includes the entire area you want to export.

1 Open the nn_homepage.fw.png file from the Lesson10 folder. This is a completed web-page mock-up.

2 Select the Zoom tool, and zoom in to the banner area. Zooming in helps you slice only the graphic and not any surrounding area.

3 Select the Slice tool, and draw a box over the entire banner. Pay close attention to the bottom edge, making sure not to select the water background image.

Note: If you do not have the fonts used in the sample file, select Maintain Appearance when Fireworks asks if you want to maintain appearance or replace the font.

A green translucent rectangle appears on top of the banner image. This is an image slice.

A slice has three main components: the slice name (user-definable), slice selection handles (for resizing a slice), and the behavior handle for adding interactivity to a slice. Red slice guides also appear, showing you how Fireworks will automatically slice up the rest of the document.

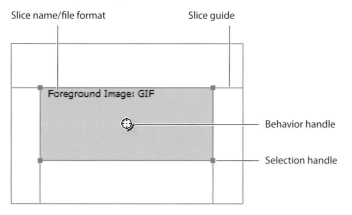

When it creates a slice, Fireworks automatically assigns the slice a name, based on the image's file name and future location inside an HTML table-based layout. These names become the actual file names for the slices when they are exported. They can be fairly cryptic, and likely won't have any relevance to you later in the web production process. We recommend that you give meaningful names to all the slices you create, in case you use the exported files in a final web page.

4 In the Properties panel, double-click the slice name to select the entire name. Change the current slice name (nn_homepage__r1_c1) to **nn_banner**. Note there are no spaces in this name. It's a good idea to use standard web-naming conventions with slices. Avoid spaces and special characters. Ideally, you should decide on and stick to a system for using upper- and lowercase letters. We keep things nice and simple by putting all web-file names in lowercase.

Note: With the exception of button symbols, a slice object is not attached to the image below it, so if you reposition the image, you also need to reposition the slice.

Now even without seeing a thumbnail of the file, you would easily know what this graphic is and where it's supposed to go on the web page.

Adjusting slice dimensions

If this is your first time creating a slice by hand, don't be surprised if you need to tweak the dimensions of the slice. When you zoom in, it should be easy to see if the slice is smaller or larger than the image behind it. If you need to make adjustments, you can either use the Pointer tool to resize the slice or change the dimensions numerically in the Properties panel.

Seeing web objects in the Layers panel

Slices and hotspots fall into the category of web objects. When you create either type of web object, Fireworks automatically places them in the Web layer of the Layers panel. The Web layer is always at the top of the Layers panel and cannot be deleted, even if it is empty.

Optimizing a sliced image

This banner is a collection of bitmaps, vectors, and text. You'll walk through the optimization process again for the banner.

1   Choose Window > Optimize to open the Optimize panel, if it isn't visible in the panel dock.

2   Set the Zoom level to 100% by pressing Command+1 (Mac) or Ctrl+1 (Windows).

3   Click the Hide Slices and Hotspots tool in the Tools panel, and then click the Preview button.

4   In the Optimize panel, choose GIF WebSnap 256 from the Saved Settings pop-up menu.

5   Study the logo. The smooth gradients in the original banner have been replaced with solid bands of color—not very attractive.

GIF files generally don't render many gradient effects very well. The status bar at the bottom-left corner reads "63.80K 10 sec @56kbps GIF (Document)." (These file sizes may differ slightly on your system.)

6   In the Optimize panel, choose JPEG – Better Quality from the Saved Settings pop-up menu. Recall that JPEG is usually a much better option for exporting an image with gradients and a wide color range.

The gradient smoothes out in the banner and reduces the file size to about 32.98K. The image quality has improved, and the file size has decreased.

7   Select the 2-Up view.

8   Select the Pointer tool, and click on the right pane.

9   Hold down the spacebar, and when the cursor changes to a hand, drag the banner to the left so that the logo is visible.

10 In the Optimize panel, change the Quality setting to **60**.

The file size decreases to approximately 19.23K. But even at 100% magnification, it's becoming obvious that the logo is losing quality. Even the text is beginning to degrade.

11 Zoom in to 150%, if necessary, and compare the banner text (Original and Preview). The panes are synchronized, so as you zoom or pan in one window, the other displays exactly the same view.

If you study the text closely in the Preview version, you will see that the background surrounding the text is not as smooth as it is in the Original view.

Tip: The JPEG format can compress areas of solid color too much, and because text is often a solid color, the quality of text can suffer noticeably. If you have large text—or a great deal of text—in your design, you can sometimes improve the text quality by enabling the Selective Quality setting (click the icon to the right of the Selective JPG slider) in the Optimize panel, and selecting the Preserve Text Quality option. Note that at the time of this writing, Preserve Text Quality does not function if the text object is locked, or if the text is part of a symbol.

What you see here is the result of the JPEG quality setting. These JPEG artifacts become more visible as you reduce the image quality of the file.

This is the fine line we've been talking about: creating the balance between acceptable image quality and small file size. 19K is very small, but the banner quality is in pretty rough shape.

12 Change the Quality setting to **70%**. The file size increases slightly to almost 24K, but the banner text is also better. This value is a good balance between file size and quality.

Adding more slices

The beauty of slices is that you can have different formats, and even different optimization settings, in a single design. This gives you the flexibility to truly optimize an entire page design in a single document, rather than having multiple separate image files. You will now add a new slice using an alternative method.

1 Return to the Original view, and select the Subselection tool. You're using the Subselection tool because this column of images is grouped, and you don't want to add a slice to the entire group, just the individual images

2 Select the kayak photo.

3 Right-click (Windows) or Control-click (Mac) the image, and choose Insert Rectangular Slice from the context menu. (Hotspots can also be created in this manner.)

Fireworks automatically adds a slice, based on the object's dimensions.

4 Set the Optimization to JPEG – Better Quality.

5 In the Properties panel, change the slice name to **img_kayak**.

Slicing tricks for working with multiple items

You will add and format the final slices for this design. First you'll use a handy shortcut to create the rest of the slices.

1 Select the Subselection tool.

2 Hold down the Shift key, and click on the remaining three graphics in this layout.

3 Right-click (or Control-click) on any one of the selected objects.

4 Choose Insert Rectangular Slice from the context menu. This time a confirmation box appears, asking if you want to create a single slice or multiple slices from the selected objects.

5 Click Multiple. All three image objects get sliced. They will all have the same optimization settings that you just used in the previous example, and each will be auto-named by Fireworks.

This time, instead of using the Optimize panel, you'll set basic optimization options in the Properties panel.

6 Change the file format to JPEG – Better Quality in the Slice Export Settings menu in the Properties panel (below the Type menu).

7 Click outside the canvas to deselect all the slices.

Naming slices

It's easy to forget to rename slices, but it's a really good idea. You will name all those new slices now, before going any further. Remember, you can change the name of any slice directly in the Properties panel.

1 Select the slice covering the lake photo, and in the Properties panel, rename it **img_lake**.

You'll rename the last two slices in a different manner.

2 Open the Web layer in the Layers panel if it is collapsed. Collapse the Optimize panel by clicking on the gray bar next to the tabs if you need to free up more room for the Layers panel to expand.

3 Select the slice covering the dog.

4 In the Web layer, locate the selected slice.

5 Double-click the slice name, and change it to **img_dog**.

6 Save the file.

Creating a hotspot

You can use the various hotspot tools to create hyperlinks within any slice object. You'll add one hotspot to this design, on top of the nn_banner slice.

1 Select the Circle Hotspot tool (⊛).

2 Hold down the Shift key, and draw a circle around the logo.

The Properties panel updates to display attributes for the hotspot.

3 In the Link field, type **http://www.adobepress.com/** and type **Visit the Website** in the Alt field.

Previewing the page in a browser (or uploading as a graphical web page) enables the link. When visitors click the hotspot, they'll jump to the URL you've entered.

4 Save the file.

Previewing in a browser

Previewing in a browser gives you the opportunity to test interactivity (rollover effects, hyperlinks) and also lets you see how your choices for image optimization look within a browser.

1   Choose File > Preview In Browser, and choose your browser from the submenu. Depending on your computer setup, the browsers listed may vary. In our case, the default (Primary) browser was Firefox.

Fireworks invokes the selected browser and loads a temporary copy of the web-page design.

2   Click on the logo text. If you have a live Internet connection, the browser will load the home page for Adobe Press.

3   Close the browser.

4   Save the file in Fireworks.

If your design has multiple pages (we'll come to that in Lesson 12), you can create links from one page to another using hotspots or slices.

More on the Hotspot tool

Fireworks provides three hotspot tools: the Rectangle Hotspot tool (⬚), the Circle Hotspot tool (⬚), and the Polygon Hotspot tool (⬚). You can quickly access the hotspot tools by pressing the J key. Like all multiple tool icons in the Tools panel, if you keep tapping the shortcut key (or hold down the left mouse button on the tool itself), you will toggle through all the available tools.

The Rectangle and Circle Hotspot tools are pretty self-explanatory, and produce fairly simple image-map HTML code when a file is exported as HTML And Images. The Polygon Hotspot tool creates precise hotspot shapes around irregularly shaped objects. But the amount of HTML markup this type of hotspot produces is significant, so it's best to use the Polygon Hotspot tool sparingly.

Exporting a single-page design

Fireworks has two main workflows for converting your visual concepts into web pages: You can export as HTML And Images or as CSS And Images.

Exporting HTML And Images

The HTML And Images export option produces a table-based HTML layout, which does an excellent job of matching your Fireworks design. It can also include hyperlinks and rollover effects. That's the good news.

Now for the bad news: This table-based layout is rigid. Removing or adding elements of the page using a web-page editor like Dreamweaver can cause the table structure—and web-page layout—to break. By default, everything in the design is exported as an image, including the text. From a best-practices perspective, you should avoid table-based, image-only layouts for your final websites, and learn how to use CSS for laying out final web pages.

That said, there is still a place for this feature in the modern designer's workflow. Many designers use the standard HTML capabilities in Fireworks for creating interactive graphical HTML prototypes for client feedback. It's a great way to test ideas and concepts without having to code any HTML right away. The client can request changes on the visual aspects of the design, and you can accommodate them without having to write a single line of HTML code—just update the design in Fireworks and export the file again. After prototype approval, you should properly code the final pages in a web editor such as Dreamweaver.

You will test out this export process now:

1   Open nn_homepage.fw.png, if it is not still open.

2   Choose File > Export, and browse to the Lesson10 folder.

3   Change the Export field to HTML And Images.

4   Set the HTML field to Export HTML File, and the Slices field to Export Slices. Make sure the following three options are selected: Include Areas Without Slices, Current Page, and Put Images In Subfolder.

5   Click the New Folder icon, and name the folder **webpage**.

6   Click the Options button, and then the Table tab.

7   Make sure Space With is set to Nested Tables, No Spacers, which maintains the layout without adding multiple transparent spacer images to hold everything together. You can leave all other settings at their defaults.

8   Click OK to close the Options dialog box, and then click Save (Windows) or Export (Mac) to create your web page.

9 Browse to the webpage folder using Windows Explorer or the Finder.

Inside the folder you will see the web page, nn_homepage.htm (or nn_homepage.html if you've previously altered the default file extension settings) and an images folder. These figures show the folder contents as displayed in the Finder (left) and Windows Explorer (right).

10 Double-click on the web page to view it in your default browser.

The page loads, and when you mouse over the buttons, the rollover effect works nicely. Other than the layout being left justified and the page background being white, this is a great proof-of-design sample for client review.

11 Compare the web page to the Fireworks PNG design; they appear very similar, if not identical. You can even click on the hotspot you created earlier over the logo and go to Adobe Press again.

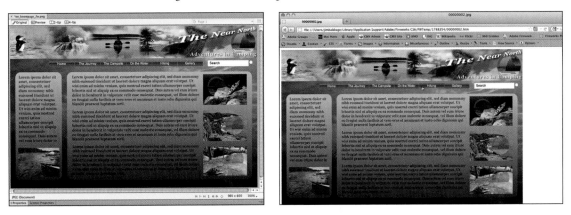

But we must stress, this is *not* a great final web page. Although everything matches the Fireworks concept, there are too many image slices, the HTML is a rigid, table-based, image-only page (no text at all, just bitmaps that look like text). The rounded rectangle containers are solid bitmaps and can't be used as flexible containers for other pages. Indeed, that kind of effect can be completely re-created using CSS3 properties—something you will be doing very soon!

12 In the main content area, try to select the text. You can't, because it's a graphic. Ideally, any text that was exported as images should be re-created as true text within Dreamweaver and styled using CSS.

13 In your browser, view the source code of the page. (In Firefox, choose View > Page Source.)

Fireworks added JavaScript to the head of the document and the inline code in the body of the document that is necessary for the image swap for the button rollover effects. Note also the rather complicated table structure.

14 Close the browser.

15 Open the images folder within the webpage folder.

Fireworks exported 33 images, 12 of which are just for the buttons. For the Fireworks-generated HTML to display properly, *all* these images are needed.

● **Note:** A Swap Image behavior is a prebuilt JavaScript used by Fireworks (and Dreamweaver) to create a rollover image effect. Behaviors do not require the user to know any JavaScript and can be customized using the Behaviors panel.

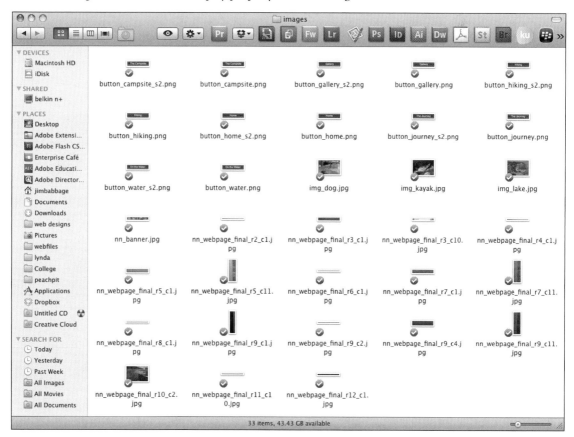

If you were to build this page in a web editor such as Dreamweaver or export as CSS And Images from Fireworks, however, only eight of those images are truly

Tip: You can also customize the file names for states. You can set this up by choosing File > HTML Setup and clicking the Document Specific button. A file must be open in Fireworks in order to access this menu item. You can also click the Options button when you are exporting a file, and then click the Document Specific button.

Note: When you export all states of a multistate file, Fireworks—by default—appends the file names with _s1, _s2, and so on, including the main state. This ensures that the graphics on other states are not overwritten. You can create your own custom state names in the Export dialog box by choosing Options > Document Specific and selecting Custom from the State names drop-down lists.

necessary—and three of that eight weren't even exported in a form you could use on other pages in the design. The necessary images are:

- img_kayak.jpg
- image_lake.jpg
- image_dog.jpg
- img_canoe.jpg
- nn_banner.jpg

along with these three missing images:

- The background image
- Up button with no text
- Over button with no text

From a mock-up perspective, this export is fine: it shows the client how the page will look and that it's interactive. However, from a practical, end-user perspective, you would want to build the final web page in a web-page editor.

16 Go back to Fireworks, and save the file.

Creating a sprite sheet

New to Fireworks CS6 is the ability to export sliced graphics as a *sprite sheet*. A sprite sheet is a single file containing a series of graphics (usually icons or buttons) that can be called on by a Cascading Style Sheet (CSS) to display bullets or rollover effects.

You can invoke the option to export as CSS sprites in two ways:

- Select File > Export, and choose the CSS Sprites option from the Export drop-down menu.
- Right-click one of the slices, and select the option Export CSS sprites from the context menu.

The second page of the nn_homepage.fw.png file is called Sprites and contains a series of icons. You will slice those icons, optimize them and then export them as a sprite sheet.

1 In the Pages panel, choose the Sprites page.

What is a sprite sheet, and why should I use one?

A sprite sheet is a bitmap file that stores multiple, usually small, graphics, such as button background images, custom bullet graphics, icons, and even logos. This file, combined with a CSS file, lets the web browser quickly load all the background graphics (all one page, remember) and then display an image located at a specific set of pixel coordinates from within the bitmap file.

Why should I use one?

This is a good question, especially if you are stuck hand-coding the CSS for a sprite sheet containing more than half a dozen image sprites. Creating the CSS for a complex sprite sheet by hand is, to say the least, tedious and probably quite intimidating for someone new to using sprite sheets. In the image editor, each image has to be planned out in terms of its exact pixel location, and you must record those locations so that later you can hand-code a bunch of CSS classes to enable the browser to locate each individual graphic. Heck of a way to spend your evening.

Fireworks makes this process virtually painless and fast, however, thanks to the CSS Sprites export workflow.

From the standpoint of data and bandwidth, all the graphics in the sprite sheet are loaded at the same time because the sprite sheet is just one big graphic file. The browser loads the entire file into its cache, and this means the browser is not continually sending requests to the server for this file or that file; they're already all in memory. It also means there is no need for any JavaScript preloading scripts (common in the bad old days of graphical button rollovers) and means the display of images is virtually immediate.

2 Press Ctrl+A (Windows) or Command+A (Mac) to select all the icons.

3 Right-click on any of the icons, and choose Insert Rectangular Slice from the context menu.

4 When prompted, choose Multiple. Each icon gets a slice.

5 In the Optimize panel, set the optimization format to PNG 8. Set the Matte color to none, the Transparency setting to Alpha Transparency.

6 Change the number of colors to **6** by typing the value.

7 Click the Rebuild button to rebuild the color palette.

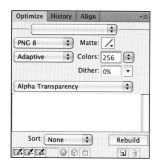

Note: When multiple objects are selected, the color palette actually clears when you click Rebuild, but when you select individual slices, you will see the color palette for each slice.

Why six colors, you might be wondering? Well, technically it's only five, as one of the colors is reserved for transparency. But other than that, it's the fine line again; four colors aren't enough because the icons start to look jagged, while eight colors look just fine but increase the file size unnecessarily.

Because the only graphics in this sprite sheet are the black-and-white icons, you can get away with minimal colors. If the color logo were in this sprite sheet, however, you'd likely have to use PNG 32 to maintain the gradient fills of the logo *and* the transparency.

8 In the Options menu for the Optimize panel, select Save Settings. This allows you to save your optimization settings as a preset, which will come in handy very soon.

9 Name the new preset **bw_icons**.

10 Click outside the canvas area.

11 Name each slice according to the object name in the Layers panel. Do this by selecting one slice at a time and matching its location with the object it covers. For example, the slice covering the icon with the axe and firewood should be named **icon_firewood**. The slice covering the picnic table should be named **icon_home**.

12 Save the file.

Exporting the sprite sheet

With the icons sliced and optimized, you're ready to export the icons as a sprite sheet.

1 Right-click (Ctrl-click on Mac) on any slice, and choose Export CSS Sprites.

In the *Export* dialog, the following options are available for CSS Sprites export:

• **Save As**: Specifies the file name with which the sprite image should be exported

• **Export**: Chooses/changes the export workflow from CSS Sprites to one of the other standard export options, such as Images Only

• **Pages**: Exports slices from selected Pages/All Pages/Current Page

- **Selected Slices Only**: Exports slices that are selected in single/multiple pages

- **Current State Only**: Exports only the slices in current state of the page (for pages having multiple states)

- **Options**: Invokes the CSS Sprites Export Options dialog, which includes options to specify the CSS Selector type (Class or ID), Prefix, Suffix, orientation of the exported sprites, and the file type/optimization of the exported sprites

Note: Slices in the Master page and other shared layers are included only once in the sprite image.

2   In the Save As field, change the name to **nn_sprites**.

3   Browse to the Lesson10 folder, and open the webpage folder you created earlier.

4   Make sure that CSS Sprites is the chosen workflow for Export.

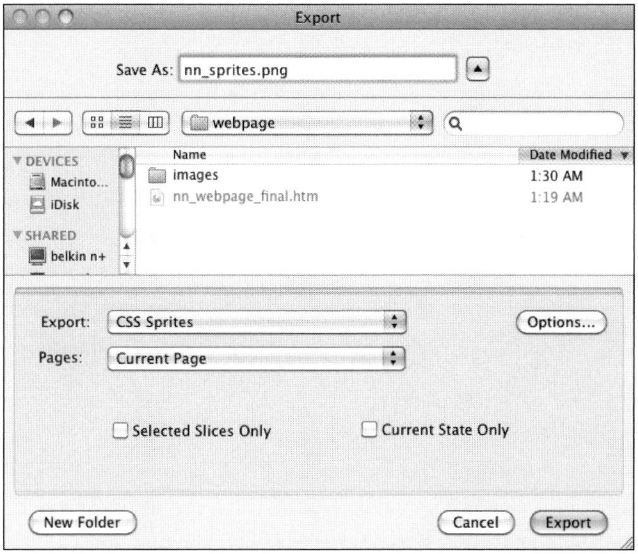

5   Click the Options button.

6   Make sure Class is selected as the selector type.

7   Leave the other options as you see in the figure below, but click the Optimization Preset list. At the bottom you will see the custom preset you created, bw_icons. Select that preset.

8   Click OK.

9   Click Export.

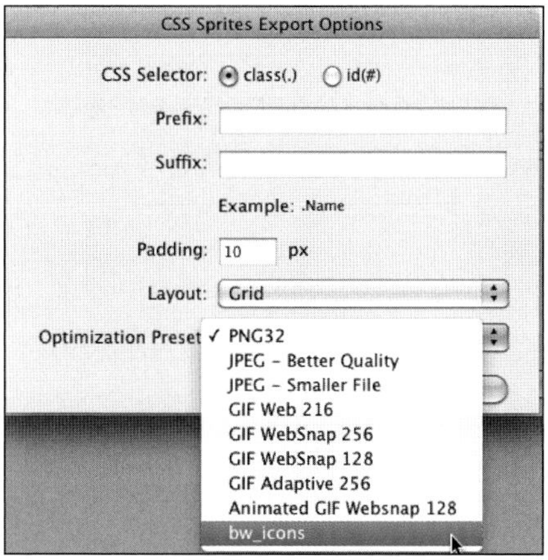

Tip: If you create a custom optimization setting, you can save it for use at a later time. Just choose Save Settings from the Optimize panel menu.

If you open Windows Explorer or the Mac Finder and browse to the webpage folder, you will see that Fireworks has generated both a CSS file and a PNG file. The CSS file specifies the displacement values for the subimages present in the exported sprite image. Feel free to open the CSS file in a web-page editor or text editor. The sprite graphic's final size is just over 1.5K.

About Fireworks and CSS

CSS files (Cascading Style Sheets) are the current standard for web-page design, and Fireworks has a couple of export workflows to help you in this regard as well: CSS And Images export and the CSS Properties panel.

CSS And Images export

Tip: For a detailed tutorial on exporting a design using the CSS And Images workflow, check out Dave Hogue's articles on the Adobe Developer Connection: http://www.adobe.com/devnet/dreamweaver/articles/turning_design_into_html_and_css_pt1.html.

Entire books have been written on CSS and its use, and this book does not pretend to be one of them. You won't be employing the CSS And Images export in this book, but we do want to give you give you some advice and preparatory information, explaining the logic behind the CSS And Images export feature. A little later, you will work with the CSS Properties panel to create specific rules that could be used in any layout.

The CSS And Images export option attempts to create an HTML- and CSS-based layout of your current design. It sounds wonderful, doesn't it? But there are a couple of caveats to bear in mind:

- Objects/slices *must not* overlap in the design. This can be more challenging than you realize at first.

- Fireworks is creating both a CSS file and an HTML file for a full-page layout, and hence, will be using naming conventions and layout schema that you may not normally use, even though they are valid HTML and CSS.

- This export workflow doesn't exempt you from learning and understanding how to use CSS in your web-page layouts! It is meant as a starting point to producing a more usable web page right from Fireworks.

- Typically, even after exporting in this manner, you will need to do some customizing in your web-page editor.

Here are some design concepts to keep in mind if you plan to export a CSS-based layout from Fireworks:

- **Keep it simple.** Overlapping slices will cause Fireworks to export a complete, absolutely positioned layout. While still valid within HTML and CSS, it is generally not good practice to produce layouts that are based entirely on absolute positioning. Elements that are set at absolute X and Y coordinates are isolated from the flow of the page and are not "seen" by other page elements.

- **Only text, rectangles, and image slices are exported.** To export as CSS And Images, any images you want to include in the web page must be sliced. Any text you wish to remain as true HTML text should not be sliced. Fireworks creates an HTML web page, using `<div>` tags to contain the text and images, according to the slices, rectangles, and text it finds in the design. A Cascading Style Sheet is also created, to handle positioning of the `<div>` tags and styling of the text.

- **Text, rectangles, and image slices are all treated as rectangular blocks.** The exporter (also called the export engine) examines the size of text blocks (the actual bounding box, remember, not the width/height of the text itself), rectangles, and slices in order to create the proper spacing between the elements. It also determines the logical placement of columns and rows, based on the position of the design elements in your file.

  Text blocks can be deceiving, because the rectangle area that defines the text block may actually be much larger than the text, causing two objects to overlap.

- **The exporter must be able to interpret where the columns and rows of objects exist.** Even though you are not using tables for layout, keep thinking in that grid-like fashion. Make it easy for the export engine to figure out where logical containers (a header, a sidebar, a main content area, and a footer) would go.

- **Use rectangles to create a specific `<div>` container around objects.** If you draw a rectangle around specific elements, Fireworks understands that the objects inside the rectangle should be in their own `<div>` container in the final CSS layout.

What is a `<div>` tag?

The HTML tag `<div>` is often used for defining a generic segment of your document. It acts as a container for other elements of a web page. With the `<div>` tag, you can group HTML elements together and format them with CSS. With the growing popularity of HTML5, many new HTML5 elements are taking the place of the `<div>` tag for certain semantic uses. For example, HTML5 includes elements such as `<footer>`, `<nav>`, `<article>`, `<section>`, and `<aside>`. These are not elements that Fireworks understands natively.

The `<div>` tag is still used for presentation purposes. For example, when you want to group elements together for the purpose of creating a design, you would still choose the `<div>` tag. The `<div>` tag is just a generic container that has no semantic meaning at all. Fireworks wraps text and images inside `<div>` tags based on the layout, which is why the placement of design elements is critical when exporting in CSS And Images format. In order for Fireworks to lay out the page using its CSS layout engine, it is important that slices do not overlap other slices, and that text areas do not overlap slices.

If Fireworks encounters any overlaps, a warning message appears, telling you where the first overlap was encountered and that the export is switching to Absolute Positioning mode. This mode is still CSS-based, but Fireworks places each object at an exact location in the web page—the elements in the page are fixed in place. If you later wish to add text in a web-page editor or other content using a content-management system, or if a user increases the size of the text for better readability, the other page elements won't shift to accommodate the extra space needed.

The CSS And Images export feature does not export rollover graphics or hotspot information. Hyperlinks are maintained for foreground images, though Fireworks displays a warning message to remind you of that fact. Image maps or JavaScript behaviors need to be added in a web-page editor. On the bright side, you would get to practice creating CSS-based rollovers!

Using the CSS Properties panel

For the longest time, creating visual elements in Fireworks (or other graphics software) culminated in exporting every visual effect as bitmap graphics. Optimization techniques can be employed, as you've already seen, but every bitmap has file weight to it, no matter how small. The CSS Properties panel virtually eliminates bandwidth for certain types of imagery, such as rounded rectangles and circles with solid, gradient, or semitransparent fills, by extracting the CSS properties of a selected object. Likewise, Fireworks can extract properties like drop shadows, transforms, and even font properties.

This panel can prove handy for anyone who is familiar with Fireworks and Dreamweaver (or a web-page editor of your choice) and wants to design for mobile deployment or to reduce bandwidth on traditional websites. Visual designers usually start designing their web pages in a design tool like Fireworks and then either send the design file to a web designer or do the web work themselves. With CSS3 gaining momentum and browser compatibility, many design aspects can be represented using pure CSS, with no need for images, such as the rounded rectangles in our web page example. The CSS Properties extension helps simplify the tedious process of hand-coding CSS for certain elements. Design properties in Fireworks, which can be represented in CSS, are now extracted using the CSS Properties panel, helping reduce the effort of having to master all browser-specific CSS properties.

Here you will learn how to use the CSS Properties panel, but we won't be discussing the fine details of Cascading Style Sheets.

● **Note:** For more information on the CSS Export feature, be sure to check out the Adobe Fireworks Developer Center at www.adobe.com/devnet/fireworks.

● **Note:** To learn more about CSS, be sure to visit the Adobe DevNet Center at http://www.adobe.com/devnet/dreamweaver/css.html.

About the CSS Properties panel

The panel has two sections. The top section lists all the attributes of a shape or text that can be converted to CSS, and it shows the specific CSS property and value for each. You can sort the properties and values in the upper window by clicking either the Property or Value headers. Doing so toggles the order of the properties or values alphabetically, in descending or ascending order. You can also select individual properties from this section and use the Selected button to copy those declarations to the clipboard. Select noncontiguous properties by pressing the Command (Mac) or Ctrl (Windows) key.

The lower section displays the declarations as Fireworks will write them out. You can scroll through this list and even select and copy specific declarations. If you want to copy all the properties for the selected object, click the All button. At this time, the panel can extract properties from only one object at a time. Any time you change the properties of a selected shape, or when you select a new object on the canvas, the panel automatically refreshes with new properties.

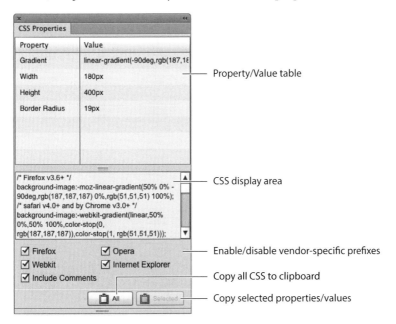

Property/Value table

CSS display area

Enable/disable vendor-specific prefixes

Copy all CSS to clipboard

Copy selected properties/values

Extracting CSS properties

You will test out the CSS properties panel by extracting declarations for the sidebar rounded rectangle, and then you will create a very simple web page using Dreamweaver to see how the declarations can be applied.

1 Return to Page 1.

2 Unlock the content layer if necessary.

3 Use the Pointer tool to select the sidebar rounded rectangle.

4 Select Window > CSS Properties. The panel appears and quickly refreshes with the CSS properties for the rectangle, including the markup needed to reproduce the gradient!

5 Use your cursor to drag the panel wider, so that the gradient rule is not clipped.

One very popular technique for containers as seen in our design is for them to be semitransparent. Currently the containers are opaque, but you can quickly change that.

6 In the Properties panel, change the Opacity setting to **60**.

The CSS properties panel updates, changing the gradient values to RGBA values. Even more impressive, Fireworks writes out vendor-specific declarations for Safari, Firefox, Chrome, Opera, MS Explorer 10, and MS filters for older versions of MS Explorer. Imagine having to hand-code all that mark up.

7 Click the All button. Fireworks copies the rules to the clipboard.

Creating a CSS rule in Dreamweaver

With the rules copied to the clipboard, you now need something to paste them into. The steps below are based on using Dreamweaver CS6 and assume you have a basic working knowledge of the Dreamweaver interface. Feel free, however, to follow along in your preferred web-page editor.

1 Launch Dreamweaver. This practice example doesn't require a site definition, as there will be no images or internal links. For a production website you will need to create a site definition, though.

For more information on creating a site definition, please review the Dreamweaver help files, available in Dreamweaver from the Help > Dreamweaver Help menu.

2 Select File > New, and from the New Document dialog window, select Blank Page, HTML (Page Type), and (none) from the Layout column.

3 Set the Doctype to HTML5, and click Create.

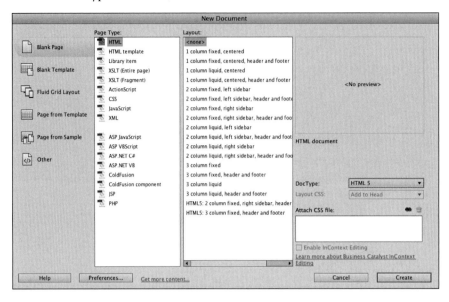

4 When the page opens, save it as **CSS3_basic.html**.

5 Switch to Split view if necessary. In Split view you see the markup on the left side of the document window and the Design/Live view on the right side.

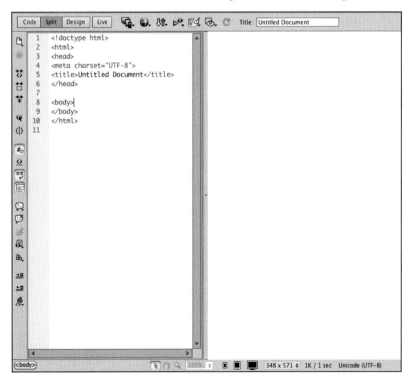

6 Select Insert Layout Objects > Div Tag.

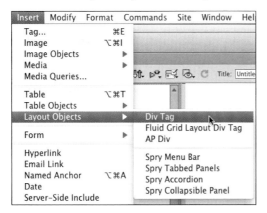

7 Give the new `<div>` tag a class of **sidebar**, and click New CSS Rule.

8 When the New CSS Rule dialog window appears, make sure the Rule Definition location is set to This Document Only. Click OK.

9 When the CSS Rule Definition window appears, just click OK. Remember, your rules are sitting in the clipboard, waiting to be pasted.

10 When the Insert Div Tag dialog box reappears, just click OK to place the `<div>` into the HTML markup.

11 In the Code pane, locate the head of the document, and then find the empty CSS rule for the sidebar class.

12 Put your cursor between the opening and closing curly braces of the rule and press Ctrl+V (Windows) or Command+V (Mac).

13 Things won't look very impressive right away, because Dreamweaver's Design view isn't capable of rendering many CSS3 properties.

Content for class "sidebar"
Goes Here

14 Turn on Live view.

The rectangle appears, complete with the linear gradient, and rounded corners. The transparency is also there, but hard to judge when the web-page background color is set to the default white.

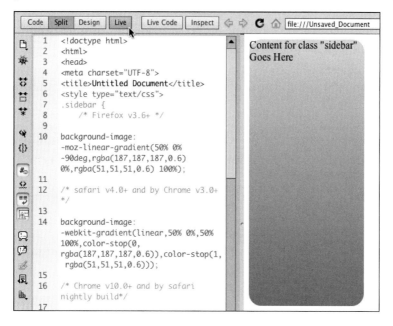

Note: CSS3 support is spotty or nonexistent in versions of IE8 and lower, so your page may display very differently from what was intended, even with the application of IE Filters.

Note: Always remember that Fireworks is, first and foremost, a design tool, and the CSS Properties panel is just a way to move you more quickly into a true web-editing environment, such as Dreamweaver.

Tip: To learn more about which fonts are safe to use on the Web without the @ font-face declaration, check out Code Style's Most Common Fonts survey results at www.codestyle.org/css/font-family/sampler-CombinedResults.shtml.

15 In the Code pane, have a really good look at all that CSS markup. Be thankful you didn't have to write it all yourself!

16 Save and close your file.

The CSS Properties panel gives you the flexibility of extracting CSS properties from vector artwork or text and can generate rules specific to the effect you are trying to create, including the entire common vendor-specific markup that is needed at this time.

Now that you see the end result, you can edit the properties by going back to Fireworks, editing the visual properties of the rounded rectangle, refreshing the CSS Properties panel, copying them again, and replacing the old styles with the updated ones. This can be a huge time-saver, when compared to the possible trial-and-error recoding of the CSS manually. Of course, you can definitely make the modifications to the CSS right in Dreamweaver if you're comfortable there.

Styling text in Fireworks

What if the text within your rectangle is too dark to be readable and isn't in the desired location? Creating a specific class within Dreamweaver that targets the color, padding, and angle of the text will resolve those issues; but just as you did for the example's circle, you can also use Fireworks for this effect, if you're more comfortable.

Simply add your text in Fireworks as you normally would when creating a mock-up, setting color, size, font family, drop shadow, and even angle. The CSS Properties panel refreshes, and you can simply click the All button to generate the CSS needed for the text effect you want. The process can be as simple as Design > Copy > Paste.

Study the css_basic_final.html markup to see how text was placed within the <div> at a specific location.

If you use a nonstandard font, Fireworks even includes the @font-face property for that font. Be warned, though, that you still must have the rights to upload that custom font to your web directory. Having the @font-face property does not give you implicit permission to use whatever font you have in your font directory. Remember to abide by copyright rules when planning to use fonts on the Web. Also remember that even purchased fonts do not always include a license to upload the font to the Web. Check out Font Squirrel for free, public domain fonts at http://www.fontsquirrel.com or investigate Adobe Typekit service for commercial fonts at https://typekit.com/.

Certain CSS properties, such as position, may need to be added or tweaked within Dreamweaver. At the time of this writing, the CSS Properties panel is converting text sizes to pixels, rather than percentages or ems. This is easily fixed in a web-page editor, though. Note also that at the time of this writing, Kerning/Tracking is not yet being converted to the CSS equivalent of letter spacing. Again, this is an easy fix in the code, though.

Review questions

1   Why should images be optimized for the Web?

2   What are the two types of web objects you can create in a Fireworks design, and how do they differ?

3   What are the main workflows for generating web pages from Fireworks?

4   What is the CSS Properties panel, and how do you use it?

Review answers

1   Optimizing graphics ensures that they are set to a suitable format and possess the right balance of file size, color, file compression, and quality. You are trying to get the smallest-possible file size (for quick downloads) while maintaining acceptable quality in the image. Optimizing graphics in Fireworks involves choosing the best file format for a graphic and setting format-specific options, such as color depth or quality level.

2   Slices and hotspots are the two main kinds of web objects you can create in Fireworks. You can add URLs to both types for interactivity. You can use slices to generate rollover effects, and you can also use hotspots to trigger remote rollover events on the web page. Slices let you cut up a larger design into smaller pieces and individually optimize each slice to get the most suitable combination of file size and image quality. Hotspots create an interactive area within an image. They do not cut up an image like slices do. They were commonly used to create image maps: a single image that has multiple hyperlinks applied to it in different areas. You can use hotspots to trigger rollover events on the web page.

3   There are two main workflows for exporting complete HTML pages:

   • **File > Export > HTML And Images.** This exports a rigid, table-based design consisting entirely of graphics. Even the text is exported as graphics. Pages created this way are difficult to edit, because removing or adding new elements to them using a web-page editor can break the layout. However, this export is ideal for creating interactive prototypes of a web page or a website. Although not suitable for a final website, the HTML pages can show the client how the site will look, and can also support rollovers and hyperlinks, so a client can interact with the prototype and request changes or approve a design before any work needs to be done on the coding side of the project.

   • **File > Export > CSS And Images.** This option can generate a more standards-based, editable web page by creating the layout using Cascading Style Sheets rather than tables. Moreover, this export option recognizes text and exports it as true HTML text. With a working knowledge of CSS, these pages are easier to edit and more flexible in terms of adding new elements within a web-page editor.

4   The CSS Properties panel generates CSS3-compliant markup of a selected vector shape or text block. The markup is then copied to the clipboard and pasted into a new or existing CSS rule, using a web-page editor or text editor. First select a vector or text object. Open the CSS Properties panel, and then copy all the CSS mark-up extracted by the panel (or select only the declarations you need) to later paste into a CSS rule using Dreamweaver or your preferred HTML editor.

11 PROTOTYPING BASICS

Lesson overview

Layout features (Smart Guides and tooltips), new symbol libraries, and the ability to switch seamlessly from vector to bitmap graphic editing make Fireworks an ideal application for building prototypes.

In this lesson, you'll learn how to do the following:

- Edit a multipage wireframe

- Share layers to multiple pages

- Use assets from a template

- Add gesture symbols

- Preview a wireframe design in a web browser

- Export a secure, interactive PDF file

 This lesson will take about 60 minutes to complete. Copy the Lesson11 folder into the Lessons folder that you created on your hard drive for these projects (or create it now), if you haven't already done so. As you work on this lesson, you won't preserve the start files. If you need to restore the start files, copy them from the Adobe Fireworks CS6 Classroom in a Book CD.

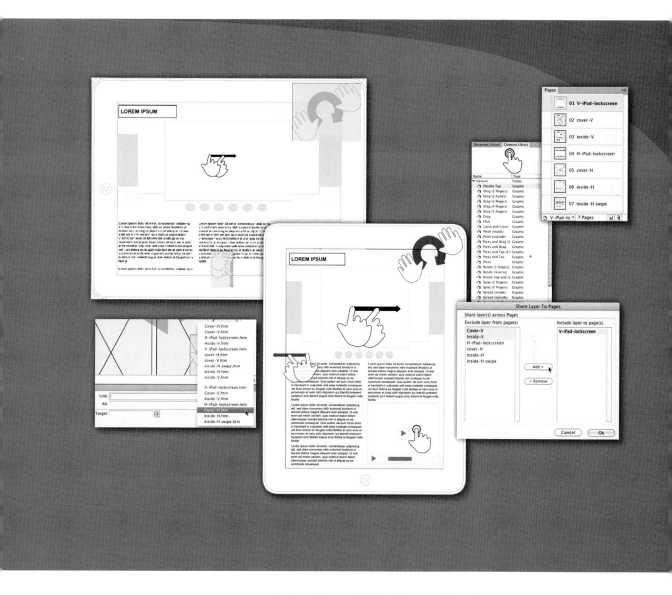

Fireworks is a graphical, rapid-prototyping tool with a multitude of features, such as the Pages panel, interactive web layers, and component symbols, making it an ideal application for building prototypes to test user interaction and nail down interface or page design issues.

The prototyping workflow

Web-page design, game design, mobile, and application design projects can all benefit from adopting some form of prototyping workflow. Developing a prototype is a good way to maintain design consistency, minimize project creep, and test functionality and design concepts before moving to the coding stage. Typically, the main phases in a prototyping workflow are:

1 Create a project concept (website, mobile application, game).

2 Create a wireframe to plan the application layout and functionality.

3 Create a realistic prototype to address the aesthetic concerns of the project.

4 Generate an interactive prototype for "proof of concept" and usability testing.

5 Upon receiving approval, build the final project.

Of course, in real life things aren't usually that simple, and a workflow may very well require several wireframe iterations or numerous design concepts before a project reaches the realistic prototype stage.

In this lesson, you get to skip the first phase and part of the second phase because we decided on the project and set up part of a wireframe for you. The project is wireframe for a tablet application, specifically a Digital Publishing Suite (DPS) interactive magazine app. The app is based on the Near North website that you have worked on in previous lessons. Your responsibility here is to build on the wireframe and add interactivity.

Note: A simplistic rendition of the final project, a wireframe can be built quickly and just as easily discarded when it has served its purpose. The goal of a wireframe is to describe an application's function, flow, and general layout, without focusing on the aesthetics of the application.

A review of the Pages panel

In Lesson 2, you learned the basics of the Pages feature. As you added content to a simple mock-up in that lesson, you learned that pages are a key prototyping strength in Fireworks. The ability to create multiple pages in a single Fireworks file makes it a great tool for creating rich, realistic multipage mock-ups. With multiple pages, you can easily generate a series of design concepts, an entire website mock-up, or an application design in one location, making it easier to keep track of assets for a specific project.

The Pages panel is the control center for adding, duplicating, deleting, and renaming pages.

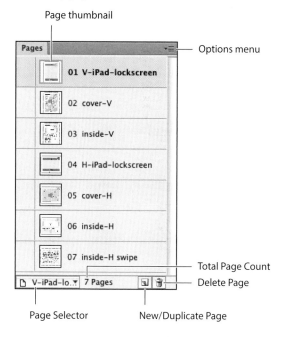

Page thumbnail

Options menu

Total Page Count

Delete Page

Page Selector

New/Duplicate Page

Each page in a document has a sequence number automatically applied by Fireworks. You can turn this numbering on and off from the Pages options menu. You can rename any page just as you can rename layers and objects; simply double-click on the page name to edit it. If your design uses a Master page for common page elements, that Master page will always appear at the top of the Pages panel.

Isolating the Pages panel

Typically, the Pages panel is grouped with the Layers and States panels, but we find it more useful to move it into its own group. You will do that now.

1   Open the Pages panel (Window > Pages).

2   Drag the Pages tab, and reposition the cursor so that it is between any two panel groups.

3   When a thin blue highlight bar appears and the panel's opacity fades, release the mouse button. The Pages panel is now in its own group.

The Master page

The Master page is an optional but useful item. Use it if you have visual elements or web objects that will be common to all pages and appear in the same physical location on each page. Because each page can have different dimensions, it's best to use a Master page only for elements that appear at the top of a design or share a common canvas color. If you are positive your page dimensions will not change, you can also include common background images or footer information in a Master page; just bear in mind that if you shorten or lengthen a page, that information may not appear in the correct position.

Each Fireworks design can contain only a single Master page.

In our sample wireframe, you'll be representing both horizontal and vertical orientations of a tablet, so a Master page will not be part of the design.

Comparing wireframe pages

By their nature, wireframes are supposed to be simple diagrams, designed to focus on function and not aesthetics.

1   Open wireframe_final.fw.png.

2   Select the V-ipad-lockscreen page.

Note: The pale blue rectangles you see covering the gesture graphics are hotspots. If you find them distracting, simply click the Hide Slices And Hotspots tool in the Tools panel.

There are three main layers plus the Web layer to this page, and its horizontal counterpart, H-ipad-lockscreen. The Web layer holds web objects called *hotspots*, which are being used for interactivity. The top graphic layer contains symbols that represent tablet gestures, the next contains the objects representing the lockscreen, and the bottom layer contains the parts that make up the iPad outline. The iPad layer is shared to the other two vertical pages in the wireframe.

The iPad layer has a small page icon appearing near the right side of the layer. The icon indicates that this layer is shared with other pages in the design—another timesaving feature.

3   Select the cover_V page.

The canvas is filled with simple shapes, and many of these shapes have been converted to symbols to make it easy to build more wireframe pages. Color issues for the final design have been deferred by using shades of gray for all the objects in the wireframe. This way, clients are not focusing on color, hue, or saturation; they are focusing on the functionality of the concept. This page contains the Web layer and three main layers, including the shared iPad layer.

4   Select the inside-V page.

5   Expand the Layers panel.

An important aspect to a touchscreen app wireframe is indicating how the user will interact with the app. Fireworks contains an entire library of symbols in the Common Library, called gesture, that covers the majority of gestures that could be used on a tablet, smartphone, or other touchscreen device.

6   Switch to the inside-H page, and note how the elements have been rearranged to represent a horizontal layout. Note also a new gesture symbol that indicates a downward swipe.

Adobe DPS publications allow the user to swipe horizontally from article to article, as well as vertically from page to page of a specific article. Here we've shown that the content continues vertically and that the user can swipe down to read the rest of the article.

Feel free to further inspect the wireframe. When you're ready, you can start adding content to a less complete version.

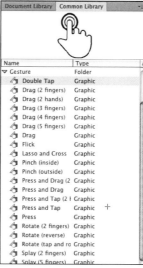

● Note: A finished wireframe would likely include far more pages than our example, but in the following exercises, you will learn all the concepts needed to create a more detailed wireframe for your own projects. It's also worth noting that these concepts (with the exception of most gestures) hold true for website wireframes as well.

Adding pages

The most expedient way to add more pages to any design is to create a duplicate of another page, if that page is similar in layout. If you have no similar pages, then creating a standard new page is the way to go. You will add a couple of final pages to the wireframe, and then use a combination of techniques to flesh them out.

1 Open the wireframe_start.fw.png file.

2 Select the V-ipad-lockscreen page.

3 At the bottom of the Pages panel, click the Add/Duplicate Page icon. Do not drag the lockscreen page to this icon; you don't need a copy of that specific page.

4 Repeat step 3 to create another vertical page.

5 Rename these pages to **Cover-V** and **Inside-V**, respectively.

6 Switch back to the lockscreen page, and in the Layers panel, select the iPad layer.

7 Right-click (Control-click on Mac) the layer to invoke the context menu.

8 Choose the Share Layer To Pages option. The Share Layer To Pages dialog opens.

9 In the left column, select Cover-V and Inside-V, and then click the Add button.

10 Click OK to return to the document.

11 Select either of the new pages. Notice that Fireworks added the iPad outline to both layouts.

Now you need to ensure new objects are visible on new layers and that nothing is added to the shared iPad layer.

12 In the Layers panel, drag the iPad layer to the bottom of the layer stack for both pages. The empty Layer 1 should now be at the top of the layer stack.

13 Lock the iPad layer. Because this layer is shared, you need to lock it only once on any page for the layer to be locked on all shared pages.

14 Save your work.

Changing Fireworks preferences

It's time to give this wireframe some substance by adding some graphic elements. Before you add any elements though, you need to change one of Firework's default preferences. In the next exercises you'll be scaling a lot of vector artwork, and you need to be sure you don't accidentally scale such vector elements as stroke widths as well.

1 Select Edit > Preferences (Windows) or Fireworks > Preferences (Mac).

2 In the General category, disable Scale Strokes And Effects, and then click OK.

As you can see, the Preferences panel has many settings. These settings are global and affect all Fireworks documents.

> **Note:** Wondering where we got the iPad outline? Fireworks CS6 comes with both iPad symbols and an iPad wireframe template. To use the template, choose File > New From Template and browse to Wireframes > iPad Sketch. This opens an extensively detailed template with a huge range of iOS user-interface components, all in vector format. To use the individual symbols, locate the wireframe-iPad folder in the Common Library and drill down to find the iPad Frame-white symbol. In the sample file, we copied the frame from the iPad wireframe template because we didn't want everything locked into one symbol.

Adding wireframe elements to the cover

You've already learned how to create graphic symbols, so for this lesson, we've gone ahead and created a couple of custom symbols for you: an image placeholder and a header placeholder. There are also several other symbols in the Document Library that came along as part of the iPad template.

1   Switch to the Cover-V page.

2   Select Layer 1, and rename it **gestures**.

3   Create a new layer, and call it **layout**.

    The gestures layer should be at the top of the layer stack.

4   Create the same layers, in the same hierarchy, on the Inside-V page. Even though you're using the same layer names, these layers will have different content on them from page to page, so you can't just share the layers to both pages.

5   Switch back to the Cover-V page.

6   Lock the gestures layer, and select the layout layer.

7   From the Document Library, drag the image placeholder symbol onto the canvas.

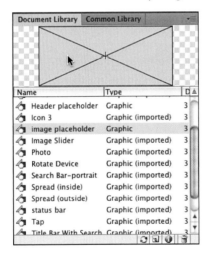

8   In the Properties panel, set the width and height to **740** and **310**, respectively, and the X and Y values to **124** and **130**.

9 Hold down the Option (Alt) key while using the Pointer tool to drag a copy of the image placeholder instance.

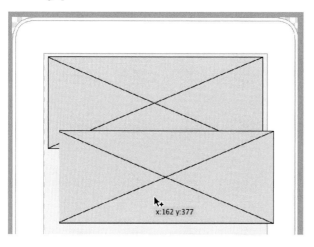

10 Set its Width to **360**, Height to **670**, X to **124**, and Y to **460**.

11 Option-drag (Alt-drag) a copy of this shape, letting Smart Guides help you align the right edge with the edge of the horizontal image.

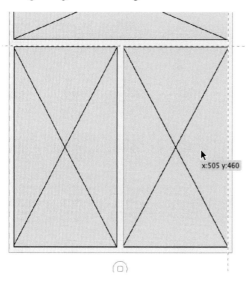

12 From the Document Library, drag the header placeholder onto the canvas and place it at the X, Y coordinates of 130, 140.

13 Also from the Document Library, drag the Audio symbol onto the canvas.

14 Use the Scale tool to resize the instance to about 360 pixels wide, and set the Opacity to **50**% in the Properties panel.

15 Align the instance to the center of the canvas.

This semitransparent icon will represent a background sound that will play when the cover page loads. Because you can't add sound to the Fireworks document, it's a good idea to indicate that sound will be part of this screen, much like a "play" icon is often used to represent video.

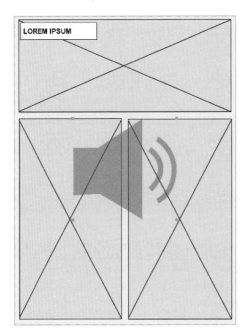

16 Before leaving this layer, name the three image placeholder objects **image placeholder horizontal**, **image placeholder vertical left**, and **image placeholder vertical**.

Adding a gesture symbol

To indicate touch interactivity, you will now add a symbol to represent a flick or swipe gesture.

1 Lock the layout layer, and unlock the gestures layer.

2 From the Document Library, drag the Flick symbol onto the canvas.

3 Use the Scale tool to resize the instance to about 270 pixels wide.

4 Place the gesture object so that it overlaps the screen and frame on the right side of the wireframe. The exact location is not crucial.

5 In the Properties panel, set the Opacity to **70**, so that you can see through the symbol slightly. While not necessary, we think this is a nice touch to indicate you're transitioning from one screen to another.

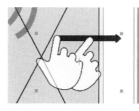

Note: Remember that many of these symbols are already in the Document Library because they have been used elsewhere in the file. If you can't find a gesture symbol, or want to use a different one, check the Common Library's gesture folder.

Creating the inside layout

The Inside-V layout is a little more complicated, but you can handle it! You'll be adding in all the elements needed to flesh out the vertical layout in this exercise.

1 Switch to the Inside-V page.

2 Lock the gestures layer.

3 Drag the header placeholder to the upper-left part of the tablet screen.

4 Position the header at X: 130 and Y: 140.

5 From the Document Library, locate the Image Slider symbol and drag it onto the canvas.

6 Position the instance beneath the header placeholder, at X: 110, Y: 210.

7 Select the Scale tool.

8 On the Canvas, drag the bottom-right control handle across to the right, stopping when the scale boundary snaps to the inner-right edge of the iPad frame. The final width should be 770 pixels. If you're off by a pixel or two, you can tweak the Width in the Properties panel.

Note: You can also find the Image Slider symbol in the wireframe folder of the Common Library.

Tip: You can also select the Scale tool by pressing Ctrl+T (Windows) or Command+T (Mac).

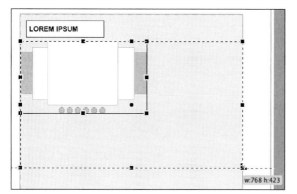

Adding text to the layout

To add the text, you'll use the Lorem Ipsum command.

1   Select the Text tool.

2   Select Commands > Text > Lorem Ipsum.

Chances are good the font styling won't be ideal.

3   With the text block still active, set the font properties in the Properties panel as follows:

Font: **Arial**

Font Style: **Regular**

Font Size: **14**

Font Color: **Black**

4   Triple-click within the text block to select the entire paragraph, and then copy the selected text.

5   Deselect the text, but stay in text-editing mode.

6   Place your cursor at the end of the paragraph, press the Enter/Return key to start a new line, and paste the copied text.

7   Press Return, and paste the text again.

8   Select the Pointer tool.

9   In the Properties panel, change the Space After Paragraph value to **8**. Now the paragraphs are broken up from each other.

10 Still in the Properties panel, set the width of the text block to **350**, X to **134**, and Y to **650**.

11 The text block will bleed out of the iPad frame, so double-click inside the text block and delete as much text as necessary to keep the column inside the screen area of the iPad wireframe.

12 Click away from this text block to deselect it, and then create another paragraph of Lorem Ipsum text. Set its width to **350**, and place it on the right side of the screen, aligned with the top edge of the first column.

13 Select both columns. In the Align panel, set the Space Evenly Horizontally value to **20**, and apply it.

Lorem ipsum dolor sit amet, consectetuer adipiscing elit, sed diam nonummy nibh euismod tincidunt ut laoreet dolore magna aliquam erat volutpat. Ut wisi enim ad minim veniam, quis nostrud exerci tation ullamcorper suscipit lobortis nisl ut aliquip ex ea commodo consequat. Duis autem vel eum iriure dolor in hendrerit in vulputate velit esse molestie consequat, vel illum dolore eu feugiat nulla facilisis at vero eros et accumsan et iusto odio dignissim qui blandit praesent luptatum zzril delenit augue duis dolore te feugait nulla facilisi.

Lorem ipsum dolor sit amet, consectetuer adipiscing elit, sed diam nonummy nibh euismod tincidunt ut laoreet dolore magna aliquam erat volutpat. Ut wisi enim ad minim veniam, quis nostrud exerci tation ullamcorper suscipit lobortis nisl ut aliquip ex ea commodo consequat. Duis autem vel eum iriure dolor in hendrerit in vulputate velit esse molestie consequat, vel illum dolore eu feugiat nulla facilisis at vero eros et accumsan et iusto odio dignissim qui blandit praesent luptatum zzril delenit augue duis dolore te feugait nulla facilisi.

Lorem ipsum dolor sit amet, consectetuer adipiscing elit, sed diam nonummy nibh euismod tincidunt ut laoreet dolore magna aliquam erat volutpat. Ut wisi enim ad minim veniam, quis nostrud exerci tation ullamcorper suscipit lobortis nisl ut aliquip ex ea commodo consequat.

14 If necessary, while both columns are still selected, use the Pointer tool and Smart Guides to align the text blocks so they are centered from side to side.

15 Drag the Video Player symbol from the Document Library and place it below the second column of text.

16 Scale the video symbol to match the width of the text block.

● **Note:** Although this wireframe is making use of some custom symbols created for the project, you are welcome to use the vector tools to create your own shapes, or build on the knowledge you gained in Lesson 10 to create your own symbols.

Adding gesture symbols

Three gestures are needed for this page: two flicks and a tap. (Hmm, sounds like a band.) You'll add those now.

1 Lock the layout layer, and unlock the gestures layer.

2 Drag the Flick symbol onto the canvas, and place it on top of the image slider instance. Resize the instance to a width of 300 pixels.

3 Add another instance of the Flick symbol.

4 Right-click (Control-click on Mac) on the instance, and choose Transform > Flip Horizontal from the context menu. This will be a cue to swipe back to the cover.

5 Place this instance on the left side, overlapping the screen and tablet frame.

6 Set the Opacity to **70%**, and scale the instance to a width of 220.

7 Lastly, locate and add the Tap symbol, placing it on top of the video playback instance.

8 Save the file.

Indicating accelerometer rotation events

One of the unique aspects of many mobile devices is that they can be rotated for viewing. Many apps take advantage of the change in orientation by adjusting the layout to accommodate the new orientation. You will want to indicate that when this app is rotated, the layout will change to suit the new orientation.

A symbol is already in use on the existing pages. You will add it to the two new pages.

1   In the Document Library, locate the Rotate Device symbol and drag it onto the upper-right corner of the tablet frame.

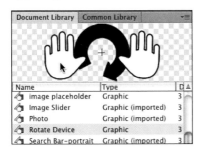

2   Change the Opacity to **70%**.

3   Rotate the instance about 45 degrees by using the Scale tool and rotating outside the bounding box. The exact angle is not crucial.

4   Resize the instance so that it's around 320 pixels wide. Reposition as necessary so that it is still in the upper-right corner.

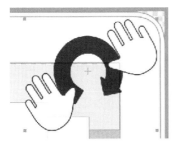

Note: You won't find the Rotate Device symbol in the gesture library; we created it by breaking apart two other symbols into their component parts, combining the parts we wanted, and then converting our new artwork into a custom symbol.

5   Before saving your work, copy and paste the instance to the upper-right corner of the Cover-V page.

Completing the interactivity

The final step is to add hotspots to the new pages. These hotspots will act as the touch points for the interactive PDF you will create at the end of this lesson.

While Fireworks can't create the sliding animation of moving from screen to screen, at least you can make the document more interactive than a basic PDF file by adding these hotspots.

1 On the Cover-V page, select the Rotate Device instance.

2 Right-click (Control-click on Mac) to invoke the context menu.

3 Choose Insert Hotspot from the menu list.

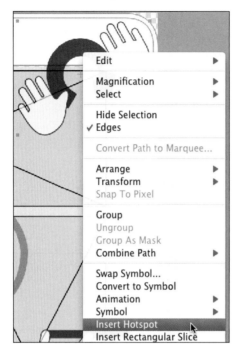

A pale blue rectangle appears on top of the instance, and the Properties panel updates to display options for the hotspot.

Hotspots are automatically added to the Web layer of the active page. Naming hotspots is not as important as naming slices; slice names become file names on export. Hotspot names are mainly just useful for understanding the interactivity within the Fireworks PNG file. Hotspots, like slices, are not linked to the underlying graphic so if you move or resize the instance, you will have to update the hotspot as well.

4 Locate the Link field, and click on the drop-down list.

As you create and name pages, Fireworks tracks this work in the background, making a list of page hyperlinks that you can call on to make the document interactive.

5 Scroll below the dividing line, and select cover-H.htm link.

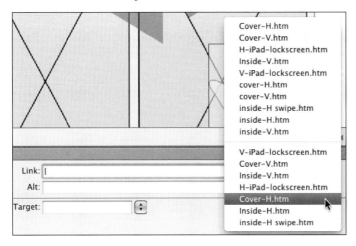

6 Click away from the hotspot to lock in the change.

7 Right-click on the Flick instance, and choose Insert Hotspot.

8 In the Properties panel, locate the inside-V.htm link. Again, be sure to select the link that appears below any visible dividing line.

9 Switch to the Inside-V page.

10 Add a hotspot to the hotspot for the Rotate Device instance, and set the link to **inside-H.htm**.

11 Right-click on the Flick instance, add a hotspot, and set the link to **cover-V.htm**.

12 Save the file.

13 Select File > Preview in Browser > Preview All Pages In to test the wireframe and have a look at how the hotspots behave. You should be able to navigate from page to page by clicking on the gestures in the wireframe.

14 Close the browser when you're done, and return to Fireworks.

Note: Fireworks not only tracks page names, but also keeps a history of which links have been used. Anything above the dividing line in the link list is just a history of previously chosen links. Unfortunately, selecting from these "historical links" does not produce a functioning hyperlink.

Note: If links don't seem to work, first check that you did indeed choose File > Preview All Pages. If you did, take the extra step of relinking the links that are attached to the various hotspots in the wireframe. Also, make sure you chose links under the dividing line, not above.

Delivering the wireframe

Now that the wireframe is complete, it needs to be sent to the client for feedback and approval. Fireworks gives you several methods for delivering designs and concepts to a client, but two of them are ideally suited for interactive wireframes: PDF and HTML And Images export.

Interactive PDF files enable the client to review the file offline and allow for direct feedback via Acrobat's commenting feature. Links placed on rectangular slices or hotspots are also supported, so the client can browse through the pages using the wireframe's built-in interactivity. Rollover or tap effects are not supported in the PDF, but for a wireframe, this isn't a huge concern. These effects can be dealt with in the prototyping stage. PDF files can also be password protected.

HTML And Images export supports hyperlinks, rollovers, and any shape of hotspot or slice, but offers no direct feedback mechanism, such as the commenting feature in a PDF. The wireframe must also be uploaded and viewed online, or you can deliver it on a CD or a thumb drive for offline viewing.

Which you choose in your own projects is up to you. For our simple wireframe, try exporting it as a secure, interactive PDF.

Exporting the wireframe

You create a PDF file from Fireworks by exporting the file.

1 Select File > Export.

2 In the Export dialog box, choose a suitable folder location and file name. To keep things neat, browse to the Lesson11 folder.

3 Change the Export type to Adobe PDF.

4 From the Pages menu, choose All Pages.

5 Make sure the View PDF After Export option is selected if you have Acrobat Reader or Acrobat Professional installed. There is no progress bar during the export; opening the PDF is the only indication that Fireworks has completed the export.

6 Click the Options button.

7 Select the Convert To Grayscale option. This reduces the size of the file slightly, and considering the wireframe is all shades of gray anyway, you won't be compromising the image quality.

8 Select the Use Password To Open Document option, and type the password **test**.

9 Click OK to return to the main Export dialog box, and then click Save (Windows) or Export (Mac).

When the PDF file has been exported, Acrobat Professional (if installed) will launch, allowing you to test the PDF and enable commenting—after you've input the correct password. If you don't own Acrobat Professional, Adobe Reader will open the file, but you cannot enable commenting with Adobe Reader.

Note: You can also password-protect specific tasks. If you choose to password-protect any of the listed tasks, you must create a different password from the one used to open the document.

Note: If you do not have Acrobat Professional, your default PDF reader will launch. Although you won't be able to enable commenting in the reader, you will be able to view the file once you've entered the password.

Enabling the commenting feature

If you have Acrobat Professional, you can switch on the commenting feature for those who own only the free Adobe Reader. The following steps can be followed if you own Acrobat Pro.

1 In Acrobat Pro, type your password in the password field. You must do this before the document can open in Acrobat Pro (or Reader).

The wireframe opens in Acrobat.

2 Enable commenting for users in Acrobat 10 (Standard or Professional) by choosing File > Save As > Reader Extended >Enable Commenting and Measuring.

3 In Acrobat 9 (Standard or Professional), turn the comments on under Advanced > Enable Usage Rights for Adobe Reader.

Review questions

1 What are the benefits of using shared layers, and how do you create them?

2 How do you create a new page?

3 What is the purpose of a wireframe?

4 How can symbols help you when building a wireframe?

5 What are hotspots, and what is one way to create them?

Review answers

1 Shared layers let you share the contents of an entire layer to specified pages, unlike the Master page, which is shared to all pages by default. Objects within a shared layer can be edited on any of the pages sharing that layer, and the edits will cascade to all the sharing pages. To create a shared layer, select the layer you wish to share from the Layers panel, and choose Share Layer To Pages from the Layers panel menu. In the Share Layer To Pages dialog box, add the pages you wish to share the layer with, and click OK.

2 To create a new page, click on the New/Duplicate page icon at the bottom-right corner of the Pages panel.

3 A wireframe is a simplistic rendition of the final project. The idea behind a wireframe is that it can be built quickly and just as easily discarded when it has served its purpose. The goal of a wireframe is to describe an application's function, flow, and general layout, without focusing on the aesthetics of the final project.

4 Using symbols when building a wireframe speeds up your work. There is no need to create new shapes on other pages for the same intended purpose and no need even to copy and paste. With symbols, you just drag and drop them onto the canvas, and if they are vector objects, scale as needed to fit your requirements.

5 Hotspots are one of two web objects in Fireworks. Hotspots allow you to create a "hot" or clickable area in your design, so that pages can be interactive. A hotspot link can link to another page in the Fireworks design, or to another external web address. One quick way to add a hotspot to a graphic is to right-click (Control-click on Mac) and choose Insert Hotspot from the context menu. The dimensions of a hotspot created in this manner will exactly match the selected graphic.

12 HIGH-FIDELITY PROTOTYPING

Lesson overview

In Fireworks, you can create complex, interactive prototypes to demonstrate how a final project will work. Fireworks is an excellent graphics editor, but it is not designed to be an HTML web-page editor, nor should you expect it to be. What you can expect is to find all the tools you need to build a realistic, dynamic prototype to whet your client's appetite.

Because this lesson focuses on prototyping, you won't be optimizing images to any great degree in the lesson, and you'll use slices only when they are needed for visual effects such as rollovers and other interactivity. In this lesson, you'll learn how to do the following:

- Create a Master page

- Import pages into the design

- Use the Slice tool for interactivity

- Trigger a disjointed rollover (emulate dynamic content updates)

- Preview an interactive web-page design in a web browser

- Export an interactive mock-up of a website

 This lesson will take about two hours to complete. Copy the Lesson12 folder into the Lessons folder that you created on your hard drive for these projects (or create it now, if you haven't already done so). As you work on this lesson, you won't preserve the start files. If you need to restore the start files, copy them from the *Adobe Fireworks CS6 Classroom in a Book* CD.

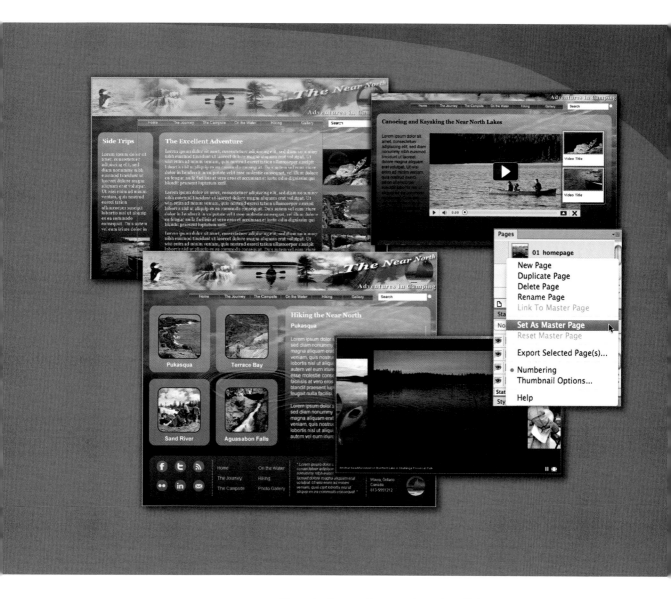

Fireworks gives you the power to create realistic, fully interactive, clickable HTML prototypes using standard Fireworks tools. Creating button rollovers and emulating pop-up windows is a snap.

Reviewing the finished prototype

Many of the concepts you learned in Lesson 11 apply to this lesson as well, so you'll have the opportunity to practice them again. To take a quick preview of where the project is headed, open our completed mock-up file; you will be building your own during this lesson.

● **Note:** The completed mock-up is a fairly complex file, so it may take a few seconds to load in Fireworks.

1   Open the completed website prototype (near_north_site_final.fw.png), in order to familiarize yourself with the final goals.

2   If you are prompted about missing fonts, simply choose Maintain Appearance for now, as you will not be interacting with this file much.

3   You may recall from the last lesson that you moved the Pages panel into its own group in the panel dock, a setup we find more useful and convenient than its default location. If your Pages panel is not still in its own group, drag to position it as such now.

Master page

As you learned in Lesson 11, a Master page is most useful if you have visual elements that will be common to all pages and in the same physical location. The pages of this sample mock-up share common elements for the header, background, and footer, so the file uses a Master page.

1   Select the Master page at the top of the Pages panel. Several graphics that are common to each page in the mock-up are present in the Master page. In particular, notice the background image and the footer.

   Since its appearance in Lesson 10, the page has been made a bit taller to incorporate a "fat footer." Unlike traditional footers, these large footers are usually chock-full of content: links, social networking, RSS subscription, links to other articles, contact information, sitemap, back-to-the-top link, categories list, recent comments, and so on. Look closely, and you will see that the background image blends into the page background color at the bottom. Fading a large background image like this is a useful technique to handle long web pages.

2 Click Show Slices And Hotspots in the Tools panel.

The banner image is sliced to provide interactivity; the banner links back to the home page when clicked.

3 Open the Web layer.

The slice for the banner appears in the Web layer. Although the button symbols are common to all pages, placing them on a Master page can cause a noticeable performance drop. For this reason, we placed the button symbols on a shared navigation layer on the index page.

> **Tip:** If you can't see your slices and the Show Slices And Hotspots tool has been selected, try clicking Hide Slices And Hotspots, then reselecting the Show tool. You can toggle between the two settings by pressing 2 on your keyboard.

Content pages

In this final mock-up, all the pages have been named using standard naming conventions. This is especially important because you will be generating HTML pages from this file. You will look now at a page that includes the Master page elements as well as its own distinct graphics.

1 Select the page named index.

2 Zoom out enough that you can see most of the document.

3 Click Show Slices And Hotspots in the Tools panel.

The slices from the Master page and the button symbols are visible, but there are no slices for the graphics on the page itself. Because this is a prototype only, slices are kept to a minimum and used only when visual effects are needed. Once the prototype is approved, the designer can come back to slice up the graphics for optimization and export for the final web pages.

Note also that you cannot select the slices or any graphic elements that are located on the Master page. Scroll to the bottom of the layers panel and you see a special layer, called the Master Page Layer. It is locked and cannot be unlocked on any of the child pages. If you need to edit Master page elements, you must return to the Master page to make those changes.

4 Click off the canvas to make sure no objects are selected, and open the Optimize panel.

The base optimization setting for this (and for all the other pages in this design for that matter) is set to JPEG – Higher Quality. Overall, this is a good choice for image quality. Although image optimization is not a primary concern for the mock-up, you want to be sure that, at the very least, all pages are set to JPEG – Higher Quality or PNG 24. Setting or leaving optimization at GIF or PNG 8 will very likely produce a poor-quality interactive prototype, due to the limited color range of GIF and PNG 8.

Note: PNG 24 could also have been used as the default optimization setting, but the resulting files would be significantly larger and might create a noticeable lag when the pages are viewed online for testing.

5 Switch to the campsite page. This page does make use of slices, but only for rollover effects and interactivity.

6 Turn off the slices and hotspots, and then click the Preview button at the top of the document window.

7 Select the Pointer tool, and move your mouse over the icons on the left side of the page. Note the subtle rollover effect. Click on any of the four icons and see the right side of the page update with new content. Not bad for a static web page! This is made possible through the use of JavaScript behaviors that you can add easily within Fireworks.

What are behaviors?

Behaviors are a quick way to add JavaScript functionality to a web-page mock-up, without having to write a single line of JavaScript code. JavaScript Image rollovers used to be pretty common in actual web pages, but now CSS-based rollover effects are the de facto standard for final web sites.

8 Switch back to Original view, and select the water page. This page content deviates from the layout of the first three pages that were roughly two or more columns of content. Here you have one large content area showing a video player. Now don't get too excited; the player doesn't actually work. The goal here is to show what that player will look like, without having to worry about its functionality.

The hiking page is very similar to the campsite page, but rather than icons, thumbnail images represent the different hiking trips.

9 Click the Preview button, and mouse over the thumbnails. Note the drop-shadow rollover effect.

Unlike on the campsite page, though, here we did not go to the trouble of wiring up any changes to the content area on the right side of the page. This isn't the actual site, remember, and we already demonstrated this planned functionality on the campsite page. There is no need to repeat the effort, if the same effect is shown elsewhere already. That is a very important concept to remember when building a prototype.

10 Select the gallery page. This last page of the prototype is a mock-up of a jQuery photo gallery, again, nonfunctional. Fireworks is not capable of producing the animated transitions that would be part of this and other jQuery or Flash-based photo galleries, so instead we focused on creating the desired look of the gallery.

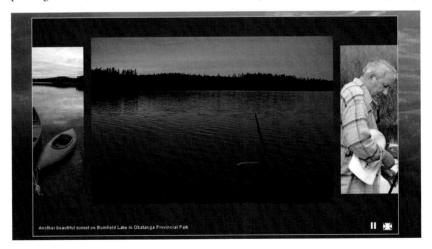

11 Close the file without saving it.

The Fireworks design community rocks!

Don't mistake building a prototype from scratch with building *everything* in the prototype from scratch. Our sample file had some help from the Fireworks design community.

This is a very open and sharing group of artists and designers, and you'll find many creators and samples out there by doing a simple Google search. And if you're a Twitter user, be sure to start filtering for the hash tag #adobefireworks for even more information about Fireworks and links to inspiring artwork.

Darrell Heath of Heathrowe.com built and generously donated to the community a Fireworks PNG file with *nine* video-player themes. One of those themes (with some photographic additions by Jim Babbage) is used in the water.fw.png file.

The artists at webportio.com are continually creating and sharing with the public everything from buttons to interfaces to icons, all built as native Fireworks PNG files. The social networking icons seen in the footer are from one of several icon packs shared by webportio.com.

Fleshing out the prototype

To expedite the lesson, we've already added some of the art for the pages. You, however, will create the Master page and two new pages, as well as add the art to the new pages. Much of your time will be spent building the interactivity for this prototype.

Creating the Master page

The site's Master page is often based on its initial web-page design. For example, the homepage you've worked on through the book contains all the main design elements for a Master page, plus the unique content section in the middle of the design. In this example, though, we did take the time to add a footer and extend the page to hold it.

1 Open near_north_site_start.fw.png. If you are prompted about missing fonts, choose Replace Fonts and select fonts on your system that look similar to any you're missing. If you don't know what a missing font looks like, search the Internet for samples.

   This version of the website mock-up is missing a lot of content, but you'll fix that in short order.

2   Select the homepage from the Pages panel, if it is not already active. It's a complete page.

3   Select the campsite page. The header, navigation, and footer content are missing for this and all subsequent pages. You need to take all the common elements from the homepage and convert them to a Master page. You'll do this without copying or pasting anything.

4   In the Pages panel, drag the homepage to the Add/Duplicate Page icon.

An identical page appears, just below the homepage.

5   Rename the copy to **index**.

6   In the Layers panel, locate each layer on the index page that holds common content: The header, footer, and background layers all need to be deleted. Deleting a layer that holds content is easy, but it takes a few steps.

7   Select the header layer in the Layers panel.

8   Click the trash can icon at the bottom-right corner of the Layers panel. This deletes the content in the layer, but not the layer itself.

9   Click the trash can icon a second time to delete the header layer.

10 Repeat steps 8 and 9 for the footer and background layers. You will be left with only the content, navigation, and Web layers.

11 Speaking of the Web layer, there's a slice for the banner image hiding in there. Select and delete it.

The index page is looking pretty sparse at the moment, but no need to worry.

12 Select the homepage, and delete the content and navigation layers (remember, it will take two clicks for each layer).

13 In the Pages panel, right-click (Control-click on Mac) on the homepage, and select Set As Master Page from the context menu.

14 Rename the Master page to **common**.

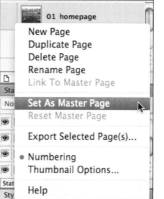

Note: You don't see the slices for the button symbols in the Web layer, because the slices are contained within the symbols themselves.

15 Select the index page. All the content you deleted earlier is now visible once again. Not only that, it's also visible on the other child pages in the file. As you click on each page, the thumbnail will update to show the Master page content.

The one thing still missing from the other pages is the navigation.

16 Switch to the index page, and right-click (Control-click on Mac) the navigation layer in the Layers panel.

17 Choose Share Layer To Pages.

18 When the Share Layer dialog box appears, select the campsite and hiking pages, add them to the Shared column, and click OK.

The Master page also gets added automatically to the sprites page, and it's not needed there.

19 Select the sprites page.

In the Layers panel, you can see the Master Page Layer at the bottom of the layer stack.

20 From the Layers panel options, choose Remove Master Page Layer.

● **Note:** Because this is a website mock-up, we chose to keep the width and height for each page at a common dimension. This allowed us to add the footer to the Master page and expedite the creation of the mock-up. If you wanted to show how the page would flow at different page lengths, you could remove the footer from the Master page, and add it manually to each page, in the desired location.

> New Image
>
> New Layer…
> New Sub Layer…
> Duplicate Layer…
> Share Layer To States
> Single Layer Editing
> Delete Layer
>
> Remove Master Page Layer
> Share Layer To Pages…
> Share Layer To All Pages
> Exclude Shared Layer
> Detach Shared Layer
>
> Flatten Selection
> Merge Down
>
> Hide All
> Show All
> Lock All
> Unlock All
>
> ▼

21 Save the file.

Adding more pages

Next you will add more pages to the mock-up. Parts of this project were parceled off to junior designers. Those files have been collected, and now you will import that content as complete pages.

1 Select the index page.

2 Choose File > Import, and browse to the Lesson12 folder. Locate the journey. fw.png file, and click Open.

3 When the Preview appears (the preview window appears for all native Fireworks PNG files), enable the Insert After Current Page option.

4 Click Open (Insert on Windows)

Fireworks imports content from the journey file and gives the page the name of the page from the journey file as well. As you can see, the Master page is automatically applied.

5 Select the campsite page.

6 Choose File > Import, browse to the Lesson12 folder, locate the water.fw.png file, and click Open.

7 When the Preview appears (the preview window appears for all native Fireworks PNG files), note that Insert After Current Page is still enabled. This option is referred to as *sticky*; once selected, it stays selected until you intentionally disable it.

8 Click Open to add the water page, complete with video-player interface, to the prototype.

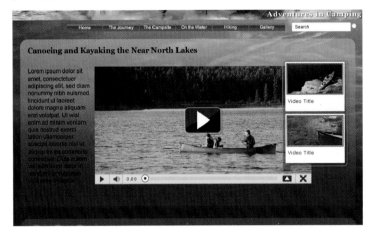

Lastly, you need the gallery page. This page has not been built yet, but you will be taking care of that soon. In the meantime, you will add the foundation for the gallery page.

9 Select the hiking page.

● **Note:** Page names become HTML file names when you export as HTML And Images or CSS And Images, so it's a good idea to follow standard naming conventions for page names, just as you would with slice names. Avoid spaces and special characters, and to keep things really simple, use lowercase letters only.

10 Click the Add/Duplicate Page icon. Fireworks generates a new page, adding the Master page content at the same time.

11 Rename this page to **gallery**.

12 Switch to the index page, right-click (Control-click on Mac) on the navigation layer and again choose Share Layer To Pages.

13 Add the new pages (journey, water, and gallery) to the Shared column, and click OK.

14 Save the file.

Creating simple rollovers

A rollover effect needs content on a separate state for the rollover to work as expected.

To show the client the intended rollover effect on the hiking page, you need, at the very least, a second *state* containing the rollover effect. In this exercise, you will create a new state with duplicate content. You'll then add a drop shadow to the thumbnail photos, add slices to enable interactivity, and then lastly apply the rollover effect.

1 Select the hiking page.

2 Open the States panel. Currently there is only a single state, the main (or *up*) state.

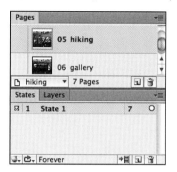

3 Click on the Options icon for the States panel, and choose Duplicate State.

4 In the Duplicate State dialog box, make sure you are adding only one duplicate state and that it is added after the current state.

5 Click OK.

The content from the up state of the hiking page is visible in the new state, but note that the content from the Master page is not visible. This is because the Master page has one state only. When dealing with multiple states and a Master page, you must be sure that the Master page has the same number of states as your child pages.

6 Select the Master page, and then in the States panel, choose Duplicate State, just as you did for the hiking page.

A stately refresher

It's been several chapters since you learned about states, so take a moment to review before going any further.

Every page in a Fireworks document contains at least one state. A design requiring no interactivity may need a single state only. Each state represents the visibility, effects, and position of objects on each layer in that particular state, of the selected page. If you require interactivity or frame-based animation, you must add new states.

There are three main uses for states:

- Create frame-by-frame animations

- Show the different states of an object, such as the normal and hover states of a website navigation button

- Control the visibility of objects based on user interaction, such as when hovering over a button displays a new button state and then clicking that button displays new content elsewhere on the page

States can include completely different content, or they can just indicate changes to certain elements that appear in both states. For example, a button may display a glow or drop shadow in a second state.

Adding the drop shadow

You need to add a drop-shadow effect to the thumbnails in the new hiking state.

1 Switch back to the hiking page and make sure State 2 is selected.

2 Select the Pointer tool.

3 Hold down the Shift key, and click once on each of the four thumbnail images. Do *not* click on the surrounding gray background.

4 In the Properties panel, click the (+) sign next to Filters and choose Shadow and Glow > Drop Shadow.

5 When the Drop Shadow properties window appears, accept the defaults by pressing the Enter or Return key.

6 Click back and forth between the two states to check the visual effect.

7 On State 1, use the Pointer tool and Shift key to select the gray backgrounds behind each thumbnail.

8 Right-click on any of the four selected backgrounds, and choose Insert Rectangular Slice.

Note: While inline images in web pages require alternate text, we're not requiring you to fill in this image description in this exercise, because this is only a prototype and not the final website.

9 When the prompt appears, choose Multiple Slices.

10 In the Properties panel or the Layers panel, select each slice and rename it, based on the label seen below each thumbnail. Otherwise, four slices of the same dimension are hard to tell apart in the Web layer.

Adding the rollover behavior

You have the two states and four slices. Now you need to add the interactive element, by adding a JavaScript behavior. Don't worry; no coding required.

Often you can immediately apply properties or behaviors to multiple selected objects, saving you precious time.

Note: A simple rollover behavior requires only two states and lets you quickly create, well, a simple rollover effect. The slice establishes the boundaries for two images: the Up image and the Over image. There must be some sort of visual difference to the sliced objects in each state, and that change must not extend beyond the edges of the slice. If the change does extend beyond the slice boundary, the rollover effect will be clipped.

1 Make sure all four slices are selected. Notice the small wheel in the middle of each slice. This is a behavior handle and gives you quick access to adding interactivity to the slices.

2 Click on any of the four behavior handles, and from the context menu, choose Add Simple Rollover Behavior.

Testing the rollover

Now it's time to test out your hard work. Well, it wasn't *that* hard, was it?

1. Select the Hide Hotspots And Slices icon in the Tools panel.

2. Click the Preview button.

3. Move your cursor over the thumbnails to check out your rollover effect.

4. Switch to the Original view again, and save the file.

Creating remote rollovers

Now that you've had a quick introduction to working with states and slices for interactivity, it's time to kick things up a notch or two, by completing the interactivity for the campsite page. First, however, study a couple of finished examples.

1. Select the campsite page.

2. Hide the slices, and then click the Preview button.

3. Mouse over the top two icons. Note that a subtle blue glow appears. This is similar to the effect that you created on the hiking page. You've got that one nailed, right? If not, no worries as you'll get more practice on this page.

4. Click each of the upper two icons. Note the change in content on the right.

Note: You will notice that the thumbnails already have a filter applied to them, and it's generically called Photoshop Live Effects. If you're familiar with Photoshop and Layer Styles, what you see here is Fireworks' ability to maintain and use those effects. Photoshop Layer Styles, though, are far more robust than the Fireworks counterpart. Our favorite effect is the Stroke effect (used here to create the border on the thumbnails). Natively, Fireworks gives you no method to easily apply a stroke to a bitmap.

This is what is often referred to as a remote or disjointed rollover. In our example, this "old-school" technique is being used to emulate a dynamic change to content. On the Web, this type of functionality can be created using jQuery and Ajax. Our main goal in Fireworks, though, is to visually show how this effect will appear to the user. In Fireworks, these effects are created using states and JavaScript behaviors. You won't have to know or write any JavaScript code though; Fireworks handles all this through the Behaviors panel.

jQuery? Ajax?
But I'm just a designer!

If you plan to go beyond design and build your own sites, getting to know jQuery would be a good idea. It's not the goal of this book to delve into web technologies, but you can learn more about both jQuery and Ajax at http://www.differencebe-tween.net/technology/difference-between-jquery-and-ajax/ and http://jquery.com/, respectively, or consult Adobe's website at http://www.adobe.com/devnet/dreamweaver/articles/introduction-to-jquery.html and http://blogs.adobe.com/adobeandjquery/.

Inspecting the states and slices

Take a look at how the states on this page make these effects possible.

1   Open the States panel.

This page contains seven states. The first three states control the icons, and the last four control the content on the right of the page. State 1 (renamed up) represents the normal view of the page. State 2 (renamed over) represents the hover state. State 3 (renamed down) represents how the icon should look when it is selected. States 4 through 7 have been renamed with logical names for the content within them.

2   Click through each state to see the changes that occur on the canvas. Note that the content area changes, but when you choose State 3 (down) the Master page content disappears.

3   Return to the up state.

Recall earlier, you had to add a second state to the Master page so that the rollover images on the hiking page would appear as expected. The same is true for the camping page. There are a total of seven states on the camping page, so you need a total of seven duplicate states on the Master page. Without these duplicates, the edges outside of the content rectangle will go dark and the content area will not appear to be as seamless as desired.

4   Switch to the Master page and from the States panel, choose Duplicate State.

5   Set the number of states to 5 (you already have two, remember), choose At the end and click OK.

6   Switch back to the camping page.

7   Turn on Slices And Hotspots. You will see slices on the top two icons, and a very large slice covering the content area on the right. Really, all Fireworks is doing is swapping out image areas under each slice with corresponding areas in different states. Slices are essential to making this effect work.

8   Click on the upper-left icon. Note the curved blue line that extends from the behavior handle and connects to the larger slice on the right. Note also this slice has a name; in the upper-left corner of the slice is the word "setup."

9   Select the slice (named reading) over the tent icon. This slice's behavior handle is also connected to the large slice (which, by the way, is named content).

The slice names are subjective/logical choices for the functionality of these different interactive areas. In your own projects, you would name these slices as you see fit, so long as there are *no spaces or special characters* in the names.

The Behaviors panel

The Behaviors panel is an interface for creating and editing several predetermined JavaScript functions, without the need for any coding knowledge. You will open the Behaviors panel now to see how it is tied to the two icon slices.

1   Select Window > Behaviors.

The Behaviors panel appears, floating on the desktop.

2   Position this panel near the icons on the canvas.

3   Select the setup slice. In the Behaviors panel you will see two behaviors linked to this slice: One controls the rollover effect, the other controls the content area.

4 In the Behaviors panel, double-click on the Action called Swap Image. A new dialog box appears. This dialog may be a little confusing at first, but once you know what to focus on, it's pretty simple.

In the scroll box on the right you see the word "content" is highlighted. This refers to the slice of the same name. All the other elements in this list are also slices; if you scroll up and down, you will see the slices named reading and setup, as well as all the button slices too. If you scroll farther up, you will see a bunch of slices with really odd numerical names. These names represent the areas of the page that we (or you) did not manually slice. Even though we didn't create slices, Fireworks still has to cut up, *autoslice*, the rest of the page so that it can be later exported as an HTML table.

On the right is a wireframe of the sliced page. The blue area shows you where the content slice is located on the page. If you click other slices (please don't), the blue highlighted area will change.

Below the slice list are the instructions to the browser, or *behaviors*, for the interactive area. You choose what state the content image slice will display when the user interacts with the icon slice. You can even browse for a completely separate file, but everything we need is right inside our Fireworks document.

You can also preload the images so the effect is immediate, rather than having a slight delay while the browser locates the image file.

The last option, Restore Image onMouseOut, is disabled. This essentially makes our choice *sticky*, forcing the new swapped image in the content slice to remain visible until a user clicks on a different icon.

5 Click Cancel to return to the document.

Adding interactivity

Now it's time to get the other two icons functional.

1 While holding down the Shift key, use the Pointer tool select the gray background shapes surrounding the campfire and picnic table icons.

2 Right-click (Control-click on Mac) on either shape, and select Insert Rectangular Slice, choosing Multiple when prompted.

With both shapes still selected, you will add one of two behaviors. This behavior will control the icons appearance as you mouse over and click on them.

3 Click on either behavior handle, and choose Add Nav Bar.

4 When the dialog box appears, all you have to do is click OK. There are no properties to change.

5 Click off the canvas to deselect everything, and then select the slice covering the campfire.

6 Rename this slice campfire in the Properties panel.

7 Drag the behavior handle for the campfire slice to the content slice. This connects the two slices. A curved blue line shows the connection between both slices, and a small Swap Image dialog box appears.

8 Click the drop-down menu, and select fire (6).

9 Click on the More Options button.

10 When the dialog box appears, disable the Restore Image onMouseOut function. This makes the image sticky, like the other two slices.

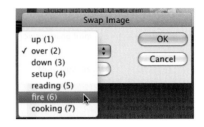

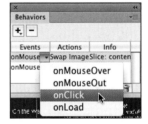

11 Click OK.

The Behaviors panel now shows both behaviors, but the Swap Image behavior is using the onMouseOver (hover) event. You need to change it to an onClick event.

12 Select the Swap Image behavior in the panel, and then click on the small drop-down menu beside the onMouseOver event.

13 Choose onClick from the list.

14 Try a quick test before you move to the final icon: Hide the slices from the Tools panel, and click the Preview button.

15 Mouse over the campfire icon. The blue glow should appear.

16 Click on the icon, and the image should change in the content area.

17 Move your mouse over another of the icons. The hover effect should appear, but the content panel should not change unless you click on a different icon. This is what we mean by *sticky*.

> ▶ **Tip:** If the Behaviors panel is getting in the way, you can either collapse it by clicking the Behaviors tab, or you can dock it with the other panel groups on the right side of the application.

18 Switch back to the Original view, and turn on the slice view again.

19 Select the picnic table slice, and rename it to **cooking**.

20 Repeat steps 7 to 13 on the cooking slice, this time choosing the cooking (7) state for the Swap Image behavior.

Completing the prototype

You have accomplished quite a bit so far—just a little more work to do before this prototype is complete.

Creating the gallery page

The last page for this mock-up is the photo gallery page. We stole your thunder in other pages, where many assets were already created for you. On this last page though, you will create the mock-up of the jQuery photo gallery, practically from scratch (we'll help out with the photos). You'll be working with bitmaps, vectors, symbols, and creative commands.

Note: Obatanga Provincial Park is a very real location in Northern Ontario, and is a short drive to the shore of Lake Superior. All photography for the Near North website prototype was shot by Jim Babbage. You are welcome to use the sample photographs for educational or personal use only.

Building the gallery shell

You'll start by building the container for the gallery.

1 Select the gallery page.

2 In the Layers panel, change the default Layer 1 name to **content**.

3 Select the Rectangle tool from the Vector toolset, and draw a rectangle.

4 Set the following properties in the Properties panel:

W: **820**, H: **470**

X: **70**, Y: **163**

Color: **#1C1C1C**

Stroke Color: **White**

Tip Size: **1**

Stroke Category: **1-Pixel soft**

Stroke Alignment: **Inside**

At the bottom right you'll add a caption for the feature image.

5 Select the Text tool and set the properties to Arial, Regular, and font size of **10**, color of white.

6 Because this text is so small, change the Anti-Alias setting to No Anti-Alias.

7 Place your cursor near the bottom-left corner of the rectangle, and type the caption: **Another beautiful sunset on Burnfield Lake in Obatanga Provincial Park**.

8 Reposition the text to approximately X: 80, Y: 605.

Near the bottom-right corner you will add some interface controls: a pause icon and a full-screen icon. Both of these graphics are symbols. The pause icon is part of the 2-D Objects in the Common Library. The full-screen icon was created for you and is in the Document Library.

9 Open the Document Library, drag the full_screen icon symbol onto the canvas, and place it at X: 854, Y: 607.

While you don't need this instance to be any larger than it already is, it's worth noting that the symbol was created with vectors, so it can be resized as often as you like, with no breakdown in image quality.

10 Open the Common Library, and expand the 2-D Objects category.

11 Locate the Media_Pause symbol, and drag it onto the canvas. Currently it's far too large and the wrong color.

12 In the Properties panel, set Width to **11** and Height to **14**.

13 With the Pointer tool, double-click on the tiny symbol to edit the color.

The graphic opens in Edit In Place mode, where the rest of the design is grayed out and inaccessible.

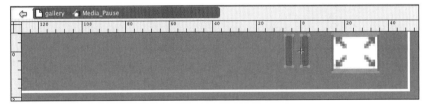

14 Select the object, and change the Fill color to White in the Properties panel.

15 Click on the gallery breadcrumb at the top left of the document window to return to the main canvas.

16 Align the pause icon with the full-screen icon.

Adding the photo samples

You will be adding three photos to the mock-up—or rather, one photo and two partial photos—to emulate how the jQuery photo gallery will treat before, featured, and after images. Even though these images won't move, the illustration should give users a good sense of how one would navigate the gallery.

But I want a *real* photo gallery!

While Fireworks doesn't natively support the creation of an interactive photo gallery, it may be possible for you to add one to the exported HTML by using a special Fireworks slice, the HTML slice, instead of building static graphics.

This process is more of a coding workflow than a Fireworks workflow, but if you're interested in learning more about adding live content to a Fireworks prototype, we recommend you check out Dr. David Hoque's excellent tutorial on the Adobe website: http://www.adobe.com/devnet/fireworks/articles/rapid_interactive_prototyping.html.

1 Choose File > Import, browse to the Lesson12 folder, and open the sunset.jpg file.

2 When the Import cursor appears on the canvas, drag the cursor until your marquee is approximately 540 pixels wide, and then release the mouse.

3 Align the image so it is centered, left to right, within the gray gallery rectangle.

4 Choose File > Import again, and import the fleet.jpg file.

5 Drag the Import cursor until the height is approximately 320 pixels.

6 Position this image on the left, 20 pixels away from the sunset photo. Don't worry that the image extends beyond the main rectangle.

7 Center it vertically. Smart Guides can help with this. There should be a 20-pixel gap between the two photos.

8 Import the last image, photog.jpg, on the right of the sunset photo, matching the height of the fleet image.

In the completed sample, both images are clipped to fit within the gallery rectangle and they are also displayed in black and white. The color change will be handled by a command, and the clipping can be done in one of two ways: masking or cropping. In this prototype, it's unlikely that you'll be changing the visible area of the gallery, so you will be cropping the images. But first, the color change.

9 Select the Pointer tool and click on both outer photos while holding down the Shift key.

10 Select Commands > Creative > Convert to Grayscale. A Live Filter is added to both images, making them appear black and white.

▶ **Tip:** You can zoom into the image while cropping by pressing the Command and (+) keys, or Ctrl and (+) on Windows.

11 Select just the fleet image.

12 Use the Zoom tool to magnify this image, but make sure you can still see the left edge of the photo.

13 Choose Edit > Crop Selected bitmap. A cropping marquee appears around the photo.

● **Note:** Remember that cropping in this manner is a destructive process. Image data is deleted when you commit to the crop.

14 Drag the center-left control handle in to the right, and when the crop line is on the inside of the white border, press the Enter or Return key to crop the photo. You may need to zoom in more to get an accurate crop.

15 Repeat this process on the photog image, but this time, crop from the right edge.

The jQuery gallery interface is complete. There are several elements to this piece of art, so we recommend that you select all the objects in the content layer and group them into one object by selecting Modify > Group. If you need to adjust individual objects in the group, remember you can select each piece by using the Subselection tool.

16 Save the file. You're almost done!

Previewing the prototype in the browser

Here's where the rubber hits the road—or the pixels hit the screen, so to speak. You are going to preview the entire prototype from Fireworks, checking functionality and links before exporting the prototype for client review.

1 Make sure the file has been saved.

2 Select File > Preview In Browser > Preview All Pages In *[your browser name]*.

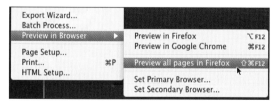

It may take a few seconds for Fireworks to generate the HTML files and export all the imagery. As soon as the process is complete, the browser will launch and load the currently active page.

3 Click on the navigation buttons to explore the entire site, making sure each page loads and loads correctly.

4 Test the interactivity on the campsite and hiking pages, as well as the banner image.

But wait, when you click on the Gallery button, the browser can't locate the file. Take a close look at the address bar in the browser.

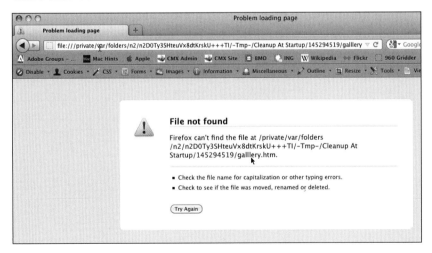

The link for the gallery page has an extra "l" in the file name. That's something you have to fix.

Notice that the black text is difficult to read at the bottom of the content areas—not very accessible, but yet another great reason to test out site designs in a prototype before jumping into the code. Now you might be rolling your eyes and cursing us for not mentioning this issue before you went ahead and built a six-page, multistate prototype. But there's actually a pretty quick way to fix this problem.

Correcting errors

You've tested the prototype and found a couple of issues: one broken hyperlink and hard-to-read text. In this exercise, you will fix those problems in less time than you might think.

1 Select any page that includes the navigation bar.

2 Make the slices visible and then click once on the gallery link.

3 In the Properties panel link field, remove the third "l" in the file name. Press Enter or Return to lock in the change.

Because the navigation bar is on a shared layer, a single change corrects the problem for all pages.

4 Save the file.

Changing the text color won't be as fast, but it will be surprisingly easy.

5 In the Panel dock, extend the Pages panel. Make the States panel just as long, in order to accommodate all the states on the campsite page.

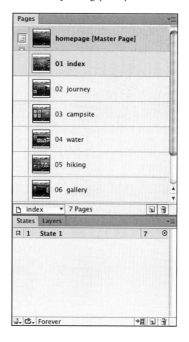

6 Select the index page.

7 Select Edit > Find and Replace.

8 From the Search list, choose Search Current Page.

9 Choose Find Color from the Find list. The panel updates to show two Fill color boxes.

10 Click the first color box, and choose black.

11 In the second color box, set the color to white.

Note: You might have noticed an option to search the entire document in the Search list. As tempting as that option may be, remember that you have many vectors in this design that also have black as their fill color. Running a search-and-replace operation on the entire document would change many objects that should not be changed.

12 In the Apply To list, set the option to Fills.

13 Click the Replace All button. It will take a few seconds, but in far less time than manually changing the color of the six text blocks requires, Fireworks replaces the text color.

14 Switch to the journey page, and click Replace All again.

15 Switch to the campsite page. This is one page where care must be taken; the icons are all vector artwork, and you don't want to change the fill colors in those icons.

16 Rather than clicking Replace All, click the Find button and watch the canvas to see what becomes selected. If text is selected, click Replace. If an icon is selected, continue to click the Find button until other text objects are selected. Click Replace whenever text is selected.

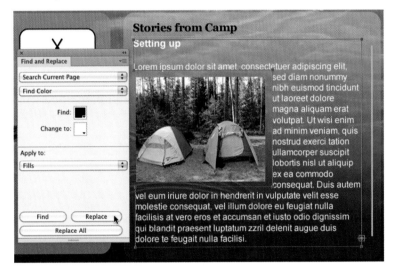

This particular page has seven states, so you will go through this Find, then Replace method until you have cleared all seven states in the page. When Fireworks moves to the next state, the active state becomes visible on the canvas, and the state itself appears highlighted in the States panel.

17 Select the water page, and use the same process as you did with the campsite page. There are no extra states on this page, but there are many vector objects that are part of the video-player interface.

18 On the hiking page, choose Replace All.

The gallery page has no text that requires changing.

19 Save the file.

Exporting the prototype

Your final step in the prototype is to export the design so the client can test drive the flow and function of the site (and of course, be impressed with your graphic design skills).

1   In the Pages panel, select all the pages except the Master page and the sprites page.

2   Choose File > Export, browse to the Lesson12 folder, and create a new folder there called **nn_website**.

3   Open (Windows) or select (Mac) the new folder.

4   Choose HTML And Images from the Export list.

5   Make sure that the HTML field is set to Export HTML File and the Slices field to Export Slices.

6   Choose Selected Pages from the Pages list, and make sure Include Areas Without Slices is selected. You sliced only a specific number of elements, mostly for interactivity purposes, and if you don't export unsliced areas, your web pages will not look right.

7   Make sure Put Images In Subfolder is selected, too, just to keep things a bit more orderly.

8   Click the Options button, and select the Table tab.

9 Choose Nested Tables, No Spacers from the Space With menu. This reduces the table complexity a little, but is by no means mandatory for the export.

HTML Setup

General | Table | Document Specific

Space with: Nested Tables – No Spacers

Empty Cells:

Cell Color: ☑ Use canvas color

Contents: Spacer Image

Cancel | OK

10 Click OK to close the HTML setup dialog box, and then click Save (Windows) or Export (Mac) to complete the export process.

There is no progress bar for this export process, but you should see the hourglass in Windows or the spinning beach ball on the Mac. The export process for this design should be finished within a minute or two.

Because the banner image on the Master page has a custom name for the slice (img_banner), Fireworks will prompt you to overwrite the file multiple times. It is fine to overwrite the image file, as it is the same on each page.

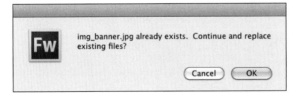

img_banner.jpg already exists. Continue and replace existing files?

Cancel | OK

11 Using Windows Explorer or the Mac Finder, locate your prototype folder.

You will see six web pages and a folder called images.

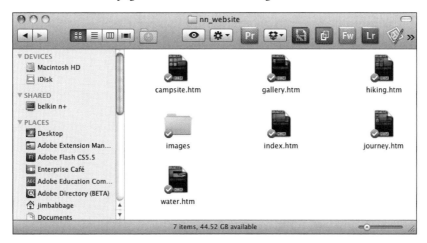

12 Open the images folder, and you will see a frightening number of graphics. As discussed in earlier lessons, Fireworks exports everything as graphics when you choose the Export HTML And Images option. Any areas that were not manually sliced are exported using the Fireworks autonaming and autoslicing process.

Again, as this is for prototyping only, it is not something you should be overly concerned about. It's also a good example of why you should not use the HTML And Images export to generate final website pages.

You're done! Feel free to double-click on the index page to launch your mock-up in a web browser, and test out the links and other interactive elements.

Review questions

1 What is a remote rollover?

2 How do you add new states to a page?

3 What are behaviors, and how do you apply them?

4 How do you edit JavaScript behaviors?

5 How do you turn a completed multipage Fireworks design into a clickable web-page prototype?

Review answers

1 When you click or mouse over an area on a web page, a visual change occurs in a different location on the same page. The effect is called a remote rollover. You can create this effect in Fireworks using slices or a combination of hotspots and slices, along with Fireworks behaviors to add in the necessary JavaScript.

2 You add new states by choosing New State from the States panel menu.

3 Behaviors are prebuilt JavaScript functions that you can add by clicking the behavior handle of either a hotspot or image slice object.

4 You can edit applied behaviors by opening the Behaviors panel (Window > Behaviors). Select the slice or hotspot that has the attached behaviors, and then select the specific behavior in the Behaviors panel. You can also add additional behaviors using the Behaviors panel.

5 Choose File > Export, browse to the desired directory, choose HTML And Images from the Export menu, and make sure that Include Areas Without Slices is selected and that Current Page Only is *not* selected.

13 IMPROVING YOUR WORKFLOW

Lesson overview

Fireworks is full of ways to save you time. From batch processing and custom automation of tasks to built-in features and integration with Adobe Bridge, you'll find many ways to speed up your project workflow without cutting corners.

In this lesson, you'll learn how to do the following:

- Use document templates

- Batch process tasks

- Locate and process files in Adobe Bridge

- Add project information to a file

- Add Photoshop Live effects

- Customize keyboard shortcuts

 This lesson will take about 90 minutes to complete. Copy the Lesson13 folder into the Lessons folder that you created on your hard drive for these projects (or create it now, if you haven't already done so). As you work on this lesson, you won't preserve the start files. If you need to restore the start files, copy them from the *Adobe Fireworks CS6 Classroom in a Book* CD.

Fireworks is all about getting the job done
professionally in as little time as possible.

Using document templates

Many designers love Fireworks because it lets them *get in and get out* quickly. Expediting your workflow is indeed a key goal of Fireworks.

One feature that may help you in the concept and prototyping stages is document templates. Fireworks comes with a number of prebuilt templates you can use to jump-start a brand-new project. The template options range from common document sizes for web and mobile projects to grid layouts for creating original web-page layouts and wireframes to iPad and iPhone wireframes and website prototype samples. You will use one of these templates to quickly generate a series of web banners to promote a website.

Opening a document template

You've been asked to create a series of web banners from some supplied artwork. This is a great chance to see how document templates can save you time.

1 Choose File > New From Template, or select the From Template option on the Welcome screen. The New From Template dialog box opens directly to the main Templates folder.

You can choose one of five default categories.

2 Open the Document Presets folder and select the Web banners template.

An untitled document opens, containing four common web-banner sizes.

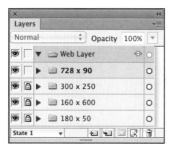

This template is already saving you time because you don't need to research banner sizes or create the banner files.

3 Lock all the layers except for the 728 x 90 layer.

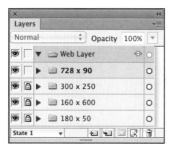

Assembling the banners

The main graphics are already created for you as separate files. It's up to you to use them in a variety of ways to create unique banners. We'll walk you through the process for the Leaderboard and skyscraper ads. A final version of the banners can be found in the Lesson13 folder. Feel free to refer to this as you work through the exercise.

Building the leaderboard banner

You will be using the Import command to speed up your workflow.

1. Choose File > Import (Ctrl+R on Windows or Command+R on Mac) and browse to the meridian_header.png file. This is a flattened PNG, with no special layers or effects.

   A preview window appears automatically.

2. Click Import, then Open (Windows) or Open, then Open (Mac), and place your import cursor at the top left of the banner rectangle.

3. Click once to import the image at its original dimensions. On the Mac, you may need to click once to set the focus to the Document window first.

4. While holding down the Ctrl or Command key, press the Down arrow key once. The image is moved behind the banner rectangle.

5. Select the Pointer tool, and click on the banner rectangle.

6. Press Ctrl+X or Command+X to cut the rectangle.

7. Select the image, and choose Edit > Paste As Mask. The banner rectangle now masks the image at the correct dimensions for the banner.

8. In the Layers panel, select the image rather than the mask.

9. On the canvas, use the blue control handle to reposition the image within the mask. Your final X and Y coordinates for the image (not the mask) should be X: –206 and Y: 32. Don't use the Properties panel to do this; use the image control handle within the image. If you use the Properties panel, you will move both the mask *and the image.*

10. In the Properties panel, reduce the opacity of the image to **50%**.

11. Save your file as **meridian_banners_working.fw.png.**

Adding a logo and a call to action

You've got your background image. Now it's time to add the logo and call to action.

1   Select File > Import, and bring in the local_logo.fw.png file.

2   Click once on the canvas to import the file at its original size.

    This file is made up of several grouped elements: a logo and three text objects.

3   Position the group at X: 30 and Y: 75.

4   Import the join_local.fw.png file at its original size, and place it at X: 490 and Y: 62.

5   Lock the layer and save your work.

Creating the skyscraper banner

You will now add content to the skyscraper banner on the 160 x 600 Wide Skyscraper layer.

1   Unlock and expand the 160 x 600 layer. The contents of this layer are grouped, and you must ungroup them to use the banner rectangle as a mask.

2   Select the group in the Layers panel, and choose Modify > Ungroup.

3   Import the file called meridian_skyline.png at the upper-left corner of the skyscraper rectangle.

▷ **Tip:** You may also want to hide the 300 x 250 layer from view to make it easier to work on the vertical skyscraper banner.

4 While holding down the Ctrl or Command key, press the Down arrow key once.

5 Select and cut the banner rectangle.

6 Select the image, and choose Edit > Paste As Mask.

7 In the Layers panel, select the image rather than the mask.

Another way to position an object within a mask is to break the link between the object and the mask. Breaking the link frees you to use the Properties panel to reposition the object, giving you pixel-precise control.

8 In the Layers panel, break the link between the image and the mask by clicking the chain-link icon between the two objects, and then select the image.

9 In the Properties panel, set the image's coordinates to X: –1118 and Y: 81.

10 Relink the image and mask by clicking between the two thumbnails for that object.

11 Import the local_logo.fw.png file at its original size.

12 Place it at X: 20 and Y: 220.

The text will be located outside of the banner area, and if you did not hide the 300 x 250 banner, it will be underneath that banner rectangle. You need to ungroup the logo so that you can place the text lower in the banner.

13 Select the logo with the Pointer tool, and then press Ctrl+Shift+G or Command+Shift+G. The objects are ungrouped but remain selected.

14 Click off the canvas to deselect the objects, and then holding the Shift key, click on the three text blocks to select them.

15 Use the Pointer tool to drag the text below the logo. The final coordinates should be about X: 20 and Y: 360. The text is in the right place, but it's too small. You will adjust this next.

16 With all three blocks still selected, change the text size to **24** pixels in the Properties panel. This will force all three blocks to overlap each other. Not to worry.

17 Open the Align panel. In the Space field, set a value of **2** and then click on the Space Evenly Vertically icon.

The text is now spaced evenly and no longer overlaps.

18 Double-click inside the first text block, and replace the comma with an ampersand.

19 Save the file.

● **Note:** Among the new templates in CS6 there is one called Miscellaneous Assets. png. It's located in the Wireframes folder and contains over 30 different symbols for ad sizes for Web, Google, and smartphone/tablet devices, along with a multitude of wireframe assets like a bar chart, spreadsheet, scroll bars, an image slider, form widgets, and even a calendar. All the assets are on their own individual locked layer within a single page.

Editing individual objects within a group

You will work with the same call-to-action file as before, but as with the logo, you will customize it after import. You will use the Subselection tool to edit individual objects in the group without ungrouping them.

1 Scroll to the bottom of the banner.

2 Import the join_local.fw.png file near the bottom of the banner.

3 Select the Subselection tool, and click on the gray circle behind the words "JOIN LOCAL." This circle is a bitmap graphic rather than a vector. You could replace it with a vector, but all that's necessary is a simple color change, so you will just edit the bitmap's live properties.

4 In the Properties panel, notice that a Photoshop Live Effect has been added to the circle. Click the *i* icon beside the filter name. The Photoshop Live Effects dialog box appears.

5 Select the Color Overlay option by clicking on the name.

6 Click the color box in the main window, choose a bright red instead of the gray currently in use, and then click OK. The circle is now red.

Photoshop Live Effects

Drop Shadow

Drop Shadow	
Inner Shadow	Structure:
Outer Glow	Blend Mode: Multiply Color: ■
Inner Glow	Opacity: 75 ▾ ▫ Size:
Bevel and Emboss	Distance: 5 ▾ ✛ Spread:
Satin	Angle: 120° ▾ △
✓ Color Overlay	Quality:
Gradient Overlay	
Pattern Overlay	Noise: 0 ▾
Stroke	☑ Layer knocks out shadow

OK   Cancel

HEX #FF0000
RGB 255 0 0

7 While holding down the Shift key, click JOIN LOCAL so both the text and the circle are selected on the canvas.

8 In the Properties panel, change the position to X: **24** and Y: **700**.

9 With the Subselection tool still selected, double-click the text block beside the circle and then triple-click the top line of text to select it.

10 Press Delete. Make sure there is no empty space left in that area of the text block.

11 Click away from the text; then, making sure the Subselection tool is selected, click once on the text block again and reposition it beneath the red line.

12 Shift-click to select the two red lines along with the text, and reposition the selection to X: 14 and Y: 760.

13 Finally, select just the horizontal red line and change its width to **150** pixels in the Properties panel.

14 Save the file.

For extra credit, study the meridian_banners_final.fw.png file and see if you can replicate those banners.

15 Save and close your file.

Working with Adobe Bridge

In this exercise, you'll help develop an art section for the Near North website. You will use another application to get started this time, however: Adobe Bridge.

Adobe Bridge can save you a lot of time by letting you view, sort, and open images you wish to use in Fireworks. You can also add information to certain types of images, such as JPEG files or Fireworks PNG files, using the Metadata panel in Bridge. If you purchased a Creative Suite edition, Adobe Bridge installs with Fireworks, which automatically links to Bridge on installation. You can also use Bridge to work with other Adobe applications, such as Photoshop, Illustrator, InDesign, and Flash.

● **Note:** At the time of this writing, if you purchase Fireworks as a standalone product, Adobe Bridge is not included. If you don't have Adobe Bridge, skip ahead to the Batch Processing exercise.

1 In Fireworks, choose File > Browse In Bridge.

2 When Bridge opens, select Filmstrip from the Workspace Switcher.

As in other Adobe applications, Bridge has a number of preset workspaces that you can use, or you can create custom workspaces to use whatever arrangement of panels you find most useful for your own workflow. For the purpose of this lesson, the Filmstrip workspace best suits what we're about to do, because you can see thumbnails of the artwork and a large preview of a selected image at the same time.

3 Click the Folders tab on the left side of the Bridge window.

4 Navigate to your Lesson13 folder in the Folders panel.

At the bottom of the Bridge window, in the Content pane, you will see a folder called fullsize and several PNG files.

Batch-processing images

The client wants to offer a variety of scenic images as wallpaper for visitors' phones, tablets, laptops, or desktops. Your job is to generate thumbnail images that can act as previews for each wallpaper image. Have a look at the images first.

● **Note:** You can change the size of the content thumbnails by dragging the slider (▬▬▬▬) at the bottom of the application.

1　Still in Adobe Bridge, make sure the Lesson13 folder is selected. Note the folder named fullsize.

2　In the Content panel, double-click on the fullsize folder. A series of ten images loads into the Content panel.

3　Select any single image, and Bridge displays a large preview.

● **Note:** If you don't see the file properties, choose Edit > Preferences (Windows) or Bridge > Preferences (Mac), click Thumbnails, and then select Show Tooltips at the bottom of the dialog box.

4　Place your cursor over the thumbnail view of the first image. After a short delay, file properties appear. The dimensions of this file are great for making a print, but far too large for a web page.

Currently, all the supplied artwork is in high resolution, at much larger dimensions than are needed for thumbnail images. You could use Fireworks to import each file and then scale the images, but this is tedious and time-consuming. Besides, you will also need actual thumbnail images for the final web-page design, not just for the prototype. What you need is a way to resize, optimize, and rename files quickly and easily.

Batch processing can take care of sizing, optimization, and even naming the needed files.

No Bridge? You can still use Batch Process

Batch Process is a native Fireworks command, so you don't need Bridge installed in order to use it. You can access the Batch Process wizard in Fireworks with these steps:

1　Select File > Batch Process.

2　Navigate to the fullsize folder in the Lesson13 folder.

3　Click the Add All button.

5 Click on the first thumbnail, and then Shift-click the last thumbnail to select all ten files.

6 Choose Tools > Fireworks > Batch Process.

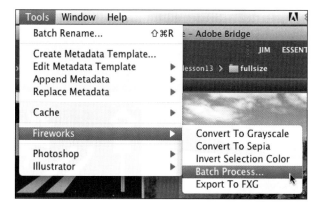

The Batch Process dialog box appears, and all the selected images are displayed in the pane at the bottom of the dialog box.

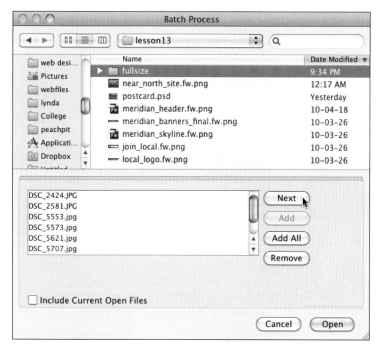

7 Click Next.

8 From the left column, select Scale, and then click the Add button to move Scale to the right column. Do the same for Rename and Export.

Batch Process	
Batch Options:	**Include in Batch:** ▲ ▼
Export	**Scale**
Scale	Rename
Find and Replace	Export
Rename	
▷ Commands	
	Add >
	< Remove
─ Scale:	
No Scaling ▲▼	
Cancel	< Back	Next >

These are the batch-processing commands you will run on the images, in the order they appear in the list. Each command in the list has editable properties. You will customize them for this project.

9 Select the Scale command from the right column, and then choose Scale To Fit Area from the Scale options list at the bottom of the dialog box.

10 Set the Max Width and Max Height to **125** pixels.

─ Scale:
Scale to Fit Area ▲▼
Max Width: 125 ▼ Pixels
Max Height: 125 ▼ Pixels
☐ Only scale documents currently larger than target size.

11 Select the Rename command from the right column, and then select the Replace option from the list at the bottom of the dialog box.

12 In the first field (Replace), type **DSC**.

13 In the With field, type **wallpaper**.

14 Select the Add Prefix option, and type **thmb_** in the text field.

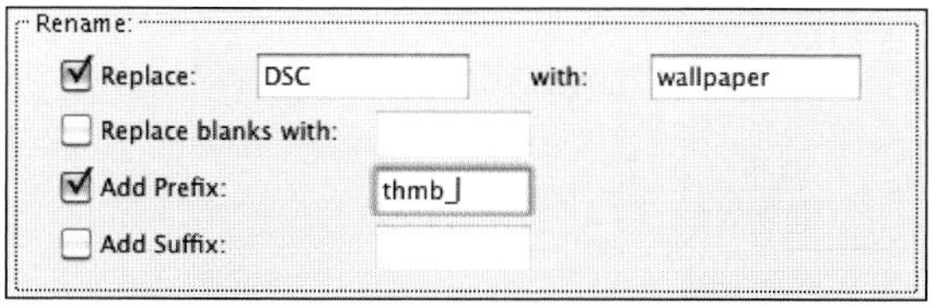

Rename:				
☑ Replace:	DSC	with:	wallpaper	
☐ Replace blanks with:				
☑ Add Prefix:	thmb_|			
☐ Add Suffix:				

15 Select the Export command from the right column.

16 Choose JPEG – Better Quality from the Settings drop-down list, and then click Next.

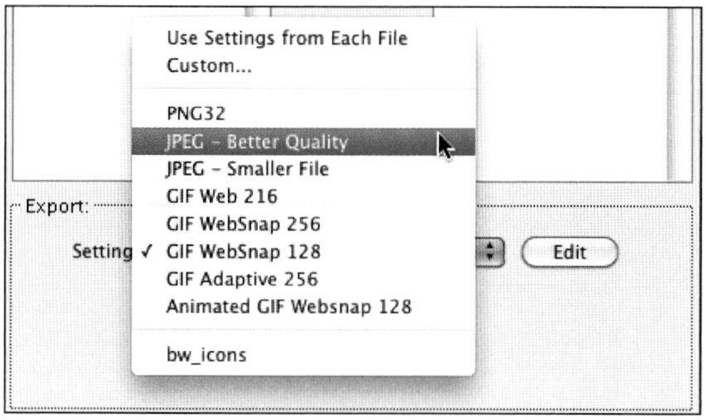

Use Settings from Each File
Custom...

PNG32
JPEG – Better Quality
JPEG – Smaller File
GIF Web 216
GIF WebSnap 256
GIF WebSnap 128 ✓
GIF Adaptive 256
Animated GIF Websnap 128

bw_icons

Export:
Setting ✓   Edit

17 Choose the Custom Location radio button, and browse to the Lesson13 folder.

18 Create a new folder called thumbnails, and open that new folder, if necessary.

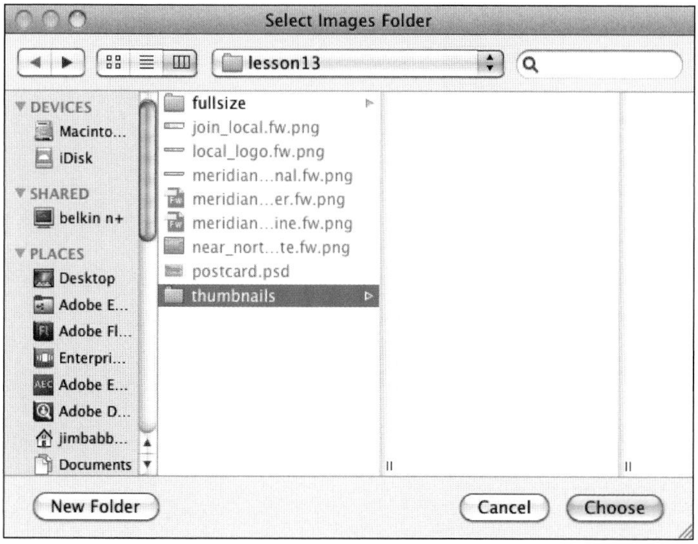

Select Images Folder

lesson13

▼ DEVICES
  Macinto...
  iDisk
▼ SHARED
  belkin n+
▼ PLACES
  Desktop
  Adobe E...
  Adobe Fl...
  Enterpri...
  Adobe E...
  Adobe D...
  jimbabb...
  Documents

fullsize
join_local.fw.png
local_logo.fw.png
meridian...nal.fw.png
meridian...er.fw.png
meridian...ine.fw.png
near_nort...te.fw.png
postcard.psd
thumbnails

New Folder   Cancel   Choose

19 Click Select Thumbnails (Windows) or Choose (Mac).

Tip: If this is a series of steps you think you will repeat again, you can save the operations as a script by clicking the Save Script button. You can then access this custom command any time from the Commands menu.

20 Click the Batch button.

Batch Process

Saving Files:

Batch Output: ○ Same location as original file
● Custom location [Browse...]
Macintosh HD:Users:jim...s:lesson13:thumbnails:

☐ Backups: ● Overwrite existing backups
○ Incremental backups

[Save Script...]

[Cancel] [< Back] [Batch]

Fireworks displays the Batch Progress box as it processes the images.

Once Fireworks is done, it will tell you that the process has been completed, and you can click OK to dismiss the progress box.

Batch Progress

10 of 10   files processed.

Batch conversion complete.

[Cancel] [OK]

In a few short steps you have scaled, renamed, and exported ten images all at once. The new images are in the thumbnails folder you just created.

Exporting a specific area

Improving workflow also means knowing how to speed up your work without cutting corners on quality.

The client for Near North Adventures is wondering about changing the font for the banner, and has asked to have a look at just the website banner. Without changing the layout at all, you can export a specific area of the page.

1 Open the near_north_site.fw.png file.

2 Choose the Export Area tool (hidden beneath the Crop tool) in the Tools panel.

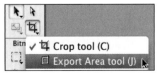

Bitn ✓ 🔲 Crop tool (C)
🔲 Export Area tool (J)

3 Draw a crop that includes the entire width and height of the banner.

4 Double-click inside the crop.

The cropped area will appear in the Image Preview dialog box.

5 Set the format to JPEG and the Quality to **70%**, if those settings are not already present. In the Image Preview dialog box, you can move around your document by clicking on the preview and dragging your cursor, allowing you to inspect the impact of your formatting choices.

6 Click the Export button. The Export dialog box appears.

7 Browse to the Lesson13 folder, and change the filename to **nn_banner**.

8 In the Type menu (Windows) or Export menu (Mac) near the bottom of the dialog box, choose Images Only.

9 Make sure Slices is set to None. An alert box may appear telling you that slices will be ignored. If it does, click OK to continue.

At this time, you want to export only the area you cropped. All other settings can remain as they are.

10 Click Save (Windows) or Export (Mac). Fireworks exports the cropped area as a JPEG file. You'll take a look at it in Bridge.

11 Back in Fireworks, choose File > Browse In Bridge. Locate the Lesson13 folder.

You'll see that the area you cropped—the web banner—has been exported as a separate JPEG file, which can easily be e-mailed to the client for feedback.

Thinking ahead: future-proofing your projects

In many situations, your files and projects aren't necessarily going to stay with you or even within Fireworks. They may take on a further life of their own. You'll want to make sure not only that other people who need to use them can access and understand them properly, but also that the files will display and behave as predictably as possible when opened within Photoshop. A key workflow for future-proofing your work is to include metadata with the original Fireworks PNG file.

Metadata is additional information about a digital file. This information can be helpful for organizing and locating a project or its assets or just sharing information across the design team. The Adobe XMP (eXtensible Metadata Platform) format lets you add file information to saved PNG, GIF, JPEG, TIFF, and Photoshop PSD files. Data such as author, copyright, keywords, contact information, and even job history can be shared and updated between Adobe applications.

Adding metadata

You can add metadata using Adobe Bridge, but it is easy enough to do right inside Fireworks as well.

1   With the near_north_site.fw.png file still open, choose File > File Info. The XMP data window opens.

Depending on the file you are working with, there may already be metadata applied to the image. This is most often the case with photographs shot with a digital camera. As of yet, the near_north_site.fw.png file contains no metadata, but you will change that.

2 In the Description tab, add the information you see in this figure.

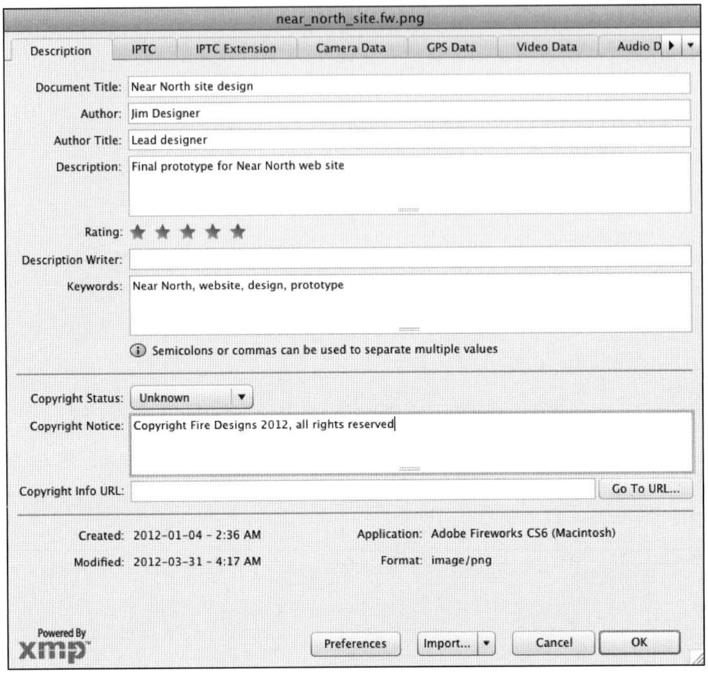

3 Click the IPTC tab to add more specific contact information, as seen here. Click on the calendar icon at the bottom of the window to set the date of creation.

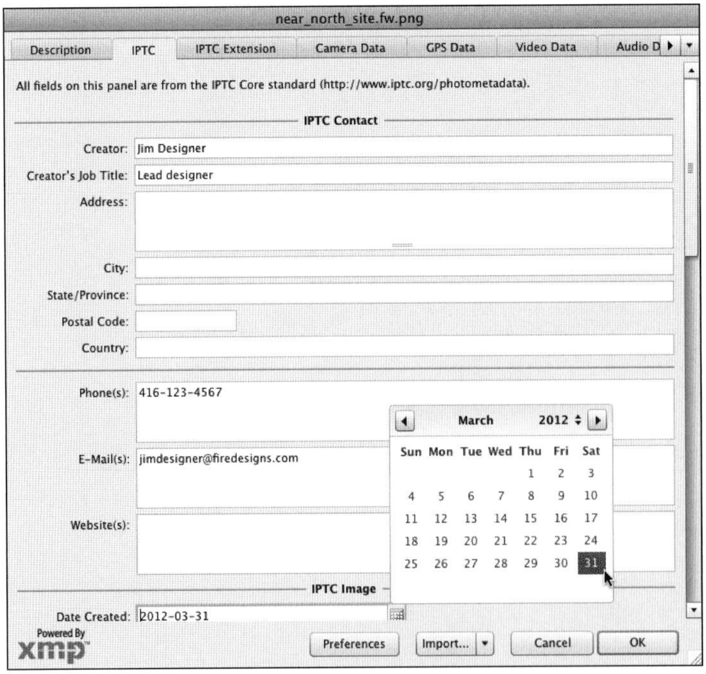

4 Click OK.

This data will now travel with the Fireworks PNG file. If you export a JPEG, GIF, or flattened PNG file, the data is automatically stripped out to reduce the web-image file size (by default, metadata can easily add 10 KB to the file size, even when there is no data added to the individual fields).

Creating a metadata template

You can automate this process even further by creating a metadata template. A template speeds up the addition of common information to project files, such as your company's contact information.

1 Choose File > File Info again.

2 Remove any project-specific information from the Description tab, such as the keywords and description.

3 Click on the Import button at the bottom of the box (to the left of OK and Cancel), then choose Export from the list. This list of options lets you import, export, browse the metadata templates folder, or apply an existing metadata template.

The Export metadata dialog box (Windows) or Save dialog box (Mac) will appear, pointing to a specific folder. All custom templates must be saved in this location.

4 Name the file **fire_designs.xmp**.

5 Click Save, and then click OK or Cancel to exit the XMP data window.

The next time you start a new design, you can select File Info and use the Import option to import your custom metadata template (or any other) into your file.

Using Fireworks files with Photoshop

Fireworks and Photoshop have a decent integrated working relationship. If you need to move your Fireworks designs to Photoshop, you'll get the best results by understanding Photoshop Live Effects, best practices for saving your file for Photoshop, and Photoshop export options.

Many elements can be preserved for editing in Photoshop. Text, hierarchical layers, layer groups, vector shapes filled with Photoshop Live Effects, solid color, many gradients, and masked objects are maintained and supported when you save a file in PSD format from within Fireworks.

Forewarned is forearmed as they say, so keep also in mind the following:

• Photoshop does not use the multiple page feature of Fireworks, so when you save a multipage Fireworks file as a PSD, the currently active page is the only page that is saved.

• Symbols and grouped objects are flattened to bitmaps, even if those objects were originally in vector format. Ideally, ungroup any grouped objects and break apart symbols to their component parts for the best editability.

• Web objects (hotspots and slices) are ignored.

• States are ignored.

What are Photoshop Live Effects?

Photoshop Live Effects are editable visual effects you can apply to objects within Fireworks. They are supported in Photoshop as layer styles. Fireworks maintains layer styles as Photoshop Live Effects when you open a PSD file in Fireworks.

The Live Effects dialog box in Fireworks is not as robust as its Photoshop counterpart, but using these Live Effects instead of native Fireworks Live Filters will guarantee Photoshop support of the effect, if you or someone else needs to edit the file in Photoshop.

If Photoshop is not part of your workflow, by all means stick to the Fireworks Live Filters or any third-party filters you may have.

Integration in CS6

Fireworks and Photoshop CS6 have tight integration in many ways. For example, hue, saturation, color blend modes, and the Hue/Saturation filter in Fireworks use the same algorithms as Photoshop to improve color fidelity and appearance.

When importing PSD files from Photoshop to Fireworks, you can force flattening of Photoshop adjustment layers from the Fireworks Preferences. This maintains the appearance of Adjustment layers, rather than just letting fireworks discard the effect.

When importing editable gradients from Photoshop, you'll get a close-to-perfect match with:

- Linear to Linear
- Radial to Radial
- Reflected to Bars

Expect an approximate match when importing:

- Diamond to Rectangular
- Angle to Conical

Likewise, when exporting editable gradients from Fireworks to Photoshop as PSDs, you'll get a close-to-perfect match with:

- Linear to Linear
- Radial to Radial
- Bars to Reflected

Expect an approximate match when exporting:

- Rectangular to Diamond
- Conical to Angle
- Ellipse to Radial
- Ripples to Radial

and only a loose match when exporting:

- StarBurst to ShapeBurst
- Contour, Satin, Waves to Linear

Saving your file for Photoshop

If your designs and comps must go from Fireworks to Photoshop for further editing and you want to retain as much editability as possible, make sure you save a copy of your file in the Photoshop PSD format. Opening a Fireworks PNG file in Photoshop *will flatten the file to a single layer*.

1   Select the campsite page.

2 Choose File > Save As, browse to the Lesson13 folder, and choose Photoshop PSD from the Save As menu. The menu name changes to Save Copy As.

3 Click the Options button.

4 To maintain as much editability as possible, choose Maintain Editability Over Appearance.

Customizing Photoshop Export options

Although maintaining editability makes the file as flexible as possible when opened in Photoshop, you may also lose certain effects or features. If the appearance is more important than the object's editability, you can customize the Photoshop export options by clicking on the Options button in the Save As dialog box.

5 Click OK to accept the settings, and then click Save to save the new file.

If you open the file in Photoshop, you will see that the file is very similar to the original Fireworks design, but as you dig deeper into the layers, you will see that groups and symbols have been flattened.

Common Live Filters

Some Fireworks Live Filters are supported by Photoshop and behave as standard Photoshop layer styles.

Photoshop Live Filters can be added while in Fireworks, or they can be supported (editable) or maintained (editable in Photoshop only) if they are added as a layer style in Photoshop.

The following Fireworks Live Filters are supported and maintained between Photoshop and Fireworks:

- Drop Shadow, Inner Shadow
- Glow, Inner Glow
- Bevel and Emboss (all)

Opening Photoshop files

The flip side to saving a Fireworks document into Photoshop (PSD) format is opening a Photoshop file in Fireworks.

A postcard illustration was created in Photoshop CS6, using the new Oil Paint feature. For visual impact, extra Saturation was added using an adjustment layer. When the illustration was optimized for the Web in Photoshop, however, the file size was still too high. What's a designer to do?

The Fireworks optimization engine often can create JPEG files that are 30% to 50% smaller in file size than their counterparts optimized in Photoshop. The postcard file has been handed off to you for eventual optimization, but your main concern in this exercise is to see how accurately the file opens in Fireworks.

▶ **Tip:** Remember that if you don't own Bridge, you can simply choose File > Open in Fireworks and then browse for the file.

1 Choose File > Browse In Bridge, and browse to the Lesson13 folder.

2 Select the postcard.psd file. Note the richness in the color of the postcard, created by an adjustment layer.

3 Select File > Open With > Fireworks CS6.

The Photoshop File Open Options dialog box appears.

4 Make sure Maintain Layer Editability Over Appearance is selected, and click OK.

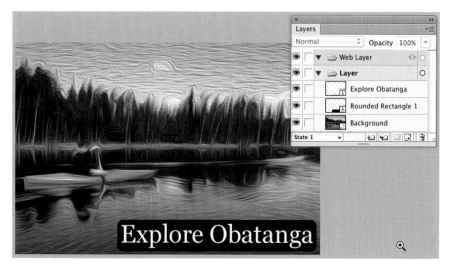

5 When the file opens, check out the Layers panel.

The image appears as it did in Photoshop, without the adjustment layer effect. Fireworks automatically discarded the adjustment when the file was opened. The image doesn't look *bad*, but it's not what the Photoshop artist created.

6   Select the text area with the Pointer tool. Notice that text properties appear in the Properties panel, and the drop shadow on the text has been maintained, using the Fireworks version of Layer Styles, Photoshop Live Effects.

The vector path behind the text has also been retained as a true path, but the Fill and Stroke settings got mixed up. You'll fix that in a minute, but first you will change how the file is converted when it is opened.

7   Close the file.

8   Choose File > Open Recent, and select the postcard.psd file.

9   When the Options dialog box opens, change the conversion setting from Maintain Editability Over Appearance to Custom Settings From Preferences, and click OK.

This time, the file looks much more like the Photoshop version! The split image clearly shows the difference in color saturation. The Adjustment Layer is still not present in the Layers panel, but its effect was flattened into the image when the file opened. The text and vector shape remain editable as well.

10 Select the vector path using the Pointer tool.

11 Click the No Fill icon in the Properties Panel, and set the stroke to Black.

12 Set the stroke alignment to Outside, and choose Basic > Soft Line for the stroke category.

13 Save the file as a Fireworks PNG file.

Common blending modes supported by Photoshop and Fireworks

Blending modes can be applied to objects or layers. When you apply a blending mode, the object's color and opacity are blended with the object beneath it in the Layers panel. Fireworks has 46 blending modes. Photoshop and Fireworks share many common blending modes (23 in total). If a blending mode in this list is applied to an object or layer, the mode will be supported and remain editable in either application:

Normal	Lighten	Hard Light	Exclusion
Dissolve	Screen	Vivid Light	Hue
Darken	Color Dodge	Linear Light	Saturation
Multiply	Linear Dodge	Pin Light	Color
Color Burn	Overlay	Hard Mix	Luminosity
Linear Burn	Soft Light	Difference	

Opening and importing Photoshop files

Opening layered Photoshop files within Fireworks is as simple as choosing File > Open or File > Import and browsing for the native Photoshop PSD file. Fireworks CS6 supports hierarchical Photoshop layers, layer groups, layer styles, layer comps, vector layers, and common blend modes, making it easy to handle files you receive from another designer.

Exceptions to this integration include adjustment layers and clipping groups. These features can either be flattened into bitmaps or ignored when you import or open a PSD file within Fireworks. Flattening retains the appearance, but editability is lost.

To globally customize how Fireworks opens or imports PSD files, change the preferences. Choose Edit > Preferences (Windows) or Fireworks > Preferences (Mac), and then select Photoshop Import/Open from the list on the left.

Preferences

Category	Photoshop Import/Open
General	General: ☑ Show import dialog box
Edit	☑ Show open dialog box
Guides and Grids	☐ Share layer between states
Type	
Photoshop Import/Open	Custom file conversion settings:
Launch and Edit	Image Layers: ◉ Bitmap Images with editable effects
Plug-Ins	○ Flattened bitmap images

Text: ◉ Editable Text
○ Flattened bitmap images

Shape Layers: ◉ Editable paths and effects
○ Flattened bitmap images
○ Flattened bitmap images with editable effects

Layer Effects: ☐ Prefer native live filters over PS Live Effects
Clipping masks: ☐ Flatten to maintain appearance
Adjustment Layer ☑ Maintain appearance of adjusted layers

(Help)   (Cancel)   (OK)

The General Photoshop Import options include:

- **Show Import Dialog Box/Show Open Dialog Box**: These identical windows give you document-level import/open control.

- **Share Layer Between Frames**: This option is important for animation or "page state" effects.

The Custom File Conversion Settings area includes the following options, organized by section.

Image Layers

- **Bitmap Images With Editable Effects**. This option is the default setting that gives you the most flexibility. Layer styles remain editable.

- **Flattened Bitmap Images**: This option flattens layer effects and blend modes to maintain the exact appearance. Photoshop layer styles are no longer editable.

Text Layers

- **Editable Text**: This option is the default.

- **Flattened Bitmap Images**: This option preserves the look and style of text, but the text is no longer editable.

Shape Layers

- **Editable Paths And Effects**: This is the default option with the most flexibility, but vectors may not render exactly as in Photoshop.

- **Flattened Bitmap Images**: When this option is enabled, vectors and effects are rasterized to bitmaps.

- **Flattened Bitmap Images With Editable Effects**: When this option is enabled, vectors are rasterized but layer effects and blend modes remain editable.

Layer Effects

- **Prefer Native Filters Over Photoshop Live Effects**: This option is recommended only if the file will not be going back to Photoshop.

Clipping Path Masks

- **Flatten To Maintain Appearance**: When this option is enabled, the mask is converted to a bitmap mask.

Adjustment Layers

- **Maintain Appearance Of Adjusted Layers**: This option flattens adjustment layers to retain the image's appearance, but you can no longer edit the effects. If this option is not selected, adjustment layers are discarded completely.

With the defaults left as they are, opening or importing a PSD file displays the Photoshop File Open Options or File Import Options dialog box. This gives you the opportunity to set options for opening a specific PSD file, overriding any options set in the Preferences panel.

Customizing keyboard shortcuts

Fireworks has its own set of keyboard shortcuts, some of which are the same as other Adobe applications and some which are not. In this exercise, you will learn how to swap keyboard shortcuts in Fireworks and also how to create your own custom shortcuts.

If you're coming from Photoshop and you prefer to use the same keyboard shortcuts you use in Photoshop, you can easily make the switch.

1 Select Fireworks > Keyboard Shortcuts (Mac) or Edit > Keyboard Shortcuts (Windows).

Interestingly, the default keyboard set for Fireworks is actually the Web Standard set.

2 Select Photoshop from the Current Set drop-down list.

3 Click OK.

Creating custom and secondary shortcuts

You can create custom keyboard shortcuts from a preinstalled set, as you've seen, and you can create secondary shortcuts to include different ways to perform an action.

Keyboard shortcuts (except for menu commands) cannot include modifier keys: Control, Shift, and Alt (Windows) or Command, Shift, Option, and Control (Mac OS). They must consist of a single letter or number key only.

1 Select Edit > Keyboard Shortcuts (Windows) or Fireworks > Keyboard Shortcuts (Mac OS).

2 Select the Photoshop set.

3 Click the Duplicate Set button. You cannot edit the master versions of the keyboard shortcuts, but you can edit a copy.

4 Enter a name for the custom set, and click OK. We called our version Photoshop Custom.

5 Select the appropriate shortcut category from the Commands list:

Menu Commands: Any command accessed through the menu bar

Tools: Any tool on the Tools panel

Miscellaneous: A range of predefined actions

6 From the Menu Commands list, select the Duplicate command (Edit submenu) as it currently has no shortcut.

7 Click in the Press Key text box, and press the desired keys for the new shortcut on the keyboard. We chose Command+D for our Mac. If you select a combination that already exists, Fireworks will prompt you to choose a different combination.

To add a secondary shortcut to the shortcut list, click the Add A New Shortcut (+) button. Otherwise, click Change to add the shortcut.

Delete custom shortcuts and shortcut sets

You can easily delete a custom shortcut set with these steps:

1   Select Edit > Keyboard Shortcuts (Windows) or Fireworks > Keyboard Shortcuts (Mac OS).

2   Click the Delete Set button (trash can icon).

3   Select a shortcut set.

4   Click the Delete button.

To delete a custom shortcut:

1   Select the command in the Commands list.

2   Select the custom shortcut from the Shortcuts list.

3   Click the Delete A Selected Shortcut (-) button.

Create a reference sheet for the current shortcut set

A reference sheet is a record of the current shortcut set stored in HTML table format. You can view the reference sheet in a web browser or print it.

1   Select Edit > Keyboard Shortcuts (Windows) or Fireworks > Keyboard Shortcuts (Mac OS).

2   Click the Export Set As HTML button beside the Current Set text box.

3   Enter reference sheet name, and select a file location.

4   Click Save.

Review questions

1 How do you access Bridge from Fireworks?

2 How do you batch-process files from within Bridge?

3 How do you crop a bitmap object that is part of a design?

4 How do you add metadata to a Fireworks PNG file? Why would you do this?

5 How do you customize the export options for saving a Photoshop file?

6 How can document templates save you time?

Review answers

1 To access Bridge from Fireworks, choose File > Browse In Bridge.

2 To process multiple files within Bridge, select the files in the Content panel, and then choose Tools > Fireworks > Batch Process.

3 Select the object, and then choose Edit > Crop Selected Bitmap. Adjust the cropping marquee to suit, and then press Enter or Return to commit to the crop.

4 To add metadata, choose File > File Info. Select the appropriate tab from the Metadata panel (choose the tab for the type of information you want to add), and fill in the areas relevant to the project and image. Adding metadata can help organize and locate content by adding contact information about the designer or company, and it can include basic data about the client, such as client name, project goals, and copyright.

5 You can globally customize the Photoshop Export options by opening the Preferences panel, or you can adjust the settings on an image-by-image basis when you choose to Save As A Photoshop PSD file.

6 Document templates can save you time by giving you a head start on the design or prototyping stages of a project. The grid templates give you several variations of grid structures to help you lay out your wireframe or even a website prototype. The Document Presets folder contains a range of files set at specific dimensions, making it easy to start designing a series of web banners at the common banner sizes, for example.

INDEX

Entries for supplemental chapter 14 are indicated by the letter "S" before the page number.

NUMBERS

2-Up view option, 189, 190
4-Up view option, 189, 191
9-slice scaling, 54

A

about this book, x
Active Buttons asset, S:8
Add Mask icon, 117
Add/Duplicate Page icon, 254, 258
Add/Union icon, 106
adjustment layers, 303, 306–308, 310, 311
Adobe Acrobat Professional, 243
Adobe Bridge, 291, 292
Adobe BrowserLab, 222
Adobe Certified programs, xiv
Adobe Community Help, xii
Adobe Design Center, xii
Adobe Developer Connection, xii, 212
Adobe Dreamweaver. *See* Dreamweaver CS6
Adobe Edge, 173, S:20
Adobe Education Exchange, xii
Adobe Exchange, xiii, S:18
Adobe Fireworks. *See* Fireworks CS6
Adobe Forums, xii
Adobe Illustrator, 63
Adobe InDesign, S:19
Adobe Labs, xiii
Adobe Photoshop. *See* Photoshop
Adobe Reader, 243
Adobe TV, xii
Adobe XMP format, 299

Ajax technologies, 264
Align panel, 50, 52–53, 171, 289
alpha transparency, 185, 186
anchor points, 96
    adding with Pen tool, 98
    basic information about, 98
    setting with guides, 100–102
animation symbols, 173
anti-aliasing
    selection edges, 69
    text, 139
Application bar, 5
Application Frame, 6, 17
assets
    jQuery theme, S:8
    wireframe, 289
Audio symbol, 234
Auto Kerning option, 140
Auto Shapes, 9, 109–110
Auto Shapes Properties panel, 110, 149
Auto Vector Mask command, 118, 121–122
auto-sizing text blocks, 132
autosliced pages, 266

B

Babbage, Jim, 116, 253, 269
background-position property, 196
backgrounds
    adding to documents, 119
    desaturating, 78
    importing images for, 54, 119
bandwidth issues, S:17

jQuery Mobile themes, S:4–S:17
    creating custom, S:7–S:9
    exporting, S:11
    limitations creating, S:16–S:17
    new features for, S:5–S:7
    previewing, S:10–S:11, S:16
    review questions/answers, S:21
    skin customization, S:12–S:15
    updating designs for, S:16

K

kerning, 140
keyboard modifiers, 74–76
keyboard shortcuts, 312–314
    creating custom and secondary, 312–313
    deleting custom shortcuts/shortcut sets, 314
    reference sheet for shortcut sets, 314
Knife tool, 92

L

Lasso tools
    selecting with, 192–193
    situations for using, 68, 77
layer comps, 309
layer effects, 311
layer styles, 263, 302, 305, 311
layers, 27, 32–39
    adding/naming, 34
    deleting, 254–255
    Dreamweaver and, S:20
    expanding/collapsing, 38
    locking, 38–39, 50
    Master Page, 31, 250
    moving objects between, 34–35
    multiple objects in, 63
    naming objects in, 32–33
    options for working with, 39
    Photoshop file, 310, 311
    protecting, 38–39
    rearranging objects in, 34
    retouching on separate, 63
    review questions/answers, 42
    sharing to pages, 35–38, 228–229, 230, 256
    stacking order of, 110

sublayers and, 38
    Web, 27, 198
Layers panel
    accessing options in, 39
    adding/naming layers in, 34
    deleting layers in, 254–255
    expanding/collapsing layers in, 38
    locking/protecting layers in, 38–39
    mask and image thumbnails in, 116
    moving objects between layers in, 34–35
    naming objects in, 32–33
    options available in, 39
    Photoshop files viewed in, 307
    rearranging objects in, 34
    Share Layer to Pages option, 36–38
    stacking order of layers in, 110
    sublayer creation in, 38
    viewing web objects in, 198
leaderboard banner, 286
leading, 140
lesson files, xi
Levels dialog box, 55
Levels Live Filter, 56, 177
lightening images, 59–60
Line tool, 95
linear gradients, 95
linked objects, 116, 124
links. *See* hyperlinks
Live Effects. *See* Photoshop Live Effects
Live Filters, 55–57
    bitmap filters vs., 57, 73
    contrast adjustments, 55–56
    drop shadows applied as, 137, 138
    masked objects and, 125–126
    saturation adjustments, 55–56
    sharpness adjustments, 56–57
    styles applied as, 148, 150
    supported by Photoshop, 305
Live Marquee feature, 70
Live Preview, Auto Vector Mask, 121
locking
    layers, 38–39, 50
    objects, 39, 50
    proportions, 11
logo files, 287
Lorem Ipsum text, 20–21, 141, 177–179
lossy format, 184

M

Mac OS
  Fireworks interface, 5–6
  importing images on, 112, 119
  starting Fireworks on, xi
Magic Wand tool, 71–77
  creating selections with, 71–73
  keyboard modifiers used with, 74–76
  situations for using, 68–69
  Tolerance settings, 69, 72, 74, 77
  undoing selections made with, 77
Main toolbar, 5
Maintain Appearance option, 140, 197, 248, 311
Maintain Editability Over Appearance option, 304, 307
Marquee tool, 68
mask icon, 124
masks, 114–129
  attribute changes, 124–125
  Auto Vector Mask command, 121–122
  banner project using, 118–128, 286, 287–288
  bitmap, 116–117, 127–128
  creating, 122–123, 127
  editing, 124–125, 127–128
  explanation of, 116
  Layers panel thumbnails for, 116
  lesson overview, 114
  Live Filters and, 125–126
  Paste As Mask command, 286, 288
  quick fades with, 121–122
  repositioning images with, 122, 123, 288
  review questions/answers, 129
  vector, 117–118, 122–125
  See also bitmap masks; vector masks
Master pages, 31–32, 228, 248–249, 253–256
matte color, 188
Media_Pause symbol, 270
Menu bar, 5
metadata, 299–302
  adding to files, 299–301
  template creation, 301–302
Miscellaneous Assets template, 289
mobile projects, S:4–S:17
  creating custom themes, S:7–S:9
  exporting custom themes, S:11
  Fireworks limitations with, S:16–S:17

  new features for creating, S:5–S:7
  previewing custom themes, S:10–S:11, S:16
  skin customization, S:12–S:15
  updating designs for, S:16
  See also jQuery Mobile themes
mockups. *See* prototypes; wireframes
modifier keys, 74–76
mouse
  highlighting objects by moving, 32
  showing tooltips by hovering, 8
  testing rollovers using, 172
moving objects between layers, 34–35
multiple documents, 16–18
Muñoz, Ale, S:18
Muse software, S:20

N

naming/renaming
  batch, 294–295
  hotspots, 240
  layers, 34
  objects, 32–33
  pages, 258
  slices, 197–198, 201–202
  states, 40, 208
  symbols, 164
navigation buttons, 168, 171
Near North Adventures website, 116
nested symbols, 162
New Bitmap Image icon, 58, 63
New Document dialog box, 4, 90, 119
New From Template dialog box, 284
New Sublayer button, 38
New/Duplicate Layer button, 34
New/Duplicate Page icon, 227, 244
No Anti-Alias setting, 139
Numeric Transform options, 54, 81–82
numerical resizing, 10–11

O

object-oriented approach, 63
objects
  aligning, 50
  editing within groups, 289–290
  grouping, 33, 53–54

Production Notes

The Adobe Fireworks CS6 Classroom in a Book was created electronically using Adobe InDesign CS5. Art was produced using Adobe Fireworks. The Myriad Pro and Warnock Pro OpenType families of typefaces were used throughout this book.

References to company names in the lessons are for demonstration purposes only and are not intended to refer to any actual organization or person.

Images

Photographic images and illustrations are intended for use with the tutorials.

Typefaces used

Adobe Myriad Pro and Adobe Warnock Pro are used throughout the lessons. For more information about OpenType and Adobe fonts, visit www.adobe.com/type/opentype/.

Team credits

The following individuals contributed to the development of this edition of the Adobe Fireworks CS6 Classroom in a Book:

Writer: Jim Babbage
Project Editor: Valerie Witte
Developmental and Copy Editor: Linda LaFlamme
Production Editor: Cory Borman
Technical Editor: Sheri German
Compositor: Myrna Vladic
Proofreader: Patricia Pane
Indexer: James Minkin
Cover designer: Eddie Yuen
Interior designer: Mimi Heft

Contributor

Jim Babbage, Solutions Consultant, Education, Adobe Systems
Jim Babbage's two passions, teaching and photography, led him to his first career in commercial photography. With the release of Photoshop 2.5, Jim became involved in the world of digital imaging, and he soon began designing for the web in addition to taking photographs. Jim is a regular contributor to Community MX (communitymx.com), where he's written articles and tutorials on Fireworks, Dreamweaver, Photoshop, and general web and photography topics. A former college professor of 21 years, Jim taught imaging, web design, and photography at Centennial College, and web design at Humber College in Toronto, Ontario, until he joined Adobe in May of 2011. Jim has spoken at a variety of technology conferences, including D2WC and Adobe MAX.

AdobePress

LEARN BY VIDEO

Table of Contents never more than a click away

Up to 15 hours of high-quality video training

Lesson files are included on the DVD

The **Learn by Video** series from video2brain and Adobe Press is the only Adobe-approved video courseware for the Adobe Certified Associate Level certification, and has quickly established itself as one of the most critically acclaimed training products available on the fundamentals of Adobe software.

Learn by Video offers up to 15 hours of high-quality HD video training presented by experienced trainers, as well as lesson files, assessment quizzes, and review materials. The DVD is bundled with a full-color printed booklet that provides supplemental information as well as a guide to the video topics.

Video player remembers which movie you watched last

Watch-and-Work mode shrinks the video into a small window while you work in the software

For more information go to
www.adobepress.com/learnbyvideo

Titles

Adobe Photoshop CS6: Learn by Video: Core Training in Visual Communication
ISBN: 9780321840714

Adobe Illustrator CS6: Learn by Video
ISBN: 9780321840684

Adobe InDesign CS6: Learn by Video
ISBN: 9780321840691

Adobe Flash Professional CS6: Learn by Video: Core Training in Rich Media Communication
ISBN: 9780321840707

Adobe Dreamweaver CS6: Learn by Video: Core Training in Web Communication
ISBN: 9780321840370

Adobe Premiere Pro CS6: Learn by Video: Core Training in Video Communication
ISBN: 9780321840721

Adobe After Effects CS6: Learn by Video
ISBN: 9780321840387

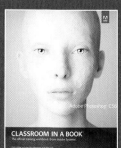